MILITARISM
IN
DEVELOPING
COUNTRIES

Militarism in Developing Countries

Edited by Kenneth Fidel

ta

Transaction Books
New Brunswick, N.J.

Library of Congress Catalog Number: 75-16479
ISBN: 0-87855-092-5 (cloth); 0-87855-585-4 (paper)

Printed in the United States of America

For Yildiz and Kerim

v

CONTENTS

Militarism in Developing Countries

1
Militarism and Development: An Introduction

Kenneth Fidel

Military organizations and personnel play a crucial role in determining the social, political and economic life conditions of a large segment of the world's population. For many living in developing nations, the military is the single most important institution shaping the quality of their existence. In some nations, the military role is explicit and public: Military leaders occupy key government positions and openly dictate national policy; military definitions of national goals prevail, dominating the mass media of communication and both public and private discussion; and military-dictated priorities supersede competing goals and policies. In other nations, the military role is less obvious but important nonetheless. Military leaders may have effective access to the highest levels of national policy-making groups. Military budgets receive priority and generally unquestioned approval regardless of other considerations or demands on limited national resources. Civilian political leadership may hold its position tenuously, dependent upon continued support from military leaders. To maintain this support, civilian leaders carefully weigh and alter all major decisions so as not to alienate military opinion. However obvious or inconspicuous the relationship to national life, there is little doubt that in most developing nations the military institution is inextricably involved not only in politics but in determining the outcome of every major social process.

The extraordinary extent of military involvement in the politics of developing nations is only partially indicated by the large number of nations having military-dominated governments. In the 1970s, that list is being continually lengthened as hardly a month goes by without new reports of coups or military discontent and unrest having the potential for culminating in revolt. In still other nations, the process of military intromission in politics and development processes is less dramatic but almost always present. The militarization of the Third World cannot be interpreted as simply a transitory phase of political evolution that will shortly be succeeded by a period of civilian political control. For while it may be possible to discern alternating cycles of military involvement and noninvolvement in the history of Third World politics, there are also indications that the present round of military power seizures is substantially different from previous bursts of military intromission in politics.

One major difference between the past and present is the sheer number and variety of nations experiencing military domination of politics. The array includes the complete spectrum of nondeveloped countries and defies any attempt to extrapolate characteristics or principles that differentiate between nations that are susceptible or nonsusceptible to military revolt and subsequent domination of government. None of the existent hypotheses delineating the characteristics of nations that have or will experience military intervention in politics is supported by events. So, for example, the hypothesis that military intervention in politics is a regional phenomena is untenable.[1] Power seizure followed by military government is true in all regions of the nondeveloped world and the time sequence of occurrence does not indicate a pattern of contagion related to geographic proximity, shared culture, common historical experience, comparable social structure or any other regional communality. Much the same can be said for hypotheses that locate susceptibility to military domination of politics in a context of historical similarity. Military power seizure and extended political domination obtains both in nations with long histories of independence and new states. In previously colonial states, the identity of the old imperial power, the form of colonial administration or the extent of preparation for independence does not provide guidelines for predicting susceptibility to military domination of politics. Indeed, in some instances, precisely those new nations that, at their point of gaining independence, were cited as models of democratic new states and unlikely to fall under the political domination of military cadres are now ruled by military men.[2]

Development-related hypotheses also fail to predict either the incidence of military revolt or the likelihood of military domination of politics.[3]/Military governments presently exist in nations at all stages of development and in nations that represent the complete spectrum of approaches to development problems and issues. The social-structural characteristics of nondeveloped nations also fail to delineate between nations that are susceptible to military domination of politics and those that are not. Military governments exist both in nations that have a full range of social-class formations as well as those with but a few distinct classes or interest groups. The political ideology of United States foreign assistance during the 1950s that viewed the development of a strong middle class as guaranteeing political democracy has proven chimeric.[4] Neither the range of class formations nor the extent of class development lessens the potential for military revolt and power seizure. This is true for both predominantly rural nations and for nations that have relatively large urban populations.

Finally, hypotheses relating military intervention and power seizure to political conditions and processes also fail to differentiate those nations that are likely to experience military domination of politics from those that do not. The hypothesis that the military does not intervene in states dominated by a single institutionalized political party is no longer tenable. Similarly, the hypothesis that the military intervenes in nations where the government lacks legitimacy is also no longer viable.[5] Nor are military revolts necessarily the result of civilian turmoil and public violence or, as some have suggested, a function of the failure of civilian political institutions.[6] While military revolt may very well occur in conjunction with any one or combination of these conditions and indeed may directly stem from events of this sort, they represent neither a suitable explanation of military revolt nor do they delineate between nations that experience military domination of politics and nations that do not.

Yet another important difference between past and present bursts of political activity by militaries in the nondeveloped world is the longevity of contemporary military regimes. In the past, military revolts were most often followed by either a new civilian regime or a temporary period of military rule. When military rule held forth, the new rulers often announced (in advance) a date for return to civilian government. Contemporary military rulers are more likely to view themselves as permanent or long-term administrators. Moreover, the transition from military to civilian government has increasingly become more a formality than a change of personnel, as military rulers are now tending to remain in office with civilian titles. In yet other instances, governmental succession is increasingly becoming a matter of one military-dominated government succeeding another. (For example, between 1967 and 1972, Dahomey experienced five military revolts and was ruled by five different military governments.)

The longevity of contemporary military regimes is intimately related to yet another difference between past and present types of military intervention in politics. In the past, the men who overthrew governments were politically or socially tied to civilian political groups. Class ties or bonds of traditional political and ideological association made military insurgents more the tool of civilian political interests than independent participants.[7] This is often no longer the case. The new military revolutionaries tend to be either completely alienated from major civilian political-interest groups or attempt to impose their leadership upon those groups that they view as their civilian constituency.[8]

The political independence of new military politicians stem, in part, from the motivational factors underlying military intromission into politics. Whereas in the past intervention in politics was most often rooted in political issues and the question of political legitimacy in particular, modern intervention is likely to be motivated by more pragmatic questions such as the failure of civilian leadership to institute and carry out acceptable development programs or the inability of the government to maintain domestic tranquility. In effect, intervention is increasingly the result of the perceived failure of civilian politics and civilian leadership. The failure of civilian rule is not viewed as a single instance or the result of the incapacity of a specific cadre of civilian leaders. Rather, new military insurgents tend to view civilian institutions and leadership as inherently incapable of dealing with questions of development and public order and that is the critical motivational difference between past and contemporary military intervention in politics.

The perceived inability of civilian institutions and leadership to deal with the pragmatic issues of the day are in large part a function of contemporary social processes. Specifically, the downward extension of the rights of citizenship and the politicization of previously nonrepresented groups. In the past, the array of political groups and participants in nondeveloped countries was limited to a small group and both the forms of political conflict and the range of potential outcomes were fairly well circumscribed and predictable. Political and social gains or losses little effected the permanent contextual character of the society or initiated processes with long-term change implications. This is no longer the case. Today, newly politicized groups are forcing themselves into the political arena and the outcomes of socio-political conflict have critical long-term implications. Gains or losses are now viewed as irrevocable and socio-political conflict has assumed a quality of desperation. The stakes are too high to even consider the possibility of losing out in the struggle for control and the right to determine the course of national history. Given these conditions, many military men are unwilling to leave the future of their nations, and indeed their own futures as well, to the whims of fortune or in the hands of leaders whose capabilities and perhaps even motives are questionable.

For many military men there are but two key issues: What are the futures of their nations to be? And, what is each one's role in both the present and future nations to be? Rather than leave the determination of the future to forces and persons over whom they have little or no control, direct intervention in present socio-political processes represents a preferred mode of action.

DEVELOPMENT AS A FOCAL ISSUE

There are numerous reasons why Third World military men have chosen development as a focus of concern and major goal of national policy. The military lives in a nationalist environment and as both a function of professional socialization and role performance are concerned with issues of national survival. As nationalists these men are primarily concerned with political autonomy and the quality of national existence.[9] For most Third World nations, political autonomy, in its outward forms at least, is not a major concern. Independence, once gained, is threatened in only a few nations. Thus nationalist concern tends to focus on the quality of national existence, which in most instances refers to the extent of development progress. Moreover, within the international arena of opinion and status, development ranks second in importance only to political independence. For the nationalist, a respectable position within the international community is an important goal as it is indicative of equality among nations irrespective of previous colonial or otherwise subordinated national status. More specifically, the goal of the Third World nationalist is equality with the great nations of the world, and while most recognize the impossibility of achieving that aim in the near future it will only be through development progress that the goal can ever be approached.[10]

There also exist important historical models of military men and institutions that significantly altered the course of national history through the imposition of development-oriented change. Ataturk, Peron and Nasser are figures well known to Third World military men, and their successes in bringing Turkey, Argentina and Egypt into the modern world argue well the feasibility of military-sponsored social change elsewhere. These examples of military-impelled change legitimate both concern with development issues and military domination of political processes as a method for attaining social goals. Indeed, military men may very well assert that within the context of the present world situation only the military is capable of effectively instituting major social change processes. Their argument is that the American, European and Russian experiences are not germane to the experience and present situation of poor countries. Rapid economic expansion through the exploitation of either external or internal resources is not an option available to most Third World nations today and population pressures are often so pressing that even a moderate rate of economic growth is not sufficient to satisfy the dual demands of increasing population size and attainment of a higher general standard of living. Therefore, gradual development programs must be rejected in favor of more focused and determined efforts that have greater promise for limited but immediate benefits.[11] And within poor nations, who are better capable of mounting an intensive program of national advancement than strong and efficient military leaders?

Military concern with developmental questions is also a function of the fact that social change or stagination vitally affect both the personal and corporate status of the military. Involvement in development and politics may be necessary for military cadres to protect or advance their position within a changing society. The essence of development is the alteration of existent interclass relations and traditional patterns of super- and sub-ordination. Specific processes include the emergence of new and intermediary social classes and interest groups, solidification of class formations and the downward extension of the rights of citizenship. Once developmental-change processes begin, the position of the military institution and military groups within the social fabric of the nation also change. And while in some nations developmental change enhances the status position of military cadres, in others changing patterns of interclass relations relegate the officer corps to a subordinated position within the newly emergent social structure. New classes and interest groups may supplant the military institution in the national power structure. Previously inarticulate and politically nonparticipant population segments may become solidified as class formations and demand a dominant role in political affairs and a more equitable distribution of income. Other groups, taking advantage of economic opportunities newly available as a result of ongoing developmental processes and programs, may establish living standards that military personnel cannot equal and thus create the conditions for status deprivation and military discontent regarding the specific path that development is taking. Soldiers may be drawn into active involvement in development as a matter of personal and corporate necessity, lest ongoing change processes get completely beyond the limits of their control.

Developmental stagnation can also be detrimental to the status of the military. To the extent that traditional patterns of interclass relations are maintained, the personal and collective ambitions of men who entered the service in search of mobility opportunity are at least partially frustrated. The maintenance of traditional patterns of governance excludes these men from participation in rule while the continuation of traditional economic systems frustrates desires for a higher standard of living.

Developmental stagnation may provide yet other compelling reasons for military intervention. A genuine concern for the life conditions of the people is one strong source of motivation. Given the absence of progress under the existent social order military men may begin to view their personal and collective role in society in terms of an historic mission similar to that assumed by other soldiers in other nations. Moreover, within the arena of international opinion, military men may be embarrassed by the maintenance of traditional patterns of rulership in their nation. This is particularly true when the nation belongs to a bloc in which other nations have already begun to undergo dramatic social change under the sponsorship of military cadres. Indeed, military leaders sometimes find themselves under pressure from neighboring states to intercede and replace the old regime with a developmentally oriented one.[12]

The corporate status of the military institution may also be enhanced by either stagnation or development. In some stagnating nations, the military presently occupies a favored position and change is viewed as potentially detrimental to the corporate interests of professional officers. Military concern with development may be rooted in a desire to oversee the nature of change so as not to dramatically alter the present condition of the officer corps and role of the military institution. While some officers adamantly oppose any change, others, seeing change as inevitable, focus their efforts on participating in change processes and retaining the capability of exercising a veto power over programs and processes that potentially force the military from their advantageous position in society. In other nations, development enhances the position of the military institution and military personnel. Where military men represent the major pool of administrative and technological personnel, the onset of development processes creates a demand for their services and places them in key administrative positions. Through control of the administration of development, the social, economic and political position of both the men and the institution benefit, at least as long as domination of access to these positions is maintained.

Internal events can draw the military into development issues in other ways as well. Development is a difficult process and while some gain, others lose. A nation caught in the throes of development may find itself incapable of dealing with the problems that always stem from dramatic and rapid social change. Political and social conflict generated by the demands and challenges newly politicized groups make on the existent political leadership often create conditions of political turmoil and widespread violence. The military institution may voluntarily or involuntarily be drawn into the role of the sole force capable of stemming violence. In this role, military leaders are not simply policemen or even arbitrators; in both the style and direction of their use of force to quell violence, they are directly participating in social change and at the same time helping to determine the outcome of development processes.[13] Once the military is so drawn into active participation in change processes it is not likely to extricate itself gracefully after restoring public order or act with equanimity towards all parties. It becomes first a participant, then a partisan and later perhaps the major acting force.

The inability of governments to function effectively is yet another entree to military intromission in politics and development. Either competing demands or gross indecision in government policy-making can lead to civil and economic chaos. The military may be the only group in the nation capable of making hard development decisions and having those decisions accepted, willingly or unwillingly, by other segments of the population. In the absence of other strong forces capable of implementing development programs, the military through the use or threat of force is likely to accept that function.

Any military claims to sole possession of concern for the national fate are of course easily refuted. Development as the primary goal of national policy is hardly the exclusive property of the military institution. Indeed, most public leaders in developing nations would agree to the primacy of progressive social change as the focal issue of their times. Yet the military appears to have an advantage in pressing its claim to developmental leadership. The tradition of military men serving in the vanguard of development-oriented cadres is not easy to ignore. In many nations, civilian success in achieving development goals is at best limited. Under civilian leadership, national unity of purpose and method seldom prevails. Civilian political institutions are often incapable of successfully arbitrating the competing demands of interest groups and sectors of the population in a manner that appears to provide maximum national benefit. If anything, civilian leaders and groups more often than not are bound into satisfying the demands of a highly specific constituency whose interests may be not only different from those of the largest segments of the population but anti-developmental as well. By contrast, both the rhetoric and self-perception of military personnel are most often in terms of the nation as a whole. And while there is usually a hiatus between rhetoric and reality the claim to best representing the interests of the nation can be made, and convincingly as well.

The numerous paths to military concern with development issues and development-related politics suggest that, despite the wide variety of conditions that obtain in the developing world and the unique characteristics of every nation, almost every possible social process potentially leads to direct military involvement in the full range of national affairs. Personal and corporate involvement in nonmilitary aspects of national life may not lead directly to power seizure, as military leaders and organizations sometimes use less obtrusive techniques of exerting their influence. However, we may suggest that, over time, military concern with development-related issues must lead either to military domination of a civilian regime or overt military government.[14] Moreover, we may also suggest that in the contemporary Third World, over a period of time, military domination of civilian regimes tends to evolve into military government.

ALTERNATIVE ANALYSES OF POLITICAL OUTCOMES

By all indications, the inclination of military men in the nondeveloped world to seize and maintain power is a trend that will continue and become strengthened in the foreseeable future. Considering present trends, we may very well soon encounter a situation in which nearly every developing nation is either governed by military cadres or subservient to its military leadership. Whether or not this situation does come to pass is, of course, a moot question, but there is little doubt that in terms of precedents, trends and the thrust of existent socio-political processes the potential for a Third World ruled by military personnel does indeed exist.

But the larger issues are not purely political. The phenomenon of military political power is just one facet of the great transformation occurring in the world today. The developing world is comprised of those nations in the process of transition from various states of underdevelopment to a developed society, and questions regarding who governs or the style of government, while important, are nonetheless subsidiary to questions about the outcome of governmental policies and development processes as gauged in terms of the life conditions of the population. The real issues of the day are developmental, and the importance of politics generally and military politics specifically lie in their relationship to development and development processes. On a broader level, the importance of the military in the Third World stems from the following observation: It now appears that if there is to be development, the military institution and military personnel are most likely to be its handmaidens. Moreover, as the military presence in developing nations is an important determinant of the societal models that are in the process of emerging and military cadres are playing a crucial role in shaping future modes of governance, trends in military governmental style and the developmental thrusts of soldier rulers are clear indicators of what the future holds for nondeveloped nations.

Analyses of current trends in military politics tend to prognosticate one of two emergent models of society and government. One line of analysis suggests that events in nondeveloped nations indicate the eventual emergence of societies characterized by shared norms of political behavior, democratic forms of government and political authority rooted in the consitutional right of a regime to hold office. Military rule, when obtained, is viewed either as a further step in the direction of emergent democratic forms of government or a temporary totalitarian interlude shortly to be followed by a return to the predominance of norms of political legitimacy. The second line of analysis provides a less sanguine interpretation of contemporary trends in military politics. The present round of military intromission in politics is viewed as indicative of future patterns of totalitarian and authoritarian styles of government. Authoritarian political styles adopted by contemporary military regimes are viewed as long-term phenomena and models for new military rulers in yet other states.

Underlying the first view is the assumption that professional soldiers are primarily interested in military affairs and their interventionist activities are first a function of the failure of civilian government to provide for national well-being and security and second a distasteful interruption in the normal course of a professional career.[15] Military intervention is interpreted as more a function of necessity than a matter of choice and design. Given conditions of relative political stability and legitimacy, general economic well-being and national security, career soldiers would be content to concern themselves primarily with military affairs and participate in politics only to the extent that their legitimate concerns require. If career soldiers in contemporary nondeveloped nations intervene in politics it is either the result of a lack of professionalism on their part or the outright failure of civilian politics and leadership. Whatever the specific cause of military intervention, the act is interpreted more as a last-resort type of response than the opening gambit of a political initiative. Under normal conditions, professional soldiers are viewed as perfectly content to live within the confines of legitimate political systems.

Going beyond assumptions about the motives of career soldiers, protagonists of the position of military politics as the politics of legitimacy find evidence for their view in the typical acts of military interveners. Once power is seized, major efforts are often made to justify both the revolt and the postcoup regime in terms of the legitimacy and righteousness of the acts and the culpability of the former regime. Public justification serves a number of important functions: First, it establishes the new regime's right to rule without destroying existent traditions of political legitimacy; second, in some instances it establishes the basis for new traditions of legitimacy where none may have existed previously; third, it pre-empts the right of potential contenders for power to attack and overthrow the new regime; and fourth, it garners popular support for the new regime.

The latter function is very important, for those who interpret politics in terms of norms of legitimacy consider popular support as critical to the maintenance of power. Indeed, they argue—in an age of widespread political awareness, mass mobilization and popular revolt—how can a regime survive without widespread support and acceptance? While force of arms may be sufficient to establish a new government, how long can a regime survive solely through the use or threat of force? Does not reliance on force as a technique of power maintenance only strengthen and solidify opposition? Moreover, recent events indicate that domination of the means of violence alone does not guarantee success in quashing popular rebellion. Advanced weapons systems, while powerful and sophisticated, tend to be of little use in low-level warfare, and even a poorly armed revolutionary force can successfully maintain itself against a modern army if it is strongly motivated and has popular support. In urban regions strikes, demonstrations and riots may get out of control, causing dissension in the regime leading to either a change of government or at the least, important policy changes. Consequently, it is argued that even a powerful military regime must have widespread recognition of its right to rule and at least a modicum of popular support.

Recognition of the importance of popular support and acceptance is often evidenced by the formation of coalitions with existent civilian political parties or the founding of broad-based civilian political organizations by new military rulers. Historically, the most successful military rulers have adopted one of these strategies as both a technique for perpetuating their rule and an efficient method of instituting reform. Within the framework of the "legitimist" argument, one might draw the distinction between reformist and totalitarian military regimes in terms of the extent to which mass political mobilization prevails and broad-based political parties are used as instruments of progressive social change.[16]

Furthermore, the history of military regimes indicates that in all but the most underdeveloped nations the military cannot rule alone. Administration of national affairs requires the active cooperation of a trained corps of government workers; despite the fact that officers may successfully fill many government positions, there are seldom sufficient numbers available or capable of carrying out the full range of necessary tasks. Thus, military government must draw upon civilian sources of assistance and participation and accept the intrusion of civilian interests and points of view.

The processes leading to civilianization are generally activated at the time of the establishment of military government. Participants in military revolt seldom share a complete range of common beliefs and opinions. Once actively engaged in governmental activities, latent disagreements and enmities are likely to emerge within the ruling circle.[17] While at first competition for power or the prevalence of an ideological view may be limited to appeals for support from other military men, eventually the politicization of the ruling group is likely to expand the sphere of political competition and draw civilian groups into active political participation. Thus, even at the height of military rule, civilian influences often play a predominant role in determining the course of events and the outcome of decision-making processes.

Civilianization of military regimes is seen as an end result of both the need for maintaining popular support and reliance upon civilian-government workers. With the growth of mass civilian parties, military rulers find their interests and concerns more closely allied with those of civilian sectors of the population than with former colleagues. The press of national problems draws military rulers into areas and issues that they were not previously interested in and exposure to public and private pressures serve to alter their points of view and frames of reference. New roles and differential exposure work to create important differences in comprehension and appreciation of national problems and politics between soldier rulers and other military men. As military regimes become more involved with civilians and more dependent upon civilian support and assistance, they may very well alienate their former comrades.[18] The final break with old military ties often comes with formal retirement and the assumption of civilian political roles and identity. In the end, military governments tend to become civilianized and dictatorial modes of rule evolve into traditional or democratic forms of government.

In sharp contrast to the view that military regimes evolve into civilian political structures whose rule is based on norms of legitimacy, the alternative line of analysis stresses the authoritarian potential inherent in contemporary patterns of military intromission in politics. This view interprets political interaction and interclass relations not in terms of the rules of the game but as systems of power and changing patterns of super- and sub-ordination. Normative rules governing political competition are viewed as meaningful only to the extent that they are mutually beneficial to all parties involved or are enforced by a dominant group for purposes of maintaining political and social hegemony. Where serious political competition is a factor, rules of the game and norms of legitimacy become fragile entities easily destroyed by any person or group for whom it lacks utility. Normative political systems are not necessarily the long-term outcome of social and political processes; indeed, with the present trends in military domination of Third World nations, they are unlikely outcomes.

This view is based less on a consideration of the history of military involvement in politics than an appreciation of master trends in the Third World and the dynamics of social organization and process. In particular, the new form of military coup and the type of government that now tends to follow upon its heels are seen as having the potential for evolving into an almost global pattern of authoritarian regimes throughout the nondeveloped world.

First, the authoritarian view of contemporary military politics rejects the idea that military men are primarily concerned with professional matters and only become involved in politics as a function of the inability or unwillingness of civilian officials to satisfy minimal demands relating to national security, political legitimacy and social tranquility. There are many routes leading from military duty to political activity and leadership. In nations that gained independence through revolution, military leaders are likely to have become politicized during the period of revolt, and once drawn into politics they are not likely to voluntarily retire from political participation, subordinate their political views to the dictates of civilian leadership or abjure personal political ambitions. Issues and conflicts arising during the period of national formation may be expected to form the basis of internal political conflict during the decade following independence. Revolutionary military leaders are inextricably involved in pre-independence political conflict, and barring either a reign of terror that eliminates potential political competition from soldiers or the establishment of an authoritarian regime in which the military is subject to close police and political surveillance, revolutionary military leaders may be expected to play an important and perhaps dominant role in national politics. The potential for revolutionary military leaders emerging as national rulers is not only present it is highly probable. The route to political leadership may be through channels of legitimate political competition or by way of a coup d'état, but that former independence fighters will be politically active is almost a certainty.

In other nations men enter the officer corps with specific political goals in mind. Political participation as a sequel to a military career is often a national tradition. Yet other men are politicized while on active duty. Political awareness, goals and ambitions may stem from interaction with other politicized soldiers or be a product of military socialization; as, increasingly, officer training includes exposure to political and social issues as well as a consideration of purely military matters. Whatever the route to politicization, there is little question that today most military men are deeply involved at both an individual and corporate level of awareness in political and social issues and it is naive to believe that politics is a secondary concern of military men in the contemporary Third World.

It is more reasonable to suggest that politics is, in many instances, the primary concern of military leaders and cadres. The salience of this topic and related issues of development and social problems is evidenced in many ways. The curricula of military schools now almost universally include courses dealing with major social issues and problems, development and development theory and politics; military journals regularly publish essays dealing with these topics; military leaders actively seek media outlets for their personal and corporate views; and political groups of all sorts are forming at military installations. Whether this represents a new phenomenon or the continuation of a long tradition of military concern with social and political issues is not our present concern. What is important is the contemporary salience of social issues, development and politics for Third World militaries and the translation of concern into personal and group action. There is little doubt but that today, military men, both singly and in groups, are psychologically available for political activity.

Availability is easily transformed into mobilization through the numerous formal and informal organizations and groups that comprise the infrastructure of any military organization; and once mobilized, politicized military groups require only a reasonable opportunity before moving to seize political power. When military cadres do intervene today the beginning of processes leading to democratic forms of political competition are not likely outcomes. As the original motivation to intervene often stems from a rejection of the efficacy of existent political systems and the perceived inability of civilian leaders to carry out important and necessary changes, new military rulers are not likely to opt for a similar political system that is dependent upon either the ephemeral allegiance of the masses or the establishment of special relationships with small interest groups. If anything, they are likely to attempt to disengage the new regime from any form of dependence upon external sources of support. In effect, claims to establishment of an apolitical regime are in reality an announcement that the regime is irresponsible and not willingly subject to the demands of groups or individuals not participating in the administration.

But military power seizure does not occur in a political vacuum and new military rulers inevitably must deal with other politicized groups, whether they be civilian or military. In their relationships with other groups, two broad strategies are generally available: Either new military rulers may attempt to establish working relationships with other groups, which implies that one side will become subordinate to the other, or they may attempt to nullify the potence of other political interest groups. The former strategy is often not possible. For, to the extent that other interest groups are well developed and viable, they may not be willing to be subordinated to military leaders. Moreover, for military rulers, the establishment of working relationships with existent interest groups may imply a return to previous political systems and thus be rejected out of hand. At present, the trend is for new military regimes to disassociate themselves from any viable interest groups except to the extent that others are willing to become completely subordinate to the new regime. Resistance to complete domination by the new regime is typically met by a harsh and often brutal response.

Thus the authoritarian view of military power seizure and its outcome presents a radically different set of conclusions than the legitimist view. The very characteristics of a developed nation lend themselves to authoritarian rule, rather than militate against its emergence. The more developed the nation in which military power seizure occurs, the greater the likelihood that an effective authoritarian regime employing a broad spectrum of repressive techniques is likely to emerge.

DEVELOPMENT AND AUTHORITARIANISM

The amount and type of opposition a new military regime encounters is a function of developmental progress prior to the revolution. Where little development has taken place, the political culture and the extent of potential opposition may be limited to a few well-developed interest groups or potentially mobilizable segments of the population. The arrest of a few men and the imposition of limited political oppression can often suffice to suppress or destroy opposition to the new regime. Once power is consolidated, threats to the regime or its policies may be dealt with swiftly and surely, with little fear of widespread repercussions or mushrooming opposition. The periods between sporadic new threats to the regime are generally characterized by a relatively loose style of governance in which the style of administration is authoritarian but not necessarily harshly oppressive.

By contrast, in a nation that has experienced significant developmental progress prior to a military revolt, both the number and potential strength of important interest groups available is greater and the political culture is considerably more complex. Enemies of the regime may be capable of mobilizing large and important segments of the population in a struggle against the new rulers. Complex systems of alliances may make it impossible to oppress one segment of the population without embroiling a host of other groups. Both major and minor interest groups may have well-developed vehicles of articulation and sophisticated spokesmen capable of accurately interpreting ongoing events and effectively presenting their views to the public. In these circumstances, the ability of a new military regime to suppress its enemies is considerably reduced and the measures necessary may be harsher and require concentrated effort over an extended period of time.[19]

In effect, there is a direct relationship between the extent of development prior to military power seizure and the emergence of a severely authoritarian regime. Given the large number of enemies and their potential effectiveness in a rapidly developing nation, a new military regime must act to suppress all political expression lest opposition to the regime grow rapidly and spread to all segments of the population. No criticism of the regime may be tolerated. Mass arrests, seizures of property and the outlawing of organizations of all types are standard procedures for destroying opposition both real and potential. If and when these techniques prove ineffective, large-scale terror campaigns with indiscriminate persecution typically occur. Thus, those nations that most closely approximate the pluralist model of a developed society may also be most susceptible to the imposition of a harshly oppressive political regime.

Both the managerial ethos and the bureaucratic structure of the military and government organization lend themselves to the effective imposition of authoritarian modes of rulership. The officer-manager has considerable experience working within a bureaucratic structure, so the transition from military activities to civil administration is relatively easy. If anything, new military rulers are more likely to further rationalize existent government organizations than introduce new patterns of traditional or charismatic leadership. With increased rationalization of government organization, the effectiveness of civil administration is likely to increase, making authoritarian rule under military leadership perhaps even more effective than it would be under civilian leadership.

The transition from civilian to military government is also eased by the bureaucratic nature of government organization. For the civil servant, the identity of government leadership is largely irrelevant. The administration of government affairs continues, regardless of the nature of the regime. However, there are often advantages for the civil service under a military regime. Military rulers may effectively end outside interference in government activities that civilian regimes either fostered or were incapable of limiting. Military rulers, formerly government employees themselves, are generally more sympathetic to the problems of the civil service than previous civilian politicians. This may result in increased salaries and benefits, provided to civil servants and their families, stricter adherence to the formal rules governing civil service employment and promotion and an enhanced social and legal status for the government employee. As a result, government organization tends to provide critical support for an authoritarian military regime and lend itself to the new leadership's purposes.[20]

Of particular importance to authoritarian military regimes is the ability to coopt the national police force. Its participation is critical to the successful implementation of programs of terror aimed at destroying real and potential opposition. For in most instances it is the police, not the military, that is given the tasks of arresting political opponents, controlling crowds or riots, political investigation and the maintenance of continuing surveillance over the population. It is often precisely the alliance with the national police and reliance on the police for the enforcement of authoritarian laws that allows military regimes to continue in power and survive the process of alienation from other sectors of the military. Authoritarian military regimes are more police states than military-dominated governments.[21]

Just as the extent of development prior to military power seizure is directly related to the potential for an authoritarian military regime emerging after a revolt, development is also related to the effectiveness of authoritarian measures a new military government may introduce. The more developed the nation, the more likely it will have a well-developed civil service with a large corps of well-trained and obedient officers. Moreover, the police organization within the civil service is also likely to be large and efficient. Once instructed to carry out a campaign of terror against the population, it may be expected to faithfully perform the assigned tasks. Other areas of the government civil service can also be expected to perform efficiently as well, providing the authoritarian regime its major buttress and mainstay of strength and longevity.

The importance of the alliance between the civil service and a military regime alters our concept of the role of force in maintaining military-dominated governments' power. We have traditionally pictured military regimes as dependent upon the literal occupation of the nation, with large contingents of soldiers permanently stationed at all key points and directly involved in every aspect of civil administration. If this were the case, then all of the observations on the impossibility of maintaining military rule through the use of force alone would indeed be accurate. But it is not the case in most military regimes. In most instances of military-dominated government, civil administration continues to function in much the same manner as it had under civilian political leadership. In fact, if anything, the scope of civil government activities is greatly expanded. Once the government has been effectively secured, the overt military presence may either return to its previous level or perhaps become even less visible than it was under civilian government. Population control tends to become the duty of the police force, which in many instances is more loyal to the new military regime than many military units.

The use of direct military force as a technique of power maintenance is most likely to obtain in response to only a limited number of conditions, such as the suppression of open and organized revolt, widespread rioting and attempts to secure for the government areas that have traditionally been antigovernment and semiautonomous.[22] Popular movements whose purpose is to overthrow a military regime seldom reach the stage of providing sufficient threat to warrant the use of military force. The potential success of popular movements is limited by a number of stringent conditions and, while there have been some instances of successful revolt there have also been numerous instances of the absolute failure of attempted revolt and insurgence.[23] The conditions that allow for the success of popular revolt include large areas of low-population density that are inaccessible to modern vehicles; outside sources of supplies, weaponry and finance; trained revolutionary leadership cadres; cohesive organization; and a revolutionary program that can successfully appeal to a large segment of the population and gain their permanent allegiance, to name but a few. Even when all of the conditons for successful revolt exist, there is still no guarantee against failure. If anything, popular revolt—or at least attempts to initiate it—has been more prone to failure than success in recent years. When revolt and insurgence do succeed, it is more often a result of the incapacities of the regime than the strength of the revolution.[24]

By contrast, an effective authoritarian regime has many

advantages in combating revolt. The use of force per se is only one technique of repression and indeed it is severely limited in its long-term effectiveness. Other techniques of repression and power maintenance that are considerably more effective, particularly in urban regions (which are the most likely source of effective opposition), include close surveillance, sporadic interrogation, arrest, property confiscation, hostage taking and exile. Once institutionalized, the various techniques of repression constitute a campaign of terror against the population which, recent experience indicates, can be extremely effective in destroying opposition to a regime, pacifying a potentially rebellious population and keeping an unpopular regime in office.[25] While these techniques are not limited to military dictatorships alone, military governments have drawn upon them sufficiently to make them characteristics of contemporary military rule.

The potential success of terror campaigns is directly related to the extent of developmental experience. Many of the societal characteristics that correlate with development also define the conditions in which terror is a viable technique of political repression and power maintenance. For example, as nations experience development, the most politicized segments of the population are increasingly concentrated in urban regions where they are directly exposed to police or military surveillance and arrest. Such groups as political leaders, union officials, the intelligentsia, media opinion leaders and students have little opportunity to form, lead or participate in revolutionary movements; unless they rapidly go undergound, all of their activities are likely to be monitored. The authoritarian regime may take advantage of the concentration of potential opposition by instituting policies of interrogation, exile, arrest and persecution that remove many of these people from the political arena. Yet others are successfully intimidated by the events surrounding them.

With urbanization there is also likely to be a breakdown of traditional bonds of group cohesion and solidarity and traditional forms of leadership that may have existed in rural areas. Previously united family, village or tribal groups may become fragmented and politically impotent in the urban setting. With the breakdown of traditional forms of group structure and cohesion, individuals may become anomic and thus more susceptible to authoritarian techniques of repression and less resistant to ongoing political trends. As individuals become increasingly personalized their concern for collective issues and well-being decreases, and in a society of individuals techniques of terror are highly effective forms of behavior control. The most salient concern of the individual becomes personal survival and well-being; and, as conformity and acquiescence represent the most successful strategy for maintaining one's present condition, participation in antigovernmental activities becomes unthinkable.

Moreover, for many in recently urbanized populations, politics is secondary to questions of personal economic status and, as long as that status is not threatened, who governs and the mode of governance are not major concerns. For some, political apathy is a long-ingrained tradition stemming from a history of lack of control over government officials and a fateful acceptance of political domination. In many instances authoritarian rule is little different from previous forms of governance and the population continues to endure its situation.

The imposition of authoritarian military rule is not necessarily met with universal civilian disapproval. Some groups, such as the urban middle class, may find military dictatorship and continuous martial law comfortable. Labor disputes culminating in strikes, boycotts or violence cease to occur. Crime rates tend to drop precipitously and price stabilization may halt a previous trend of personal and corporate economic deterioration. Thus, very often, the urban middle class may support an authoritarian military regime, at least as long as repression does not directly effect either their standard or style of life. If and when it does, however, it may, by then, be too late to become politically active in opposition to the government and the middle class may find itself helpless and impotent.

By contrast, rural populations in less-developed nations often have a much greater potential for resistance. Group cohesion based on tribal, village or family membership sometimes provides effective patterns of group leadership, succession, interpersonal and collective support, norms and values and traditional modes of response and resistance functionally suitable for dealing with terrorism and military activity directed against the local population.[26] Moreover, in rural areas local populations are often inaccessible to military and police forces on a daily basis. Military occupation of the region may be the only technique for maintaining close government control over the area and that too can be ineffective or overly costly for the government. Even in urban regions, strong corporate ties allow individuals and groups to successfully resist terrorism. Group members may provide sanctuary for hunted men, patterns of mutual assistance may provide for the families of arrestees or hostages, group organization may serve as the nucleus for resistance movements and group members may subvert police systems of surveillance and intelligence gathering. While strong bonds of group membership do not guarantee successful resistance to official terrorism, they help vitiate its effectiveness.

Events occurring all over the developing world provide greater support for the authoritarian prognosis of military rule than the legitimist view. At present, it does not appear likely that contemporary military regimes will evolve into pluralist states characterized by western-style democracy. The more likely outcome, both in states presently dominated by military regimes and those that have yet to experience military seizure of power, is the authoritarian regime employing political repression and terror as major techniques of power maintenance and goal attainment. Totalitarianism, rather than democracy, appears to be the most likely successor to traditional and colonial forms of political rule.

MILITARY RULE AND DEVELOPMENTAL CHANGE

In a wide spectrum of nations, the prospect of development overseen by authoritarian regimes has important implications for both the nature and direction of development and the emergent social structure. Military definitions of development and a soldier's view of what development ought to be may be expected to prevail. While historically new military rulers have drawn upon available expert opinion in determining national priorities and specific techniques for goal attainment, their choice of advisors, the questions they ask and their interpretation of advice is all too often fashioned by a rather limited world view that is more a product of personal experience, military education and military socialization than an understanding of development processes. The military man's perception of the nature of development is likely to be a limited one, and military determination of development effort is likely to limit the scope and nature of both the effort and the gains that accrue from it. We may therefore expect the military approach to development to be pragmatic and programmatic rather than ideological or innovative. Taking existent military regimes as models, we may make predictions regarding the direction of development in states ruled by authoritarian military governments.

Development goals are most likely to be defined in primarily economic terms. Specific types of goals may consist of attempts to increase gross national product, greater exploitation of natural resources and the acquisition of control over sources of income presently controlled by foreign interests. Capital investment is likely to take precedence over investment in noneconomic goods and show-piece projects may be inaugurated. In particular, the latter often include grand-development schemes like steel mills or gigantic irrigations systems, even though these may be uneconomical. In most general terms, the goal of the economic program is likely to be achievement of economic self-sufficiency in a short period of time, regardless of the costs. While the goal is common to all developing nations, the means for achieving it differentiate the authoritarian military regime from other states. But the real difference between the authoritarian state and other nations is not in its approaches to economic issues, it is in its effects on social structures and the human condition.

In structuring models of development, the social aspects are likely to be subordinated to economic questions. In a number of areas, aspects of social development may coincide with the general economic-development program. In particular, health and education are often viewed as concomitants of economic development, especially in those nations that are plagued by endemic, disabling diseases or where the shortage of technical personnel is critical. In response to these social-economic problems, programs of public health and expanded educational effort are often instituted. Where these problems are not critical, little may be expected of the authoritarian military regime. In fact, in those nations previously characterized by widespread student-and-faculty political activity and agitation, educational effort is typically contracted in non-technical areas.

While there may be some attention to public aspects of social development, there is not likely to be very much effort devoted to changing traditional aspects of interpersonal relations. Authoritarian military regimes are more likely to attempt to strengthen traditional patterns of interpersonal relationships and traditional modes of public behavior. Modes of dress and personal appearance become regulated; the traditional authority of parents and teachers is reinforced; and compulsory religious affiliation and observance are reinstituted. The regime may also seek to control the overt aspects of individual morality. Laws prohibiting pornography, promiscuity, petty crime, public disorderliness, juvenile delinquency and infidelity are strengthened and strictly enforced. Traditional husband-wife relations may also be strengthened by making divorce more difficult to obtain. So far, all the evidence indicates that authoritarian military regimes are typically conservative in their approach to interpersonal and public aspects of behavior.[27]

Considerably more important are the conservative effects authoritarian military regimes have on interclass relationships. While some military regimes do destroy previously superordinate social classes, authoritarian rule, for the most part, solidifies existent interclass relationships and creates a new super-ordinate class of higher-level government managers.

Social classes most vulnerable to destruction by the new type of military regime are the landed rich, the urban wealthy and minority middle-class groups. These three classes share a number of important characteristics that make them particularly dangerous to new military regimes and thus a special object of repression. First, these groups tend to be politically and financially powerful, and if they oppose the regime they constitute a serious threat to its continued existence. Their power may be rooted in traditional patterns of repressive interclass relationships based upon land or business ownership and consequent community leadership, their control of available private capital, a monopoly on the ability to provide requisite services or the extent of their internal cohesion and ability to resist the new regime. Typically, these groups have an important stake in maintaining the old order and their position within it; thus, they are not only a threat to the new regime but provide an easily distinguishable target as well. In most instances programs of repression, directed at nullifying the potence of these groups, are justifiable in terms of nationalist or developmental goals. Whether or not these policies actually achieve their publicly stated aims is, of course, another question.

Where the landed rich pose a threat to military regimes, a typical mode of response—land reform—has emerged. Through land reform, breaking up vast farm holdings and distributing the property among previously landless peasants, dictatorial regimes have an effective technique of power maintenance. The landed rich are deprived of their source of wealth and power, while newly established small farm holders are in many ways bound to the new regime. First, the new small farmer must support the government, as a return to the old regime almost inevitably insures the loss of their newly acquired property and a return to their previous landless status. Second, as new small farmers can seldom manage their farms unassisted, they are dependent upon the government for seed, machinery, loans and marketing services. Without massive government assistance, the small farmers would quickly become bankrupt and lose their new status. In terms of interclass relations, the peasants' previous subordination to the landed rich is replaced by subordination to government managers, and there is little change in their corporate status within the national class structure. Indeed, subordination to the civil service may be more oppressive in that there is no recourse to an alternative source of authority.

Expropriation and seizure of property has also become a typical mode of dealing with opposition in the industrial and commercial sectors of the nation. In these instances, property tends to fall to the government itself. The effect, however, is similar to that which is prevalent in rural areas. Government managers replace owners as the controllers of business and industry. For the working class, there is little change in its social condition. If anything, its position is made worse, for as government employees they are likely to lose whatever rights they had in the private sector of the economy. In particular, they generally lose the right to unionize and strike.

In those areas of interclass relations in which the authoritarian military regime does not directly intervene, the position of the various classes, vis a vis one another, tends to become solidified. With increased government control over the economy and the growth areas in particular, mobility opportunity becomes severely limited for individuals and groups outside of the civil service. Control over public behavior generally insures the continuation of traditional patterns of interpersonal relations. This is particularly important at the points of social-class interface. Relations between employee and employer, professional and client and buyer and seller become ossified in their traditional modes. The relationship between the individual and the government or its representatives also becomes solidified in a traditional mode; the individual has no means of pressing grievances and claims against the government or government employees acting in their official capacity.

Indeed, if interclass relations are at all altered by authoritarian military regimes, the major direction of change is the rise to power of the civil service and the higher levels of government management in particular. While the lower levels of society are little changed, the higher level managers fill the vacuum of authority and status created by the destruction of previously super-ordinate groups.

In both urban and rural areas, the effect of eliminating previously super-ordinated classes is to create a two-level model of social status and power. The individual, generally barred from participating in any form of organization that can effectively represent his interests to the administration, must face the full force of government authority and power unassisted. The product of a two-party power model in which resources are distributed in a one-sided fashion is, inevitably, the permanent subordination of the disadvantaged group. In this instance, the civilian population as a whole is relegated to a subordinate position in relation to the government and its employees. While class differences within the civilian population may continue to exist, the overriding fact of interclass relations in an authoritarian military regime is the one-sided relationship between the individual and the state.

In sum, the developmental outcomes of the new type of authoritarian military regime are likely to be contradictory in nature. While nations ruled by military regimes may very well experience important economic gains, the economic condition of the individual is not dramatically altered. While traditionally super-ordinate classes and interest groups may be destroyed, traditional patterns of interclass relations are likely to be maintained. In the near term at least, the model of society most likely to emerge as characteristic of authoritarian military regimes appears to more closely resemble the fascist state than the Western political democracy.

NOTES

1. Explaining civil-military relations and patterns of military power seizure in specific regions of the world in terms of shared historical, cultural and political characteristics was the first step in the attempt to develop a general theory of military politics in the underdeveloped world. Some of the many works employing this approach are Edwin Lieuwen, *Arms and Politics in Latin America* (New York: Frederick A. Praeger, 1961); John J. Johnson, *The Military and Society in Latin America* (Stanford, California: Stanford University Press, 1964); Manfred Halpern, *The Politics of Social Change in the Middle East and North Africa* (Princeton: Princeton University Press, 1963); Morris Janowitz, *The Military in the Political Development of New Nations: An Essay in Comparative Analysis* (Chicago: University of Chicago Press, 1964); and more recently Ernest W. Lefever, *Spear and Scepter: Army, Police, and Politics in Tropical Africa* (Washington: The Brookings Institution, 1970).

2. Perhaps the best examples are those former British holdings in Asia and Africa where serious attempts were made to develop effective civil administrations. Nigeria is, of course, the most obvious case in point.

3. This and a series of other, related hypotheses are perhaps best stated in Edward Shils, "The Military in the Political Development of New States," in *The Role of the Military in Underdeveloped Countries*, ed. John J. Johnson (Princeton: Princeton University Press, 1962).

4. Scholarly expression of the tenets of the American position on the emerging social structure in developing nations and the role of the military in politics and society may be found in Manfred Halpern, "Middle Eastern Armies and the New Middle Class," in *The Role of the Military*, ed. Johnson and Johnson, *The Military and Society*.

5. This hypothesis is presented in Janowitz, *The Military in the Political Development of New Nations*. Contradictory evidence can be cited for a number of nations but the best contemporary example is Egypt where a single institutionalized party has dominated politics since the destruction of effective party competition in the late 1950s. During the period 1970-73, there were a number of attempts, by military groups, to overthrow the regime there.

6. See Gino Germani and Kalman Silvert, "Politics and Military Intervention in Latin America," in *Political Development and Social Change*, eds. Jason L. Finkle and Richard W. Gable (New York: John Wiley and Sons, 1966).

7. This was the case in the 1960 Turkish revolution. While some of the military insurgents were politically independent, the group of officers that came to dominate the postcoup government was in the main tied to the Republican Peoples party.

8. Perhaps the best example is the actions of the military government that came to power in Greece after the 1967 revolution.

9. See Maury D. Feld, "Professionalism, Nationalism, and the Alienation of the Military," (paper presented at the Working Group on Armed Forces and Society at the Sixth World Congress of Sociology, Evian, France, September, 1966).

10. See Irving L. Horowitz, *Three Worlds of Development: The Theory and Practice of International Stratification* (New York: Oxford University Press, 1966).

11. Ibid.

12. For many years, Egyptian leaders pressured military men in other states in the region. More recently, Libyan leaders have become the chief protagonists of military insurrection in the Middle East and Africa.

13. In both Greece and Turkey, the military were called upon to stop uncontrollable violence. Greece has since become a military dictatorship and Turkey appeared to be on the verge of complete military power seizure in 1971.

14. Military domination of an ostensibly civilian regime was for many years the case in Argentina and, during the period 1971-73, characterized the political situation in Turkey.

15. See Samuel P. Huntington, *The Soldier and the State: The Theory and Practice of Civil Military Relationships* (Cambridge, Mass.: Harvard University Press, 1964).

16. See José Nun, "A Latin American Phenomenon: The Middle-Class Military Coup," in *Latin America: Reform or Revolution?* eds. James Petras and Maurice Zeitlin (Greenwich,

Conn.: Fawcett Publications, Inc., 1968).

17. The phenomenon of ruling juntas fragmenting over issues of government policy and administration is neither new nor unusual. For example, after the 1960 revolt in Turkey, the National Unity Committee was hamstrung in its attempts to formulate a government policy. Resolution of this crisis in rulership came after the expulsion of 14 members of the committee. Argentina, Algeria, Egypt and numerous other nations provide similar examples.

18. Even Nasser was eventually forced to rely more upon civilian support than former military colleagues. Indeed, we might speculate that were he not so personally popular his regime might have fallen to a military coup.

19. On this see Hannah Arendt, *The Origins of Totalitarianism* (New York: The World Publishing Company, 1958); and David H. Bayley, *Public Liberties in the New States* (Chicago: Rand McNally & Company, 1964).

20. Successful alliances between the civil service and new military rulers have been realized in many countries. Perhaps the most notable instance is Egypt.

21. For some detailed accounts of the role of the police in military-dominated states see Bayley, *Public Liberties.*

22. One case that combines all of the conditions likely to elicit an armed response from a military regime is the Kurdish revolt in Iraq.

23. While revolutions that fail are often deprived of publicity, we still can cite numerous instances. There have been unsuccessful revolts in Greece, both after World War II and the 1967 military coup. In Turkey, Bolivia, Sudan, Yemen and elsewhere, attempted popular revolts have failed.

24. The success of Fidel Castro in Cuba is more readily attributable to the incapacities of the regime than the force of the revolutionary movement.

25. This is certainly the case in contemporary Greece.

26. For example, despite the use of force against village populations, Kurdish resistance to Iraqi military units was maintained over many years. In the northwest territories of Pakistan, tribal values and organization are strong enough to allow continuous revolt despite armed intrusion by government forces.

27. The conservative, moralistic bent of authoritarian military regimes can be observed in the laws and policies of military governments in Libya and Greece and the influence of military moralists on the government of Turkey.

2
Center and Periphery in Developing Countries and Prototypes of Military Elites

Moshe Lissak

Many policy-makers and political scientists have toyed with the idea that a group of "young Turks" are able to drastically change social, political and economic scenery. The few successes and the many failures raise many interesting questions about the relationship between modernization and military coups. To begin to answer this question, it is methodologically advisable to refer to more specific issues:

1. A great difficulty in this context is that military takeovers occur in dissimilar societies and under different regimes. As well as differing in their structure and organization, these societies have achieved different levels of economic, political and social development. If such is the case—and there is ample statistical evidence to substantiate it—any logical relationship between processes of modernization and frequency of military intervention in domestic politics is itself suspect and must be further probed.

2. If such a relationship is found to exist, yet another question

Author's Note: This chapter was prepared with the help of a fellowship from the Center for International Affairs, Harvard University. I am grateful to Professor Samuel P. Huntington for his help and encouragement.

must still be borne in mind: Can any uniformity in the role expansion[1] of the military be shown? If not, are there any unpredictable variations or are all variations explicable?

3. Another question refers to the conditions conducive to the emergence and rate of proliferation of various types of role expansion (if and where role expansion exists). Why is the military inclined to role expansion in certain circumstances, reluctant in others (but nevertheless active) or enthusiastic in the performance of this function (of role expansion) in yet others?

4. Not all attempts by the military to take over civilian control are successful. When does the military exceed the "anticipatory stage," make its breakthrough and actually gain control? Can any predictions be made?

5. Under what conditions and in what circumstances does the military relinquish its power to an acknowledged and indisputable civilian elite?

Before proceeding to a detailed discussion, a digression is necessary in order to do justice to some classical and modern scholars who have dealt with these specific issues, albeit from another angle.

A discussion of military takeover cannot be exclusively confined to problems of modernization in developing countries. The study of revolution is far older than both the issue of modernization and that of military takeovers in developing countries. Suffice it to mention such names as Hegel, Marx, de Tocqueville and Brinton, whose studies greatly enriched our knowledge of the phenomenon. A review of some general conditions promoting violence in society seems called for. Moreover, since military revolutions constitute but *one* type of violent or illegitimate activity, it is important to refer to general theories of military revolution.

General theories of revolution are concerned with four main subjects: (a) the definition of the concept of revolution and its various subtypes; (b) the elaboration of paradigms and schemes aimed at locating the direct and indirect causes of different types of revolutions; (c) within the above context some students of revolution deal with those factors responsible for the nonoccurrence of a revolution, when all indicators would predict it as inevitable; (d) analyses of the aftereffects and the byproducts of different types of revolutions.

The concept of revolution boasts dozens of definitions and in most cases distinctions between them are semantic. Relevant and most appropriate to this study is the following one:[2]

It is change, effected by the use of violence in government and/or regime, and/or society. By *society* is meant the consciousness and the mechanics of communal solidarity, which may be tribal, peasant, kinship, national and so on; by *regime* is meant the constitutional structure—democracy, oligarchy, monarchy; and by *government* is meant specific political and administrative institutions.[3]

The common denominator of most definitions, according to Lawrence Stone, is the lack of harmony between social and political structures. This lack of harmony becomes intensified when some subsystems are deprived as a result of radical changes or rapid economic growth and/or technological changes, or even significant transformations in metaphysical beliefs. These circumstances, either alone or in combination, need not lead to violence or to attempts at illegal takeover. Much is contingent upon additional conditions, such as the behavior of entrenched elites and their intransigence manifested by their blocking any means of expression to the opposition. Other accelerators (or precipitating elements) are the emergence of a charismatic leader or the creation of secret revolutionary organizations. In an effort to summarize the numerous factors involved, Chalmers Johnson states that "power deflation, plus loss of authority, plus an acceleration provide revolution."[4] Power deflation is mainly caused by pressures created by a disequilibrated social system; loss of authority stems from the inability of the leadership to offer changes that would prevent further deterioration. The accelerator, according to Johnson the direct and last cause of the revolution, "is some ingredient, usually contributed by fortune, which deprives the elite of its chief weapon for enforcing social behavior (e.g., an army), or which leads a group of revolutionaries to believe that they have the means to deprive the elite of its weapons of coercion."[5] Some writers, although accepting (in general) these three conditions, do not see revolution as inevitable, even at that stage. They note several factors that might prevent it or at least mitigate its intensity if it were to erupt. Recent studies on internal war have enumerated these preventive factors. Harry Eckstein names the following: (a) ruthless, efficient repressions; (b) diversion of energy (foreign war or religious movements may serve as the opiate of the people: bread and circus); (c) timely political concessions.[6]

One has to bear in mind the combination of conducive factors and mitigating mechanisms that might change the potential, preconceived and intended character of the revolution as giving rise to different types of revolutions. The military coup is only *one* possibility among a number. Role expansion initiated by other groups, the government or the party, the bureaucracy, oligarchic elites or popular movements are daily occurrences. This study is restricted to a specific field of role expansion within modernizing societies. Reference is necessary only to those factors related to the de facto emergence of the military as the central or exclusive factor within the political arena.

Definitions of modernization are multidimensional. They refer to sociodemographic, structural and value-system changes as well as to the capacity to adjust to new situations. Every multi-faceted phenomenon raises questions about the compatibility and the internal harmony of its various indicators. For a long time, questions of compatibility and positive correlation between the various indices of economic differentiation, communication, urbanization and political development remained unquestioned.

Many quantitative analyses have been devoted to this issue.[7] The findings based either on quantitative or qualitative data were unsatisfactory and not always convincing. Doubts ensued, traces of which are noticeable in numerous studies.[8] Great encouragement was given to this development by the newly found concern with the problem of retraditionalization and by the confrontation with the breakdown of political systems in various developing societies. These two phenomena, often unrelated, indicate that a linear and parallel development of the various indices of modernization is not necessarily the salient pattern. The uneven development of indices of modernization, one of the most crucial questions concerning instability in the developing countries, can be approached at several levels: from reflections upon the unevenness within the status of individuals or small groups through a comparative study of the modernization of specific institutional spheres (the polity, the economy and so on), ending with the examination of the relationship between the center and the periphery.

Particular emphasis need not be placed upon the significance of the concepts of center and periphery, since these have been so ably dealt with by Edward Shils.[9] Their prime importance is the capacity of the center (capacity here being equivalent to strength) to cope with the problem of social mobilization in the periphery and within the center itself. Social mobilization means substructural differentiation encouraging the crystallization of new social groups or the recrystallization of older (and disintegrated) groups and thereby creating a new balance of power. On a more abstract level, the interaction between the center and the periphery reflects the actual state of uneven development and the low level of sustained growth. Concepts such as *strength* of the center and *differentiation* are complex and must be defined more precisely. For the sake of both simplification and clarity in the presentation of a number of hypotheses, two main dichotomies leading to the formulation of four prototypes are suggested. These two dichotomies are: (a) the strength of the political center (strong versus weak) and especially its capacity to deal with the direct and indirect consequences of modernization; (b) the degree of institutional differentiation, a process that produces numerous new social, economic and political power centers, which become the foci of new demands and claims (high versus low).

These dichotomies give rise to four types, which are presented in Chart 1.[10] This is a very crude typology and will necessitate further elaboration.[11] Despite its simplified appearance, the chart offers four *prototypes* of situations or different stages of modernization (although not necessarily according to the order presented here).

Two basic assumptions are connected with these prototypes.

First, the extent of *stimulation* and temptation to institutional or noninstitutional, legitimate or illegitimate role expansion of the military or other groups differ according to the specific prototype. Second, the ability of the ruling elite to cope with the various groups' *predisposition and propensity* toward role expansion, varies from one prototype to another according to the character and magnitude of the problems and the *power* of the groups concerned.

The stimulus, the propensity and the power to intervene may serve as independent (or intervening) variables.

THE STIMULUS TO INTERVENE

Stimulants must be discovered from among the whole complex of ongoing processes together with the current effort to modernize the society in question. The character and scope of the problems to be faced will differ in each of the prototypes of powerbalance between the center and the periphery. The intensity and direction of these stimulants on the attitudes of the military will differ in each case. The four prototypes are:

1. A situation in which an *optimal* balance of power between the strength of the center and the differentiation of the periphery have been reached.[12]

2. A situation in which the power of the center is inferior to the task, i.e., it cannot cope with demands and pressures stemming from the accelerating process of differentiation, formation and consolidation of new groups within the periphery.

3. A situation in which the power of the center is overwhelming, leading to complete domination of the periphery.

4. A situation in which the power relations between the center and the periphery are more or less balanced. This is due to the weakness and retardation of both the center and the periphery.[13]

The importance of investigating whether there is any systematic relationship between these four prototypes and the various types of military elites suggested by various pieces of research should be noted.[14]

THE PROPENSITY TO INTERVENE

The propensity to intervene is contingent upon the general atmosphere prevailing outside the military establishment. It is eventually determined by the interpretation lent by the officer corps to developments outside the military establishment. This interpretation is inevitably dependent upon the structural and functional features of the military establishment.

Four prototypes are suggested to deal with issues included under the heading of the military's propensity to intervene. They are based on the assumption that many officer corps, especially in developing countries, are faced with a dilemma: the choice between emphasis on intensive pursuit of higher levels of technological, administrative and logistic standards on the one hand, and promotion of a *separatist* ideological identity and sense of exclusive corporateness on the other.

Type A: There is an optimum coordination between technological-logistic achievements and the scope of social cohesiveness and normative identity. This is the classical professional approach of the officer corps in democratic societies (see Chart 2).

Type B: The integrative and pattern-maintenance aspects are overemphasized. An example of this type would be partisan units, although this type can also be found in regular armies.

Type C: Internal balance is expressed by large-scale efforts on the part of the military to improve the professional level without maintaining internal cohesiveness and a satisfactory value system.

Type D: It is characterized by very low achievement in the logistic and technological spheres as well as in the cohesiveness-ideological sphere. These features were very typical of Latin American armies in the nineteenth century, of some Middle Eastern armies in the twentieth century and probably also of a number of contemporary African armies.

The possibility of linking the elements of the first set of variables to various types of interdependence between civilian and military elites was noted earlier. A similar suggestion is possible with regard to this second set of variables. Besides the already-mentioned typologies, the literature includes some rarer classifications dealing not with interdependence, but rather with analyses of the functions and orientations of military elites in connection with general issues and particularly with problems of development and change. To achieve a more comprehensive classification concerning the attitudes of the military elites towards change analysis should be founded on three basic variables.[15] The first is *entrepreneurial qualities of the military*. This refers to the degree of innovativeness inherent in the military's programs and actions when compared with the social structure as conceived of by the civilian elites (see Chart 3). Such innovative and entrepreneurial efforts may be exerted in different spheres, such as the political, the economic or the educational. The second variable is the degree of *ideologically articulated rationalization* evident in entrepreneurial activities. Four prototypes are produced by setting up these two dichotomized variables in a typology:

In the first case (type A), entrepreneurial traits in conjunction with their ideological rationalizations are at play. These attributes might cover a wide array of activities in the economic, political or in the education-socialization spheres.

Type B displays entrepreneurial traits too, although they are of less intensity and less steadfastly adhered to. Activities undertaken in the different spheres lack any clear ideological justification.

Type C does not usually reveal any tendency to initiate new organizational frameworks but concentrates on the best available means to allocate the flow of qualified manpower into its ranks. Identification (e.g. with the colonial heritage) provides the necessary ideological justification.

In type D, the principal motive of the army, or of its most powerful cliques, is consumption of the rewards of economic and political power together with social prestige. There is hardly any incentive to create new economic institutions and new general values.

The third variable is *effective power*. Here the focus is on the existence (or absence) of an absolute or relative advantage of the military as against other power centers, resulting from the control of resources available for use against real or potential adversaries.

These three sets of variables serve as the point of departure for a number of hypotheses. For example, a military establishment classified in the category I-B (see Chart 4) with regard to *stimulation* (i.e., the stimulation derives from a situation where a weak center is unable to respond and control the pressures from the periphery) would probably be of type II-B with regard to *propensity* all other things being equal (i.e., relatively neglecting purely professional achievement and overemphasizing social and ideological cohesiveness and solidarity). If the officers feel that they are indeed significantly superior (and therefore placed in category III-A with regard to other power centers) an attempted takeover of the political center would be almost inevitable. A study of this specific profile might help predict the character and scope of precoup role expansion and patterns of coping with national issues arising from the seizure of power.

Another hypothesis formulated with the aid of the chart might run as follows: where the military establishment becomes strengthened as a political power in a society in which the political and symbolic strength of the center is far greater than that of its adversaries (potential and real) outside the ruling elite (therefore belonging to type I-C),[16] the military will (at least initially) tend to emphasize the administrative and logistic aspects of the military system. In some cases, pseudo-ideological separateness might be promoted, and the officer will therefore be classified in type II-A or II-B. Here the relative superiority of the military is not guaranteed and, therefore, a great number of abortive coups are to be expected. This particular type of officer corps would probably not exhibit any entrepreneurial zeal or would restrict any such activities to the political sphere alone. Conspiracies would stem more from personal feuds. The successful junta would seek to establish a "praetorian regime."

When discussing theories of revolution, a distinction should be made between revolution and rebellion. One of the most erudite discussions of this issue is that of Johnson.[17] He accepts Hannah Arendt's definition that a *rebellion* is not involved in the challenge of authority or of the established order, but is always a matter of displacing the person holding the position of authority, either by replacing a usurper with a legitimate king, or a tyrant who had abused his power for a lawful ruler. Johnson also distinguishes between a simple rebellion and an ideological rebellion. The former is "not motivated by an ideology; the goal structure of such a movement is actually a fully elaborated structure of values that the rebels believe is still capable of organizing their communal life." The salient feature of an ideological rebellion is that is espouses "the revival or reintroduction of an idealized society that allegedly existed in the society's own past." These movements advocate the creation of a pattern of social organization which the rebels justify by a claim to traditional values, although they may actually break with tradition in many of the institutions that they seek to establish. The definition of *ideological rebellion* raises the question of its differences from the phenomenon of *revolution*. Johnson's answer is that only "when the goal culture of an insurrectionary ideology envisions the recasting of the social division of labor according to a pattern which is self-consciously unprecedented in the context of a particular social system, then we should use the term 'revolution.' " Johnson[18] further distinguishes between simple revolution and total revolution. In the former case, the revolutionary ideologies are restricted to fundamental changes of only a few values. In the case of total revolutions, the aim is to supplement "the entire structure of values and to recast the entire division of labor." In these definitions the ideological criterion is central to differentiate between the main types of revolutions. It would be insufficient, however, for specific typologies. Johnson's analysis is helpful in this respect too.[19] He contends that the concept of force and the wielding of force may be clarified if they are reviewed "in terms of the levels of socio-political organization upon which they impinge." He refers to three levels—the *governmental*, the *regime* and the *community* levels—suggesting that one add to the ideological criterion the target of the attack.[20] Other relevant criteria are the duration of violent activities, domestic violence and position with regard to mass participation. All these criteria (the general and the more specific) are helpful in distinguishing between different forms of violence directed against the ruling elite.[21] From these few examples, it is apparent that the analysis is not restricted to revolutions sponsored and led by the military. Scholars engaged in a

CHART 1

Strength Of The Center

	+	−
Extent of differentiation of the periphery +	A	B
−	C	D

CHART 2

Cohesiveness-Ideological Identity

	+	−
Technological and logistic achievements +	A	B
−	C	D

CHART 3

Level of Entrepreneurial Activities

		+	−
Level of ideo− logical articulation	+	A	C
	−	B	D

CHART 4

	I Stimulation: to interfere		II Propensity: to intervene		III Effective Power
	Center	Periphery	Logistic	Cohesiveness	Relative Superiority
A	+	+	+	+	+
B	–	+	–	+	–
C	+	–	+	–	
D	–	–	–	–	

study of military revolutions or rebellions suggest more specific typologies:

1. "Palace revolutions" or governmental coups, involving violence that is narrow in scope and objective: The main aim of the conspirator is to reestablish the authority of the government, which had been eroded by corruption, ineptitude or arbitrariness. This is done by changing the ruler without modifying the institution.[22]

2. Revolutionary coup: "It differs from the governmental coup not in the initial seizure of power but in the postcoup efforts to make basic social and economic changes and to alter the underlying distribution of power within the political system by subordinating some groups and adding or strengthening others."[23]

3. Reform coup: This type "falls somewhere between the first two. A combination of military and civilian groups seizes power intending to make reforms in the political, economic or social structures. They usually do make some reforms, though they do not instigate a convulsive revolutionary process."[24]

These three types chiefly define the conspirators' initial intention (or their strategic programs). They express neither the tactics nor the role and status of the revolutionaries within the military.[25] Another deficiency of these typologies is that they do not deal with the attitudes of the military towards the character, direction and rate of the mobilization of societal resources before the coup. It is important to carefully check the absence or existence of entrepreneurial qualities and the extent of ideological sophistication. Some fresh hints as to why and when officers resort to a particular type of force against the ruling elite may be gleaned from assessing the relative weight of each of these elements in the molding of the general objectives of the military.

The type of revolution eventually carried out, and the kind of regime imposed upon the population, are not the sole dependent variables to be sought for in this type of research. Another important dependent variable is the degree of success (or failure) of the revolutionaries in consolidating their power and establishing (or reestablishing) an effective and dynamic political and cultural center. In order to understand the reasons leading to the military's success (or failure) one must try to locate and analyze their main advantages and disadvantages as an agent engineering change and/or modernization.

The scope of either the success or failure of the military is primarily a function of the gravity of the problems faced. In this respect, there is no difference between military or civilian elites. Nonetheless, other things being equal, the military has some advantages and less disadvantages than do other groups.

What are the potential positive qualities attributed to the military which enable it to deal with the particular situations with which this study is concerned? Three main advantages can be cited:

1. Certain achieved qualities, absent or very insignificant in other sectors (especially in pretechnological societies) are customarily found in or attributed to the military. For example, the military is often a pioneer in the technological field. Willingness to develop and maintain a modern army compels even small and primitive armies to promote a trained cadre equipped with technological know-how, rarer in other sectors. Such experience is usually acquired through training in institutions in the more developed countries. One central result of graduation from an alien military (or civilian) institution is the adoption (albeit a selective one) of the norms prevailing within the foreign institution and society. It is therefore natural that the officers return, eager to inculcate in their soldiers some of the norms to which they have been exposed. The military, a social organization combining traditional structural features (ritualism, rigidity, hierarchy and so on) with a division of labor based on universalistic principles, provides a setting for absorbing unorthodox norms by people raised within a traditional framework.[26] One of the advantages of the military is the blending of traditionalism and innovation to restructure social life.[27] The innovative spirit is not merely a function of a different type of professional education, but is also linked to

the fact of belonging, both chronologically and mentally, to a younger generation. The officers can thus more readily capture the youth and identify with their sense of impatience.

2. Another advantage, attributed particularly to the officer corps but also to the entire military establishment, is that in the fragmented and already split societies it may serve as a new focus of solidarity and even as an embodiment of respected and sacred symbols. At face value, it would seem that the military is irreplaceable as a nation-builder. In fact, the implementation of such a project is fraught with many problems.

3. Even in societies where the military is less respected or prestigious, it still has the advantage of being the most highly organized and efficient system within the society. The fact of having at its disposal the resources and means to guarantee its establishment as an alternative elite enhances the likelihood that the military will become a more productive elite, if only in terms of providing a substantial level of security and stability.[28]

Many cases can be cited where these advantages did not lead to any gains. For instance, where the military had not become a focus of solidarity and suffered from internal cleavages with insignificant technological contributions to the backward sectors of the society. For this reason, so-called advantages of the military may not be unequivocally stated but must rather be termed *potential advantages*, which need not materialize in every case. Also, some potential advantages will probably be neutralized by potential disadvantages. When studying these disadvantages, one may find that a number of current assumptions are in need of reexamination and perhaps some myths may even have to be discarded.

One example of such a myth is that of the military's efficiency. Many armies in developing countries are small. Their limited size and the lack of serious challenges to their security (which is also indicative of a lack of opportunity for testing their skills) are reflected in a rather simple or even primitive administrative and logistic structure. The experience acquired by the officers, whether gained in field commands or in staff assignments, is limited even in comparison with experience accumulated by administrators in civilian occupations. In many cases, the officer corps is unable to handle problems of a complicated administrative nature efficiently, let alone to establish an administration which would be more effective than the existing civilian bureaucracy.[29]

Collaboration between civilian and military administrators may temporarily ease the burdens imposed upon the officers. But in the long run, such collaboration undermines the already shaky administrative framework due to vagueness in the interpretation of the flow of information. One inevitable result is a thinning out of the upward feedback which eventually leads to a distorted view of reality. The inability to cope with economic and administrative problems stems from inadequate training or qualifications and also from the fact that military expenditures often represent a severe drain on an impoverished economy. A defense budget is a burden to any modern economy, let alone a backward economic structure.

There is some correlation between a low rate of economic development and military intervention, but caution must be exercised in assuming a similar correlation between military rule and accelerated economic growth.

Another myth is to view the military as mediator between opposed groups. Administrative and economic knowledge is achievable, but does not contradict the basic tenets activating the military-bureaucratic network. This does not hold true for so-called "political know-how." The crucial weakness in the military's attitude is its inability to adjust to political bargaining. Analysis has revealed a varied list of direct and indirect factors attributed to this potentially debilitating characteristic of the military. Some scholars emphasize the psychological aspects of officer socialization in exclusive and closed training schools. The isolation of these institutions does not promote sensitivity to current public opinion. On the contrary, the typical graduate from military institutions is inclined toward dictatorial behavior and to a lack of tolerance towards "flexible interaction and interrelations of manifold power elements within the society."[30] As a complementary explanation, some refer to structural causes. Janowitz asserts that armies that have not yet achieved that level of technological, managerial and logistic development promote a mental affinity between military and civilian sectors and are less capable of dealing with civilian affairs and especially of promoting political communication.[31]

To summarize the above discussion on the shortcomings of the military in their efforts to extend and redefine their classical roles, we suggest the following hypothesis: The main weakness of armies, caught up within the process of modernization, is that because they are usually eager to ensure that reforms will be pursued at a faster rate and without any serious interruptions, they may destroy the societal networks involving the leaders of public opinion, vital to a two-way political interaction. On the other hand, officers are beset with almost insurmountable obstacles in their efforts to suggest alternatives to such social networks of opinion. The military ruler would find it difficult to articulate both manpower and ideas and to mold them into a new social movement intended to support military rule. A good example of these suggested alternatives are what might be called *nonpolitical models* of power relations. They are nonpolitical in the sense that they have few provisions for mediating conflicts and reconciling incompatible interests. They promote cohesion without consensus by balancing social forces against each other.

When considering the potential deficiencies of military rulers in the technological-managerial sphere, and particularly in the realm of political communication, we find that skills acquired in the army are not easily transferable to civilian life. The training undergone by the officer makes him more competent to prevent the exercise of political rule than to exercise it. In some cases, while in the throes of revolution, the military may be able to open up bottlenecks within frozen and rusty social frameworks. New bottlenecks follow rapidly, however, because of the military's ineptitude at providing new infrastructures designed not only to mobilize material assets but also to crystallize new contractual, i.e., technical reforms, guaranteeing basic defense, improvement of physical means of communication, and so on. Such reforms have some indirect repercussions on traditional political and social patterns, but they do not frustrate or confuse the officers, since they are still on familiar terrain. To the extent that the military is slipping outside of its domain—either voluntarily or pushed by circumstances—into the realm of more fundamental decisions (which might bring about important changes in the contractual principles uniting the society), it is treading on foreign grounds. Officers are most disturbed by the impact of circumstances compelling them to change their original professional image. This professional image was, in the first place, quite different from the so-called "classical" professional image and in some cases it must undergo even more radical alterations in order to accommodate to the military's role, namely to head a political system and provide a new kind of legitimation for contractual relations within the society.

The brief survey of the potential advantages and shortcomings of the officer corps as a ruling elite was aimed at underlining the fact that any analysis of the chances of success of military coups must take into account this ambiguous potential and test it against the background of the general conditions in which the coup takes place. There is no guarantee that each of the advantages will indeed materialize, and by the same token all the potential failings may not be revealed to the same degree or act to curb the army in similar ways. Coups are staged in different circumstances and their initial aims are not all identical. Bearing in mind the "natural" capabilities and weaknesses of armies as agents of modernization, it is possible to predict the chances of a particular military establishment in given circumstances. In order to improve predictability, a more sophisticated typology is needed. The main conditions (and their variations) conducive to military intervention should likewise be further defined.

This brings us back to the character of the center in terms of its complexity and the strength and character of the periphery in terms of its differentiation and fragmentation. There is a relationship between the success or failure of the military on the one hand, and the type of deposed elite or the political apathy of the masses on the other hand. This leads to the hypothesis that the military's chances to consolidate its power are greater in the early phases of the radical praetorian society, due to such factors as the limited pressure of the nonurban population at this stage.[32]

Finally, some remarks about an additional dependent variable should be presented. This dependent variable might be called the prospect of transferring from military to civilian rule.

There are two major types of transfer from a military to a civilian type of regime:

1. *Abdication* (or disengagement from overt military rule). Here the military (or the ruling junta) willingly—or unwillingly—hands the reins of power to civilian elites.

2. *Recivilianization.* In this case, the original military elite has gradually become civilianized. This shift in emphasis is both symbolic (such as the wearing of civilian clothing) and constitutional. The new constitution, following this transition, is supposed to redefine the separation of functions and of power between the military and other executive branches of government. It also should forbid soliders and officers on active duty to participate in partisan politics. The civilianized military elite takes over the leadership of a civilian political movement.

The above are two principal paths of "return to the barracks." In practice, there exist many in-between ways. One middle-of-the-road pattern (recently frequently adopted) is for the military to become, sometimes even formally, a functional group alongside other functional groups such as political parties, trade unions and so on. In their new capacity, the officers take on active and *legitimate* part in partisan politics. Most often, the military becomes a partner in a coalition government. This pattern, also typical of a precoup situation, may prevail in the period preceding the full restoration of civilian rule.

The interesting question here is: Under what conditions does this civilianization of military rule follow either the extreme patterns or some combination of them? Part of the answer lies in the character of the ruling military elite as it is challenged to redefine its public image.

We may distinguish between four types of military elites: (a) the entrepreneurial-ideological; (b) the non-ideological-entrepreneurial; (c) the ideological-nonentrepreneurial; and (d) the non-ideological-nonentrepreneurial.

From here it can be hypothesized that the military elite that evolved in the first place as an entrepreneurial and ideologically articulated system, while consolidating its power, will reveal more than any other type of elite a reluctance to relinquish its political control and return it to civilian hands. Such an elite would tend to civilianize itself and find proper ideological justification for so doing. This kind of elite would often argue that there is no place for alternative social theories nor for other competing social and economic programs. Its own programs appear to this particular type of elite as the only way to redeem the society from its agonies. One may hope here that personal motives, such as an urge for power, are only marginal and latent factors. The official and undeclared position, when encouraging such a policy, would be based upon the strong belief in the policy's diagnostic and therapeutic value.

Paradoxically, and for entirely different reasons, the nonentrepreneurial and nonideological military ruling elites will also probably prefer to become civilianized rather than give up their monopoly of power to civilian counterelites. In contrast to the case cited above, their major motives to pursue such a policy would be dictated by the desire to continue the personal enjoyment of the various rewards involved in a monopoly of political power.

For the two remaining types of military elites, it is reasonable to hypothesize that they will be inclined toward some kind of abdication or cooperation with the influential civilian partners. The ideological, nonentrepreneurial elite is generally conservative. It tries to introduce social reforms very gradually and for this reason it needs civilian partners. Such an elite will be ready to abdicate altogether when it feels that the civilian alternative would pursue more or less similar policies of gradual reform.

In the opposite case, officers who are enterprising in the economic and political spheres, but happen to be ideologically "sterile," might seek an adequate ideology among civilians, who might then become the chief partners in the government.

Empirical evidence supporting or disproving these hypotheses is unfortunately very meager. In the past there have been a number of instances, particularly in Latin America, of army withdrawal and "return to the barracks." These cases were all of one type, namely provisional abdication. No sufficient evidence is available of military elites of all four types who changed their constitutional status or who may be expected to do so. It seems nonetheless worthwhile to test these hypotheses, even if only a limited number of case studies can be examined.

NOTES

1. For reasons to be specified at a later stage, the broader concept of *role expansion* is preferable here to the narrower one of *intervention*, the application of which is generally restricted to the political sphere.

2. See also Raymond Tanter and M. Midlarsky, "A Theory of Revolution," *The Journal of Conflict Resolution* 2 (1967): 267.

3. Lawrence Stone, "Theories of Revolution," *World Politics* 18 (1966): 159.

4. Chalmers Johnson, *Revolutionary Change* (Boston, Mass.: Little, Brown, 1966), pp. 103-6.

5. Ibid., p. 91.

6. Cited in Stone, "Theories of Revolution," p. 167.

7. For the relationship between urbanization and exposure to mass media and level of education and exposure to mass media see Daniel Lerner, "Communications Systems and Social Systems: A Statistical Explanation in History and Policy," *Behavioral Sciences* 1 (1956). Also see Arthur S. Banks and Robert B. Textor, *A Cross Polity Survey* (Cambridge, Mass.: MIT Press, 1963). Matrix 45/29. On the level of education, income and industrialization, see Lerner "Communications Systems and Social Systems," and Karl W. Deutsch, "Toward an Inventory of Basic Trends and Patterns in Comparative Politics," *The American Political Science Review* 54 (1960): 54. On the rank order correlation between technological, economic and demographic indicators of modernization and the extent of urbanization and metropolization, see Leo F. Schnore, "The Statistical Measurement of Urbanization and Economic Development." *Land Economics* 37 (1961): 234. On the relationship between economic and political development, see Gabriel A. Almond and James S. Coleman, *The Politics of Developing Areas* (Princeton, N.J.: Princeton University Press, 1960), pp. 532-76; Seymour M. Lipset, "Some Social Requisites of Democracy, Economic Development and Political Legitimacy," *The American Political Science Review* 53 (1959); 87-90 and Lerner "Communications Systems and Social Systems," pp. 271-73.

8. A more or less complete list of those who oppose the previous approach can be found in C. S. Whitaker, Jr., "The Dysrhythmic Process of Political Change," *World Politics* 19 (1967): 193-99; David E. Apter, *The Politics of Modernization* (Chicago: Chicago University Press, 1965), p. 61; Samuel P. Huntington, "Political Development and Political Decay," *World Politics* 17 (1965): 387-93; and Deutsch, "Toward an Inventory of Basic Trends," p. 495.

9. Edward Shils, "Centre and Periphery," in *The Logic of Personal Knowledge: Essays Presented to Michael Polanyi on His Seventieth Birthday* (London: Routledge & Kegan Paul, 1961).

10. A number of other schemes, which may be of similar utility to the present one may be found in other works. The most useful and relevant to the problems raised here are those of Huntington, "Political Development and Political Decay," and Lipset, "Some Social Requisites of Democracy."

11. Further elaboration is required, especially in two particular directions: (a) more variables should be added (e.g., the rate of strength-consolidation or the decay of the central political power), (b) a simple dichotomization of the two dimensions is to be avoided.

12. The fact that each prototype may have some variations is being ignored here.

13. Another interesting typology is to be found in Samuel E. Finer, "The Military in Politics: Further Reflections on a Theme," unpublished, p. 2. Finer maintains that the military might find the justification to intervene in two entirely different situations. In the first instance, a lack of consensus regarding the rules of the political game is combined with a high rate of mobilization within various voluntary associations (e.g., in relatively developed countries). The second instance is when both the rate of mobilization and the degree of consensus are low.

14. There are a number of other examples of typologies. One typology, based on the distinction between military elites subjugated to a "subjective control" and those subjugated to an "objective control," is to be found in Samuel P. Huntington, *The Soldier and the State* (New York: Random House, 1957), ch. 4. A typology that classifies all civil-military relations into four major models—aristocratic, democratic, totalitarian and garrison state—may be found in Morris Janowitz, *The Military in the Political Development of New Nations: A Comparative Analysis* (Chicago: University of Chicago Press, 1963), Appendix. Janowitz also

distinguishes between the military as the instrument of sovereignty, the military as a partner in a political bloc and the army as a ruling group. Finer suggests four levels of military intervention: influence, blackmail, displacement of the civilian government and the supplantation of the civilian regime. See Samuel E. Finer, *The Man on Horseback: The Role of the Military in Politics* (London: Pall Mall Press, 1962), p. 139. Other typologies may be found in Irving L. Horowitz, "The Military Elites," in *Elites in Latin America*, eds. Seymour M. Lipset and Aldo Solari (New York: Oxford University Press, 1967); Davis B. Bobrow, "Soldiers and the New States," *The Annals of the American Academy of Political and Social Science* 358 (1965); and David C. Rapaport, "A Comparative Theory of Military and Political Types," in *Changing Patterns of Military Politics*, ed. S. P. Huntington (Glencoe, Ill.: Free Press, 1962).

15. Moshe Lissak, "Modernization and Role-Expansion of the Military in Developing Countries: A Comparative Analysis," *Comparative Studies in Society and History* 9 (1967): 250-51.

16. This is characteristic of personal autocratic regimes, based on a traditional elite rather than upon mass parties or other political groups.

17. Johnson, *Revolutionary Change*, p. 136.

18. Ibid., pp. 138-39.

19. Stone, "Theories of Revolution," p. 159.

20. For criticism of this approach see Ibid.

21. Ibid. As an addition to the general distinction between the two types of rebellion, there is another typology consisting of six types: (a) the Jacqueries; (b) the Millenarian rebellion; (c) the Anarchist rebellion; (d) Jacobin Communist revolution; (e) conspiratorial *coup d'etat*; (f) militarized mass insurrection. Other typologies are suggested in William Kornhauser, "Revolution and National Development," (Evian, France: paper presented at the Sixth World Congress of Sociology, September, 1967).

22. Ibid.

23. Samuel P. Huntington, "Patterns of Violence in World Politics," in *Changing Patterns of Military Politics*, ed. Samuel P. Huntington (Glencoe, Ill.: Free Press, 1962).

24. Ibid.

25. The question of tactics is not a relevant issue here. More important are the role and status of the coup leaders within the military. At least five main types may be noted. See Eliezer Be'eri, *The Officer Class in Politics and Society of the Arab East* (Tel Aviv:

Sifriat Paalim, 1966), p. 179.

26. See Lucien W. Pye, "Armies in the Process of Political Modernization," in *The Role of the Military in Underdeveloped Countries* ed. John J. Johnson, (Princeton, N.J.: Princeton University Press, 1962); and William Gutteridge, *Military Institutions and Power in the New States* (London: Pall Mall Press, 1964).

27. John H. Kautsky, "An Essay in the Politics of Development," in *Political Change in Underdeveloped Countries: Nationalism and Communism*, ed. John H. Kautsky (New York: John Wiley, 1962); and Irving L. Horowitz, *Three Worlds of Development: The Theory and Practice of International Stratification* (New York: Oxford University Press, 1966) p. 268.

28. Ibid.

29. Keith Hopkins, "Civil-Military Relations in Developing Countries," *British Journal of Sociology* 17 (1966): 172.

30. Ibid.

31. Janowitz, *The Military in the Political Development of New Nations.*

32. Samuel P. Huntington, *Political Order in Changing Societies* (New Haven: Yale University Press, 1968).

33. Finer, *The Man on Horseback*, pp. 190-204.

3
Political Style of the Guatemalan Military Elite

Jerry L. Weaver

During the final hours of March 30, 1963, a delegation of Guatemalan army officers led a contingent of soldiers to the *Casa Crema* (presidential palace). Entering the building without resistance, the officers confronted President Miguel Ydigoras Fuentes with an ultimatum that he resign to make way for an armed forces seizure of the government. After a brief pause to allow the president to collect his personal belongings, Ydigoras was escorted to a waiting air force plane and was quickly on his way to exile. Guatemala City awoke to discover that Ydigoras's minister of defense, Colonel Enrique Peralta Azurdia, had been declared chief of government in what was officially designated the *Gobierno Militar* (military government).[1]

Overthrow of the Ydigoras government was just another instance in a long line of political interventions by the Guatemalan armed forces. While military involvement in national politics dates from the

Field work in Guatemala (May 1965–June 1966) was made possible by a fellowship from the Henry L. and Grace Doherty Charitable Foundation, Inc. The author wishes to express thanks to the participants in the Study of the National Social Structure of Guatemala project for sharing their data and ideas with him. Special gratitude is owed Dr. Richard N. Adams, project director, and the Institute of Latin American Studies, The University of Texas, for support and encouragement throughout the preparation of this chapter.

1821 struggle for independence, 1944 marks the emergence of the contemporary political style of the Guatemalan armed forces. In 1944, elements of the armed forces joined with students and young progressives to oust dictator General Jorge Ubico. In 1949, disgruntled officers led an unsuccessful revolt against Guatemala's first democratically elected civilian president, Juan José Arévalo. But not until 1954 and the disaffection of many of its civilian supporters were the armed forces able to overthrow the revolutionary regime and Arévalo's successor, Colonel Jacobo Arbenz. The officer corps was instrumental in the destruction of the Arbenz government by refusing to defend it against Colonel Carlos Castillo Armas and his Honduras-based counterrevolutionaries.[2] Only three years before his overthrow, President Ydígoras barely survived a demand for his resignation and accompanying rebellion by elements of the armed forces.

The pattern of military intervention in national politics common to Guatemala is likewise found in many, perhaps most, Latin American nations, yet little is known about the ways, means and reasons of military intervention. Why do officers move against established governments? How do military-dominated regimes build and retain support? What are the characteristic means of maintaining control employed by officer-politicians? What role does the civilian politician play in military-dominated regimes?

The merits and demerits of military rule have been argued by many writers,[3] but few scholars have produced studies analyzing basic political processes in military-dominated societies. In this chapter, we will analyze military-dominated politics through the study of political decision-making during Guatemala's *Gobierno Militar* of 1963–1966. At the outset, this effort necessitates the identification of individuals and groups who controlled decision-making—the political elite.

DECISION-MAKING AND ELITENESS

Carl Beck and James M. Malloy point out that there is basic agreement in modern elite studies that the phenomenon of *power* is central to the notion of an elite.[4] But Robert A. Dahl argues that to state that "A" has power to do something by no means says that

"A" actually accomplishes it. that the concept *power* implies a static quality adhering to an individual or group and that for eliteness to have analytical utility a distinction must be made between power as a potential and the reality of politics. Dahl further suggests that it must be demonstrated that an individual or group actually exercises *control* over decision-making in order to meaningfully apply the label "elite."[5]

If the political elite is defined in terms of persons who exercise control over political decision-making, the focus of analysis becomes the decision arena. Here again the distinction between potential and actual control is central. Dahl points out, in his study of New Haven, that the identification of social or economic notables in a community is not synonymous with defining the operational elite structure. Dahl then suggests analysis of actual decisions as an effective index for determining the scope and intensity to which an individual or group exercises control.[6]

Thus our analysis of the Guatemalan political elite is made in the context of specific decisions made during the *Gobierno Militar*.

GUATEMALAN POLITICAL ELITE

Three basic policy questions continually recurred during the *Gobierno Militar* and they serve as foci for analyzing the political elite. First was a series of issues concerning the suppression of a small-scale but vigorous insurgency inherited from the Ydígoras regime. Numbering no more than 300 and split by ideological differences into two separate organizations, the insurgents nevertheless confounded all attempts to destroy them in the rural areas and to interrupt their campaign of terror in Guatemala City. Second, the *Gobierno Militar* dealt with a number of alternatives designed to reverse the economic decline continuing from the previous administration. Fiscal and monetary policy, administrative reorganization and public assistance to the private economic sector were repeatedly items on the policy-making agenda between April 1963 and July 1966. Third, the elite made a number of decisions affecting the scope and intensity of governmental intervention in and control of economic, social and political activities. Representative programs that were initiated by the *Gobierno Militar* and concerned the definition of public-private spheres including comprehensive public planning, tax reform, nationalization of the coffee industry and suppression of middle-sector political organizations.

Analyzing decision-making in the three policy areas reveals that the political elite of the *Gobierno Militar* was a complex coalition of military officers, economic notables and technocrats. Within the elite structure a series of subcoalitions formed as particular issues appeared and then dissolved as decisions were reached. No single coalition continually dominated a policy area or controlled an extensive range of issues. Disputes and sharp differences of opinion arose among the officers, economic notables and technocrats who composed the elite, but a thorough commitment to maintaining the existing mass/elite boundaries—reinforced by an elaborate communications network—and a willingness to compromise encouraged extensive intra-elite bargaining. Thus potentially disruptive intra-elite conflict was minimized and the grand coalition of officers, economic notables and technocrats prevailed.

Military Officers

The primacy of military officers within the elite coalition is reflected in their occupation of key executive, advisory and administrative positions. Senior military officers held the offices of chief of government; minister of the interior, defense and public finance; director-general of the customs service, national police, national prison, national ports; and several major autonomous public corporations. Likewise the 22 governors of Guatemala's administrative departments were senior officers. Other officers were found in executive positions throughout the public bureaucracy.

But this military cadre was no monolith. Factionalism within the armed forces produced a pattern of conflict for supremacy that mirrored the social, political and economic antagonisms of the greater Guatemalan society. Fratricidal violence occasionally appeared between the factions during the 20 years prior to the overthrow of Ydígoras. In 1949, for example, the followers of Colonel Francisco Javier Arana, army chief of staff and candidate of the conservative faction in the struggle to succeed President Arévalo, turned their troops and tanks against the supporters of Arbenz, minister of defense and heir-apparent to the presidency. In 1960, elements of the armed forces rebelled against President Ydigoras, himself an army general from the Ubico era. From this rebellion grew the insurgency that plagued the *Gobierno Militar*. The leaders of the two insurgent groups, Marco Antonio Yon Sosa and Luis Augusto Turcios Lima, were both young army lieutenants when they joined the 1960 rebellion.

Factionalism was produced by several factors: personality, ideology, opportunism, but none was more significant than the alignment of "officers of the school" vs. "officers of the line." The latter had received their commissions directly from the ranks, usually in return for supporting a senior officer or politician at some crucial juncture in a political struggle. On the other hand, the "officers of the school" were graduates of the National Military Academy. School officers indicated that line officers were uneducated, boorish, uncultured and "unprofessional," fit only to command ignorant recruits in remote garrisons. For their part, line officers, usually of marginal lower-middle-sector rural origins and older as a group than academy officers,[7] reacted defensively to what appeared to be snobbishness and punctiliousness by portraying school officers as too "liberal" and unaware of "communism." As proof of their accusations, line officers stressed that many academy graduates had been educated during the Arévalo–Arbenz regime (1945-1954) when the academy had been under the control of the "Reds." Verification of this "Red" tint was suggested by the fact that many of the 1960 rebels were academy-trained. Moreover, both Yon Sosa and Turcios Lima, as well as other insurgents, were academy officers (and graduates of United States Army training installations as well).

Factionalism found expression in partisan politics during the 1965-66 campaign to elect a successor to the *Gobierno Militar*. This campaign suggests that we might conveniently view the Guatemalan officer corps as an alliance of three competing factions: the Economic Reformers, the *Duristas* and the Moderators. Not all officers fell into one of these camps, some maintained independent positions; but those officers who demonstrated eliteness during the 1963-1966 period were firmly committed to one faction. In the

1965-66 political campaign, each faction advanced its candidate and two of the original three appeared (with a civilian) on the presidential ballot.

The Economic Reformers

One faction within the Guatemalan officer corps continually advocated major development programs and reforms to ameliorate the society's impoverished condition. Closely associated with Major Jorge Lucas Caballeros, minister of finance during most of the *Gobierno Militar*, this group supported the introduction of program budgeting, tax reform, public planning, administrative reorganization and reform and associated programs.

Cabballeros advocated measures that called for a more aggressive and expanded role for government in the economy. Similarly, he introduced and supported measures designed to protect Guatemala's infant industries and to nurture domestic enterprises through subsidies, tariffs and licensing restrictions that discriminated against foreign competitors. Caballeros eagerly solicited the support of moderately left-wing progressives and reformers while he attempted to create political organizations among the middle and lower sectors. In essence, Caballeros and his supporters offered a program of economic nationalism and a direct challenge to the prevailing social and political status quo. This program attracted many graduates of the military academy who were oriented toward national change and development. But at the same time, Caballeros repelled senior officers who looked forward to enjoying the fruits of the status quo. When Caballeros spoke of social justice as the prerequisite for national development, he raised the spector of *change*, an issue that divides many Latin American military establishments.[8] Not surprisingly, few senior officers were numbered among the reformers: the Economic Reformers reflected enthusiasm and innovation rather than seniority and status.

The response to the reformers' program among economic elites from mild support to outspoken condemnation. Businessmen and manufacturers struggling for credit or competing with foreign concerns for domestic markets responded favorably to pleas for protective tariffs, expanded public credit and related measures. On the other hand, planters, exporters of raw materials, financiers and others tied to external markets saw little profit from increased taxes, higher minimum wages, agrarian reform or expanded government support of and control over the national economy.

Individuals and organizations favorably disposed to economic reform and development reflected a new element within the economic elite: men concerned with profit and loss and technical innovation as opposed to traditional norms of social prestige and *patronismo* (patronage). These supporters of reform typically had emerged from the established middle sector, often since 1944, and many still faced a protracted struggle for survival. Characteristically, these individuals saw government as a positive instrument to be used for their personal advantage in contrast to the notion held by many established economic elite that government's business was restricted to punishment and protection. Many civilian supporters of Caballeros had been followers of President Arévalo. They had retained their commitment to progressive reforms and national development even after becoming disenchanted and finally alienated by the extremism and violence of the Arbenz regime.

Alone among the prominent officers of the military government, Caballeros looked to the middle and lower sectors for political support. While the elite structure generally was determined to preserve its hegemony by excluding new groups and interests from political participation, Caballeros joined hands with the Christian Democrats and the Guatemalan Socialist Party, two moderately progressive vehicles of nonestablishment politics. Major Caballeros seemed intent on offsetting his lack of following in the military hierarchy with support from elements of the new middle sector—men interested in genuine social and economic reform who were effectively disenfranchised by the status quo members of the political elite.

The *Duristas*

While Caballeros spoke about combating insurgency and unrest with basic social and economic reforms, another faction within the officer corps urged vigorous suppression and expanded military operations against all opponents of the government. During the

1965-66 presidential campaign, Colonel Miguel Angel Ponciano emerged as the principle spokesman of the *Duristas* (hard liners). As chief of staff, Ponciano repeated the theme of restoring discipline and order to Guatemala. The general theme of defending Guatemala against "communism" easily expanded into attacks upon labor leaders, intellectuals, reformers and anyone who happened to disagree with the status quo. Specifically, the *Duristas* sought to drastically reduce the scope of public control of the economy and governmental services to the lower sector.

The *Duristas* counted among their ranks a disproportionate number of senior and retired officers. Some of Ponciano's associates had supported the Ubico dictatorship; perhaps they saw in Ponciano the image of Ubico—the colonel's references to the sanctity of private property and the necessity of discipline compared closely with the doctrine of the former dictator. Other *Duristas* had risen to prominence after the 1954 overthrow of the Arbenz regime. Ponciano inherited most of the followers of former President Carlos Castillo Armas, the leader of the "Liberation Army" that had ousted Arbenz. Ponciano enjoyed the status of being both anticommunist and divorced from the military faction that had deposed many of Castillo Armas's followers after his 1957 assassination. The chief of staff appeared a restoration candidate with a strong possibility of success.

Among civilians the *Duristas* drew support from the (dogmatically) anticommunists, from many who had suffered expropriation or reprisals during the Arévalo-Arbenz regime and from the defenders of the status quo who repudiated even limited attempts at socio-economic reform. The hierarchy of the Catholic Church (but not many parish priests) firmly but quietly supported the candidacy of Ponciano. Joining the Catholic hierarchy were many retail and import-export interests, owners of large plantations and processors of export goods. All had a vested interest in the existing distribution of values, saw nothing to be gained from expanded welfare and public services, felt no compulsion to subsidize infant and generally inefficient industries and considered the proper role of government limited to providing physical protection to themselves and their property.[9] Subjective concern for the existing elite structure permeated the conversations of many supporters of the *Duristas*. Often this concern was expressed openly by statements of fear of the emergence of the mass-mobilizing style of politics practiced during the revolutionary era, 1944-1954.

The Moderators

Separating the two militant wings of the officer corps was a third faction, the "government party," that supported Chief of Government Enrique Peralta. Peralta eschewed factional identification and attempted throughout the *Gobierno Militar* to remain above factionalism. He even refused to endorse formally a successor, preferring to vindicate his oft-made pledge that his successor would be democratically and openly selected. The public spokesman of the "government party" was Colonel Juan de Dios Aguilar, Peralta's friend and advisor.

Johnson has written that military officers in Latin America do not find public control of the economy objectionable because they are bureaucrats themselves and because they come from essentially nonindustrial families.[10] While this proposition seems only partially valid for the Guatemalan officer corps, Colonel Peralta and the Moderators did accept many of the programs expanding the role of government in formenting and directing economic development advocated by the Reformers. With Peralta's support, a social welfare program was established as an autonomous executive agency; administrative, fiscal and monetary reforms were instituted; and military civic action was given official encouragement and was expanded in the areas of adult literacy training, hot lunches for school children and medical assistance to remote regions —particularly areas of insurgent activities.

At the same time, Peralta publicly adopted a vigorous anti-insurgency, anticommunist posture. In his speeches and interviews, Peralta's position seemed indistinguishable from that of the *Duristas*:

> We feel profound respect for all institutions, public and private, and we acknowledge and assure the fundamental human rights. But this does not mean that we are going to tolerate disrespect to authority or disorder, nor that

demagogues and criminals will enjoy leniency. Security and order are indispensable prerequisites for the realization of the values of economic and social evolution. Who disturbs the public order will be energetically reprimanded, and those who attempt against the security of persons, goods, institutions or the state will suffer forceful sanctions . . . Those who intend to bring communism to Guatemala will be destroyed without pity.[11]

Collectively the followers of Peralta incorporated many of the attitudes while avoiding the dogmatisms of the *Duristas* and reformers. Thus Peralta was able to play the role of moderator and honest broker since almost all of the officer corps recognized some level of philosophical identity with the chief of government and members of the "government party." Where compromise could not be attained on the philosophical plane, Peralta's following within the officer corps and the government enabled him to extract moderation and compromise in the cabinet. Lacking Peralta's support, neither of the two doctrinaire factions could muster a winning coalition since rarely could the militants unite to produce a majority. Occasionally Moderators broke rank and supported a militant position; this accounts for unexpected radical swings sometimes taken by the government. Two dramatic and unusually militant decisions accountable to temporary defections of Moderators were the placing of striking hospital employees under martial law and nationalization of the coffee producers' association. Such temporary dislocations occurred often enough to demonstrate the dynamic and flexible quality of intra-elite coalitions.

Informants close to the decision-making reported that the cabinet of the *Gobierno Militar* operated on a unanimity rule. When serious objections arose, the issue under consideration was tabled while informal discussions were conducted. Similarly, informants stated that when the chief of government expressed what he felt to be an equitable compromise, opponents gave way.

The fastidiousness with which the chief of government and his followers pursued compromise and the willingness of their more dogmatic colleagues to comply suggests that the military elite recognized that the unity of the officer corps was prerequisite to other individual and group values. Indeed, recent Guatemalan history demonstrated that fracture of the corps was followed by rapid erosion of valued privileges and rewards. In 1944 and in 1949 the officer corps had become irreconcilably divided and civilian politicians displaced senior officers in the political elite while established leaders of the corps were either replaced or forced to share control with junior members. The civilian/junior-officer coalition that arose from the intra-corps strife of 1948 (i.e., the Arbenz government) nearly succeeded in displacing the armed forces from their invaluable position as sole possessors of the means of violence early in 1954 when attempts were made to create an armed peasant and worker militia.[12]

As Guatemala's best-organized institution[13] and commanding unequaled political resources (disciplined and organized subordinates, arms, communication systems, wealth and, perhaps most importantly, experience in politics), a unified officer corps pre-empted political power. As long as this situation existed, the material privileges enjoyed by the armed forces could not be effectively diminished. These privileges included access to duty-free imported goods and discounted domestic merchandise, subsidized housing, government-provided servants, doctors, cars and other luxuries; preference in obtaining positions in the diplomatic corps and the public bureaucracy; and liberal retirement benefits. In addition, active and retired officers enjoyed virtual immunity from civilian judicial authority—an immunity that approached if it did not equal the ancient estate of *fuero militar* (military privilege).

But perhaps the most significant and basic privilege possessed by the armed forces was that of ultimate arbiter of national political affairs.[14] Three weeks before the formal ouster of President Ydígoras, the then minister of defense, Colonel Peralta, announced that, contrary to the verdict of the Guatemalan Supreme Court and the stated policy of President Ydígoras, the armed forces would not permit former President Arévalo to return to power if he won the upcoming scheduled election. President Ydígoras remained firm in his support of the court's decision. Within three weeks, Ydígoras was living abroad in exile.

A similar exercise of military sovereignty occurred after the victory of the lone civilian candidate in the presidential election of

March 6, 1966. Amidst rumors of a *golpe* (coup) by disgruntled officers to prevent the inauguration of the civilian government, a series of meetings took place between Colonel Peralta and high-ranking officers. Peralta declared that the armed forces would respect the decision of the electorate *if* the president-elect agreed to permit the officer corps a free hand over internal military matters (selection of the minister of defense, chief of staff, garrison commanders, budgets, and so on), to retire no more than 200 of the 400-plus colonels on active duty and to exclude all "radicals" (i.e., followers of Arévalo, members of the Revolutionary Democratic Union [URD] and other revolutionaries) from the new government. Consultations with the president-elect produced a pledge to honor these demands and it was publicly announced that the armed forces stood ready to guarantee a peaceful and orderly transfer of authority.

The moderate reforms introduced by the Peralta government were supported throughout the established middle sector: bureaucrats, owners of middle-sized plantations, retail, professional and service interests. This segment of the population with deep roots in Guatemalan history had developed an accommodation with the political elite. In return for forfeiting their political ambitions and accepting the status quo, the middle sector received jobs in the public bureaucracy, schools for their children, economic and personal security and the status that came from exercising the powers and privileges delegated them by the ruling elite. This comfortable arrangement was rudely disrupted and temporarily suspended during the revolution. Representatives of the lower sector were given traditional middle-sector jobs in the public bureaucracy and were recruited into the cadre of revolutionary political organizations. Reforms were instituted with the aim of enfranchising the lower sector. Thus the revolution's socio-economic reforms openly and directly challenged the economic security and social-political status of the established middle sector. Not surprising, therefore, was the established middle sector's support of the Moderators' emphasis on limited economic reform within the context of preserving the post-1954 distribution of political power and influence.

The Guatemalan economic elite was divided in its support of the

Moderators and the "government party." Interests concerned with expanding local consumption and developing domestic industry preferred the more aggressive policies of the reformers. Other economic elite fearful of "communism" and "totalitarian" government appreciated Ponciano and the *Duristas*. Nevertheless, Peralta and the Moderators drew widespread, if not enthusiastic, support from the economic elite. It was commonly thought that a victory at the polls by either the reformers or the *Duristas* would plunge the nation into civil war. Correctly or not, many economic elite believed that the reformers would never submit to the reactionary *Duristas* and vice versa. Insuring a victory of the Moderators by supporting the "government party" seemed the surest means of preventing civil war. Aside from these speculative reasons, economic elites supported the Moderators because business acumen dictated that economic interests should cultivate favorable relations with the existing government since Guatemalan regimes typically practiced self-perpetuating politics. By early 1966, Moderators and their civilian allies had created an imposing political organization, thanks in large measure to their access to the vehicles, funds, talent and jobs of the public bureaucracy. Colonel Peralta's disclaimers notwithstanding, many economic elite foresaw a continuation of the *Gobierno Militar*—especially as embodied in the candidacy of Aguilar and the "government party." For whatever reason, a number of prominent industrialists, lawyers, financiers and planters publicly associated themselves with the policies of the Moderators and supported the presidential candidate of the "government party."

Economic Elite

Guatemala's economic elite—industrialists, retailers, financiers and planters—constituted the second element in the political elite of the *Gobierno Militar*. Unlike Latin American elite structures of the nineteenth and early twentieth centuries, the Guatemalan economic elite was not synonymous with the country's social nobility or "old families." Representatives of this preindependence landed aristocracy were found among the economic elite but were far outnumbered by men whose wealth and power was less than a century old. Indeed, counted among the economic notables were not only individuals who had risen from the local middle sector but also members of ethnic minorities (Jews, Lebanese, Chinese) as well as late nineteenth- and twentieth-century European immigrants, especially Germans. North Americans quietly but effectively operated within the political elite, either as owners or managers of business enterprises. Sons of the middle sector, immigrants and foreigners were not counted among the uppermost social strata, but as advisors, ministers and spokesmen of associations that exercised widespread control over the formulation of economic policy.[15]

Members of the economic elite exercised control over political decision-making continuously but their involvement was restricted to issues which they perceived to directly affect their personal or group interests. For example, during the debate within the government over the introduction of comprehensive national planning, notables were very much in evidence and actively attempted to legislate their preferences. On the other hand most economic elite ignored the formulation of the various counter-insurgent programs—although they certainly opposed the insurgency—until the terrorists began kidnapping wealthy industrialists and blackmailing businessmen.

Presence of economic notables within the ruling elite was clearly useful to the Peralta government. First, as civilians, the notables provided legitimacy to a de facto government. As Finer has pointed out, governments coming to power (illegitimately) must defend themselves against one challenge after another, and only by securing the cloak of legitimacy do such governments effectively slam the door of morality in their challengers' faces. Not only does legitimacy act as a bar to the challengers, it also facilitates acceptance by subjects of commands set down by rightful authority. Finer suggests the analogy of the schoolmaster who controls his charges without constant resort to force because obedience is secured by recognition of the authority vested in his office: it is socially sanctioned to obey the schoolmaster, and so they do so.[16]

At the same time, the economic notables brought the government much needed expertise: managerial skills, professional experience, technical competence and the invaluable heritage of experience in dealing with civilians. Little wonder that members of the economic elite were found in the cabinet, on policy-making boards and commissions and in executive positions throughout the bureaucracy. Furthermore, the notables associated with the *Gobierno Militar* provided Peralta and his colleagues with convenient and regularized points of contact and channels of communication to individuals and groups controlling wealth, social status, skill, information and other politically relevant values.[17] By dealing continuously with a number of notables, the Peralta administration was able to assess the views and to anticipate reactions of a politically significant segment of Guatemalan society. Through repeated and prolonged dialogue the government built and retained the support of individuals who had experience in politics and a personal stake in the community. Consequently, the presence of the civilian economic elite reduced the potential of an effective antigovernment movement. Civilians who might become or sponsor counter-elites were provided ample opportunity and procedures for airing their views. Indeed, they were able to exert influence, to exercise power and even to shape policy in areas of their concern. Whether consciously or not, the military officers materially strengthened their control by involving managers of the economy in political decision-making.

The reciprocal of this arrangement was the expression of the interests of economic elites in public policy. For example, the reformed tax laws enacted by the *Gobierno Militar* provided generous exemptions to industrialists and planters, but weighed heavily on shopkeepers, self-employed professionals and other middle-sector interests not counted within the elite. Similarly, the government's investment program emphasized electrification, highway construction and other capital improvements of direct benefit to the economic elite to the exclusion of social-welfare and public-service programs.[18]

While not all economic interests were equally successful in exercising control over policy, financier and planter, retailer and industrialist alike benefited indirectly from the programs of the Peralta government. They benefited in the sense that the status quo allocation of political power and the existing demarcation of governor and governed were assiduously guaranteed. The government took no action to upset the hegemony of the employer over labor, the predominance of the planter in the local rural community or to revoke the powers delegated to the established middle sector. Thus, even where direct control was denied certain economic elites, the *Gobierno Militar* continued the post-1954 policy of permitting notables and officers to define the scope and content of national politics.

Technocrats

The third element of the 1963-66 political elite was the technocrats—engineers, economists, managers of large business operations and others whose main stock in trade was technical skill and expertise. Emphasis on economic development during the Peralta administration stimulated the demand for technical skill and sophisticated advice at top-level decision-making. Few officers or economic elite possessed such attributes and the established coalition had to look beyond its membership for assistance. Consequently, the doors to decisional arenas were opened to various technocrats. Minister of Finance Lucas Caballeros as much as any single individual was responsible for the initial recruiting of technocrats and officers of the Bank of Guatemala, economists, agricultural specialists and bureaucrats and advisors from other agencies were drawn into planning and evaluation of specific programs. Thus the Peralta administration witnessed the appearance of technical skill and experience alongside wealth and the means of violence as bases for political eliteness.

Experience and skill enabled technocrats to exercise a degree of control over decisions concerning fiscal and monetary policy, specific programs and priorities, and in negotiations with foreign governments and business interests. Significantly, however, this competence was restricted to implementive or tactical decisions; questions of major policy remained beyond the technocrat's grasp. The relatively limited demands for technical expertise generated by the primitive Guatemalan society and the unwillingness of the officers and economic notables to expand full membership in the political elite combined to deny the technocrat a full role in elite circles.

Nevertheless, advent of the technocrat as a member, albeit only a junior member, of the political elite represented a basic change in Guatemalan politics. Where the traditional political elite had recognized only wealth, social status and control of the means of violence as criteria for eliteness, the events of the 1963-66 period introduced a new dimension, a new basis for entry into political decision-making. The traditional mass/elite boundary was significantly modified. This redefinition of elite recruitment criteria did not indicate a complete departure from closed decision-making, but the officer-notable coalition clearly admitted a pragmatic tolerance toward admission of new elements into the elite structure.

Perhaps more significant for the political development of the society, the technocrat differed fundamentally from his colleagues in defining solutions to Guatemala's basic problems. Characteristically, the technocrat attributed Guatemala's ills to economic disharmonies and proposed solutions based on economic reforms. The insurgency and general social unrest should be checked by programs that expanded the economy such as agrarian reform, industrialization, fiscal and monetary measures. Jobs and land, not bullets and prisons, were the technocrat's answer to the communist threat.

The technocrat also saw necessity for new political procedures in order to produce the essential social changes he sought. Engineers, technicians, college-educated administrators and other members of the new middle sector complained, during the 1965-66 presidential campaign, that they had no legitimate alternative. Only parties acceptable to the status quo political elite had been granted a place on the ballot. Unlike members of the established middle sector, the technocrat was unwilling to forego politics: indeed, he was highly politicized and demonstrated familiarity with international as well as domestic issues. Furthermore, the technocrat saw organized labor and lower- and middle-sector political organizations as useful and manageable political vehicles. Unlike the officers and economic elite, the technocrat was confident that these organizations could be directed and made to serve the interests of the new middle sector. Consequently, the technocrat favored expanding the national political participation to include middle- (if not lower-) sector interests.[19]

Few in number, with neither political vehicles nor organized bases of support, technocrats emerged during the *Gobierno Militar* as a force for change. In the political arena, no less than social and economic systems, the programs and ideas of the technocrat stimulated developments which in turn produced even greater reliance upon technical skills and experience. Still, the technocrat had far greater impact on the economic system than on the political life of Guatemala. As Carl Beck has pointed out in another context, although technical experts advance into the political elite, one cannot assume the result will be rationalization of the political system.[20] Specifically, throughout the Peralta administration, technocrats were either forced or persuaded to accept a restricted exclusive form of political participation for themselves and the middle and lower sectors.

CONTROL TACTICS OF THE POLITICAL ELITE

Assimilation of technocrats into the elite structure posed a problem common to every political elite: how to maintain intra-elite stability while continuing to control the society. Each elite evolves its own norms and procedures for meeting what is in essence a two-fold control requirement. Such methods involve the interaction of tradition, immediate past experience, ideology and elite perspectives of the situation. For example, an elite realizing its existence is being threatened might resort to such tactics as secret police, concentration camps and random terror to maintain control of the situation. On the other hand, an elite committed to democratic procedures would be forced by the tenets of its ideology to abjure terror and arbitrariness in favor of nonauthoritarian measures such as consensus building and demand satisfaction. The tactics employed by an elite to maintain control define the elite's political style.

Elite-Mass Norms

Until the revolution of 1944, the Guatemalan political elite exercised control over the nation through a system of delegated responsibilities: that is to say that, within each social subsystem, the national elite was represented by an agent. In the traditional Indian communities, the *caciques* (elders) formed the link between the elite and communal constituencies. Outside interference was unknown as long as the traditional leadership continued to meet certain well-definied obligations. These entailed providing labor gangs for plantation work and public construction, seeing to it that the preference of the national elite was reflected in local election returns, reporting to local officials the presence of labor organizers, political agitators and other undesirables and generally reflecting disapproval of innovation within the traditional community.[21]

On plantations and in the fledgling industries of the pre-1944 era, the *patrón* wielded authority limited only by his personal values. Vagrancy laws replaced debt peonage but the effect on the lower sector, and particularly the Indian, was the same. Resistance or violence brought reprisals from which there was no appeal.

In the administrative realm, the pre-1944 national elite was represented by the government, which in turn was represented on the local level by the *jefe político* (political boss). The effect of this relationship between elite and government was to provide the local official not only the authority base of the government but also the support and resources of local planters and other notables.[22]

The revolution of 1944 destroyed the traditional mass-elite relationships.[23] During the Arévalo-Arbenz regime, revolutionaries made determined efforts to mobilize and politicize Indians, labor and the middle sector. Political organizations, *campesino* leagues, hundreds of labor unions and scores of cooperatives were created and came to play a major role in developing political awareness and participation. A labor code, agrarian reform laws and welfare programs were enacted to free the lower sector from the traditional elite. Labor courts became decidedly pro-labor. Representatives of revolutionary political parties and reform-minded bureaucrats urged landless peasants to press for the expropriation of plantation holdings. Labor organizers led strikes to obtain higher wages and better working conditions. Reforms and policies of the revolution replaced the *patrón, cacique* and *jefe político* with governmental institutions receptive to the demands of the citizenry. Mass manipulation and demand satisfaction became the instruments of the revolution in the lower sector while the remnants of the traditional elite were ignored.

The counter-revolution of 1954 proved that the followers of Arévalo and Arbez had been overly optimistic in evaluating their strength in the lower sector and unwisely permissive with their upper-sector opponents. The revolutionaries had succeeded, however, in mortally wounding the traditional mass-elite control system. Agrarian reform committees and labor unions had created irreparable hostilities and animosities between *patrones* and laborers. At the same time, new industries had been created and new crops introduced—cotton, for example—that placed the premium on profit, not the social status of "owning" a large number of residential workers. And ten years of politicization had awakened segments of the middle and lower sectors to the realization that improvements could be obtained through political action. New means of reestablishing control had to be devised by the post-1954 elite.

Initially, Castillo Armas's so-called "Liberation Government" relied heavily on detention, censorship and the threat of denunciation to control the society.[24] Armas's successor, General Ydígoras Fuentes, lifted the most repressive features of the Liberation regime, choosing to indulge the lower sector with public housing, expositions, school construction and other impact projects. Liberalization of the Ydígoras period emptied the public treasury, but failed to meet Guatemala's basic social and economic problems. Ydígoras's ineptness succeeded only in exacerbating the frustrations of progressives and conservatives alike.[25]

Following the Ydígoras administration and inheriting social unrest, economic decline and growing demands for political participation from the middle and lower sectors, the *Gobierno Militar* sought to protect the established mass-elite boundary by an attitude of resistance to demands for reform. Occasionally, resistance was reinforced by limited repression of especially vigorous antigovernmental elements. Characteristically, the Peralta administration followed a policy of strangling actual and potential counterelite organizations.

Through bureaucratic procedures and a hostile public attitude, obstacles were placed in the path of any organization with the potential for becoming what S. N. Eisenstadt calls a "free-floating resource": an organizational vehicle for political action that is not dominated by the established elite.[26] Informally, the creation of such organizations was discouraged by the attitude of the elite and its representatives. When a senior bureaucrat was asked in 1966 about the presence of a public administration association or society, he replied that none existed. "When you talk of societies *they* think you are plotting against the government, so you go to jail. We tried to form a public administration society a few years ago, but no luck. Most people were too frightened." When asked to identify "they" the bureaucrat replied: *"Los políticos"* (the politicians).

Formal steps were taken to restrict and discourage popular political participation. An electoral law was decreed that required organizations desirous of the designation "political party" and a place on the ballot to submit petitions signed by at least 50,000 eligible voters. Two pre-1963 parties, the Movement of National Liberation (MLN–Castillo Armas's party) and the Revolutionary Party (PR) along with a newly formed "government party," the Institutional Democratic Party (PID), were speedily certified. Both the MLN and the PID were controlled by the elements of the officer-manager elite. PR had supported the ouster of President Ydígoras and had collaborated with the *Gobierno Militar* by participating in local elections and the assembly's drafting of a new national charter. Within the framework of Guatemalan politics, PR was left of PID and the reactionary MLN, but was still decidedly conservative.

Nascent political organizations that attracted the support of intellectuals, labor leaders and organizers, young professionals and other reform-minded individuals were barred from the ballot. Leaders of the most radical party, the Revolutionary Democratic Union (URD), were exiled shortly after the advent of the *Gobierno Militar*. Throughout the 1963-66 period, the party's local cadre was harassed by the *judiciales* (secret political police) and *comisionados militar* (members of local military reserve detachments charged with internal security duties). The Guatemalan Christian Democrats (DCG) submitted petitions containing over 57,000 signatures to the Electoral Registry. After weeks of review, legal status for the DCG was denied on the grounds that only 49,275 eligible voters had been confirmed. This decision was handed down shortly after the deadline for submitting applications, thus effectively preventing a follow-up petition that would have contained the necessary 725 signatures. Similarly, the Guatemalan Socialist Party (PSG) was prevented from gaining a place on the ballot by a bureaucratic *fait accompli*. The director general of national security refused to permit the certification of the PSG because, he declared, its rolls contained the names of 734 persons found in the "Black Book" of suspected subversives.[27]

During the Arévalo-Arbenz regime, labor organizations played a major role in politicizing the middle and lower sectors. Just prior to Arbenz's fall, the labor movement claimed over 500 organizations enrolling 100,000 urban workers. All unions were disbanded by Castillo Armas and many of their leaders jailed. While the Peralta administration continued the liberalized policy of the Ydígoras government and desisted from physical attacks on unionists, procedural handicaps reinforced by a hostile official attitude effectively undermined efforts to revive the union movement. All prospective unions were required to register and receive official sanction—a process that typically consumed six months—before they could engage in any type of activity. Union officials were restricted by law to a single two-year term, thereby effectively disrupting continuity of leadership. Procedural handicaps were augmented by a decidedly anti-labor, pro-management attitude in the Ministry of Labor and throughout the government. When unions or individual laborers were involved in legal actions, it was extremely difficult for them to secure lawyers or to receive speedy hearings. In the face of the official policy of studied indifference, the Guatemalan labor movement of 1966 was able to muster four score organizations totaling no more than 25,000 members.[28]

The history of the cooperative movement in Guatemala parallels that of organized labor. During the 1944-1954 period, considerable attention was paid to the formation of cooperatives—both credit and marketing. Scores of coops with thousands of members were created during the revolution. Not only were these organizations instrumental in improving the economic conditions of their members, they also served as nuclei of political socialization. Along with labor leaders, members of agrarian reform committees and revolutionary politicians, leaders of cooperatives were arrested in 1954 and their organizations were abrogated.[29] The post-liberation political elite sought to discourage organizing activities among the lower and middle sectors. Even after the declaration of the Alliance for Progress with its emphasis on self-help and community development, the Guatemalan elite scarcely supported the formation of cooperatives.

During the Peralta regime, efforts at reestablishing cooperatives were made by local Christian Democrats, U.S. Peace Corpsmen, individual priests and an occasional representative of the government. The US/AID mission in Guatemala City advocated coops and made loans and technicians available to communities interested in forming an organization. By the end of the *Gobierno Militar*, the advocates of coops had succeeded in establishing about 150 organizations with a total membership of about 12,000 individuals. Not all cooperatives, however, were active.[30]

The limited success of the coop movement reflected a complex of factors including official hostility. For example, on February 1, 1965, the Guatemalan press carried the story of the expulsion from the country of a Spanish priest, Father Luis Guniarón. Father Guniarón was being transferred from Guatemala at the request of the government after he had been charged by a departmental governor with "teaching communism"; Father Guniarón had been instrumental in the formation of several cooperatives among his Indian parishioners.

The government's attitude toward cooperatives was explicitly demonstrated in its support of the administrative agency charged with assisting the formation and supervising the development of cooperatives. The cooperative section of the Ministry of Agriculture was grouped with the Department of Poultry Production, granted a total appropriation of $23,280 by the national budget of 1965 and stripped of travel funds.[31]

Official indifference and occasional outbursts of hostility towards unions, parties and cooperatives only partially explain their limited success. The attitudes of the government must be viewed against the background of the persecution and violence of the liberation to understand fully why anti-establishment movements languished.

Many of the individuals responsible for the post-liberation repressions and terror were closely associated with the *Gobierno Militar*, either as officials or members of the political elite. To be denounced as a "communist" meant detention and imprisonment as well as registration by the National Security Archive. Furthermore, during most of the Peralta administration it was unclear who would control succession: the likelihood of a victory by the *Duristas* and their allies weighed heavily in the minds of potential activists and leaders of the lower and middle sectors. The election of Colonel Ponciano, it was said, might well signal the return of violent repression and terror.[32]

Where legal obstacles and administrative delay, indifference and hostility failed to discourage counter-elite activities, the Peralta administration resorted to limited and generally moderate repressive measures.[33] The vehicles of this policy were the secret political police, the *judiciales* and the *comisionados militar*. The former infiltrated and spied upon middle- and lower-sector political parties, unions and associations and kept a particularly close surveillance over student organizations and activities. In the rural areas of Guatemala, these services were performed by *comisionados*.

Comisionados and their deputies were found in every population center—towns, villages, hamlets and even among the scattered settlements of plantation workers. Ostensibly, *comisionados* commanded local military-reserve detachments and served as local draft boards. During the military government, however, these unpaid agents undertook many local security tasks: observing and reporting the presence of insurgents, political organizers and strangers; accompanying military patrols seeking out insurgents; questioning, detaining and ordering the arrests of suspects. During suspensions of constitutional guarantees (i.e., state of alarm or siege) *comisionados* exercised authority limited only by their subordination to the military hierarchy—in other words, limitless authority vis-a-vis civilians. Individuals ordered arrested by *comisionados* were held by the armed forces and were, in effect, beyond the scope of civilian courts and due process of law.

While the *comisionados* were formally responsible to departmental reserve commanders and the military hierarchy, in reality local notables (planters, managers, politicians, retired military officers, and others) controlled the selection and deployment of *comisionados*. This informal arrangement made the local commissioner a truly powerful individual: he wielded public authority as well as influence derived from his close association with the local elite structure.

Occasionally the connection between the *comisionado* and the local elite was publicly verified. For example, during the 1966 harvest season, newspapers carried an account of a local reserve detachment being ordered into the fields to pick cotton. On another occasion, the local military commissioner acted as a labor contractor for a plantation having difficulty securing workers: a detachment of armed reserves visited nearby hamlets and forcibly persuaded Indians to climb aboard trucks destined for the fields. Other reports appeared of *comisionados* arresting union organizers and harassing URD, PSG and DCG meetings. Critics of the Peralta administration pointed out that draft levies were filled with Indians and members of families associated with labor or leftist organizations while the sons of local notables or supporters of the MLN or the PID were almost never selected for service.

The enrollment and extent of the *comisionado* system was a closely guarded secret, but an idea of its nationwide scope may be gathered from data concerning the department of Jutiapa. In this eastern region during the summer of 1965, some 971 *comisionados* and assistants were employed: a ratio of one agent to every 50 adult males.[34]

Elite Etiquette

V.O. Key coined the term "elite etiquette"[35] to describe the rules by which elites regulate their behavior, the norms that govern elite-elite relations and the customary techniques employed to control and avoid intra-elite conflict.

In pre-1944 Guatemala, intra-elite relations were characteristically tranquil and orderly—in large measure a reflection of the social homogeneity of the tiny membership. The prevailing elite etiquette was deferent to the prerogatives and spheres of interest of each segment and individual members of the elite: the Church, the armed forces, the planters and the businessmen.

Revolution and the 1950s precipitated the expansion of the elite structure, in terms of both individual membership and interests. The Arévalo-Arbenz regime encouraged the growth and development of domestic industries; new agricultural commodities and processes were launched; and retail and commercial service facilities—such as transportation, marketing and maintenance—expanded the wealth of

the society. By 1954, Guatemala had been shaken from the lethargy
of plantation agriculture. This economic transformation brought
large numbers into the political elite and heightened the potential
for conflict of interests and intra-elite friction.

No longer could the elite rely on face-to-face communications
and the informality associated with social intercourse to negotiate
and resolve differences. Where once a plantation-based economy had
fostered a wisespread identity of interest in social, economic and
political institutions, the post-1954 elite contained elements unable
to see the profit or prestige in maintaining 70 percent of the nation
at a subsistent level of consumption. When members of the political
elite advocated social and economic reforms as instruments of
national development, they made demands for expanded public
services. Spheres of control that had been historically defined and
traditionally respected came under increasing challenge and were
considered by many elites atavistic irrelevances.

By 1963, disregard for traditional elite etiquette and newly
emerging intra-elite competitiveness pushed the evolution of new
modes of conflict resolution and control within the political elite.
Where once a simple system of face-to-face communication had
sufficed, during the *Gobierno Militar* the political elite moved to
formalize communication through a complex network of channels
and points of contact. Throughout the Peralta administration the
central device in maintaining intra-elite contact with decision-making
was the associational-interest group. Reliance on communication via
these associations was a basic feature of elite etiquette.

The 60-odd associational interest groups of the Peralta era grew
out of and reflected the politics of the 1944-1954 period. Prior to
the revolution, only a handful of associations existed. These
organizations were loosely knit social clubs with little or no political
role.[36] During the Arévalo-Arbenz regime, a score of associations
sprang up. This development occurred in response to Arévalo's
efforts at fomenting industrialization and economic expansion
through government incentives—protective tariffs, tax concessions,
ready public credit. Individual entrepreneurs found that associations
facilitated public-private intercourse while enabling interested parties
to keep abreast of relevant technical and political developments.
Where Arévalo's policies encouraged industrialists and businessmen,

Arbenz's programs and public statements frightened the upper sector. Lands were expropriated, industries were struck and social reforms were inaugurated. Close friends and advisors of the president visited communist capitals and denounced capitalism and its imperialist supporters. In the face of this growing militancy and radicalism, planters, industrialists and businessmen looked to associations for leadership and public expression of their dissatisfaction with the government. Thus the Arbenz government stimulated the organization of sectoral and industrial mutual-protection societies.

But the associations of the revolutionary period received neither support nor encouragement from the regime. Arévalo and Arbenz were concerned with the organization of the lower sector in order to create politically aware and active supporters of the revolution. Between 1945 and 1954, the official attitude towards upper-sector organization moved from tolerance to hostility. The liberation reversed this trend and restored the officer-manager political elite. The accompanying pro-business, anti-labor disposition of Castillo Armas and his willingness to cooperate with the newly established economic elite produced a veritable explosion of association building. Between 1954 and 1964, more than 40 new business associations were formed. And within organizations of general or national scope, regional and specialized associations were formed. The national Chamber of Commerce incorporated 20 separate industry-wide associations; the National Coffee Association (ANACAFE) encompassed 17 regional organizations.

These associations became instruments for the articulation of views of the economic elites. In the traditionally prestigious coffee industry, the National Coffee Association published a monthly bulletin, *Revista Cafetalera*, in editions of 4,000 copies. *Revista* circulated technical information and editorial opinion throughout the industry and was delivered to government offices, other associations and the mass media. The industry received both scientific and political enlightenment. The government and other members of the political elite were informed of the views and attitudes of the socially and economically prestigious individuals who controlled the association.

While association meetings, conferences, newsletters and other communications techniques were continuously employed to express positions and influence decision-making, the primary function of the associational-interest groups was the nomination of representatives to office boards, commissions and councils. According to a 1962 decree, the board of directors of ANACAFE was empowered to establish domestic coffee-production quotas, collect export taxes, collect and distribute industry-wide statistics and appoint delegates to negotiate Guatemala's national production quota at conferences of the International Coffee Organization. These delegates were further authorized to sign the international coffee-quota treaty in the name of the Republic of Guatemala.

Nor was statutory authorization of decision-making competence peculiar to the coffee association. The 1957 decree establishing the National Municipal Development Corporation (INFOM) placed a representative of the National Municipal Association on the corporation's board of directors. The *Gobierno Militar* was merely following post-1954 policy when it created a Council of State to advise the chief of government and established its membership as representatives from the Chambers of Commerce and Industries, the Agriculturalists' Association, the private financial sector and one member from the legally chartered labor unions.

Without formal legal sanction, but nevertheless producing the same decision-making formula, was the government's policy of appointing representatives from the relevant associations to advisory and supervisory boards and commissions in such fields as public health, education, agricultural research and development, the peaceful uses of the atom and the Central American common market as well as a host of *ad hoc* delegations and conferences.

This policy of dealing almost exclusively with representatives of economic-interest groups and of delegating to them decision-making competence was not uniformly accepted within the political elite. Some economic reformers and technocrats wished to expand the scope and level of political participation. No doubt they understood that only by expanding the scope of conflict could they muster winning coalitions. In any event, technocrats and reformers took the lead in attempting to redefine the role of associations.

The outstanding instance in the battle to modify the existing interest-group style of politics was the struggle to nationalize

ANACAFE. This engagement merits consideration since it was not only a major decision during the Peralta administration, but also because it involved several diverse interests, spilled over into the public press and, consequently, provided an opportunity to witness a case of interest-group politics in detail. The swirl of men and charges and organizations presented an insightful picture of the political style of the Guatemalan elite.

INTEREST-GROUP POLITICS

As we noted above, ANACAFE had been invested with wide authority to control the coffee industry. This situation did not go unchallenged, reformers and their allies being especially critical of what they saw as an abdication of a sovereign prerogative (negotiating and signing treaties). Furthermore, reformers claimed that the association quotas discriminated against owners of middle-sized and small plantations. To retrieve national sovereignty and weaken critics of their programs, reformers urged that the association be made a public corporation subject to governmental control.

ANACAFE and its allies vigorously opposed nationalization—a position cited by reformers as proof of its domination by a small clique of coffee barons. The association and its supporters argued that if the government were not blocked, other organizations would fall under public control: the sanctity of private property and the spectre of emerging socialism were oft-heard themes.

Representatives of PID and the moderate faction were found on both sides of the nationalization issue, but Colonel Juan de Dios Aguilar and top officials of the PID argued that a massive disaffection of economic elites would result from nationalization, a disaffection likely to ensure PID's defeat in the upcoming presidential elections in 1966.

During December and January (1965-66), the economy of Guatemala suffered a sharp reversal, in part as a result of the flight of funds and delayed purchasing precipitated by terrorist kidnappings and extortion. Several of the government's principal economic advisors used this occasion to press for nationalization. Guatemala was faced with an acute economic crisis, the advisers argued, and it was necessary to establish complete control over the nation's principal producer of foreign exchange. At the height of the agitation for nationalizing the coffee association, Colonel Aguilar decided to abandon his presidential campaign for a brief vacation in Mexico. Less than 72 hours after his departure, Colonel Peralta signed *Decreto-ley* 417: ANACAFE was nationalized.

Breaking with normal procedure, opponents of nationalization took their case to the public press. Their strategy was to convince the government that not only coffee interests but also industrial, financial, commercial and other agricultural associations repudiated 417. In open letters, interviews and full-page advertisements, anti-417 forces attacked the government. Not since the weeks preceding the overthrow of President Arbenz had Guatemala witnessed such public displays of elite opposition to a regime.

The antinationalization material was rarely endorsed by individuals, although certain prominent agriculturalists did sign protests. Rather, associations were the vehicles of protest. Besides ANACAFE, the national associations of cattle, cotton and sugar producers as well as the General Association of Agriculturalists published attacks against the government. And these national organizations were joined by regional associations: the Eastern Coffee Growers Association, the West Association of Agriculturalists, and so on.

As newspapers ran their charges, anti-417 leaders held prolonged meetings with the minister of agriculture, other cabinet members and high-level bureaucrats. Leaders of PID attended these meetings while conducting their own private discussions with agriculturalists from various associations. The strategy of the anti-417 forces was to persuade PID officials that unless they were able to convince Colonel Peralta to repeal 417, the party would receive precious little support from agricultural interests in the March elections. PID was vulnerable to this strategy because the candidate of the MLN, Colonel Ponciano, had stated unequivocally his support for ANACAFE.

After little more than two weeks of discussions and public pronouncements, Decree 417 was a dead issue. In April 1966, the government formally announced what was already widespread knowledge: ANACAFE was being returned to private status. Furthermore, to help repair the damage done to the government's rapport with coffee interests, the new decree, no. 449, established an export tax on coffee from which ANACAFE would derive its operating capital.

But although Decree 449 represented a major retreat by the government, it was not a complete capitulation. Indeed, the cause of economic nationalism was considerably strengthened since the government retained the authority to nominate delegates to international quota-fixing conferences and to establish all domestic production quotas. As had been the procedure in post-revolution politics, this expansion of public jurisdiction was supplemented by a proviso formally incorporating a representative of the newly created governmental constituency in official decisional arenas: Decree 449 established a Council of Coffee Policy composed of the president of ANACAFE as well as the ministers of agriculture, economy, public finance and foreign relations. Thus while the coffee industry nominally fell under public control, its official spokesman was incorporated in the industry's governance.

The short-lived nationalization of the coffee association points to the most distinguishing characteristic of Guatemalan political elite etiquette: maintenance of the existing elite through moderation and compromise. Colonel Peralta had accepted nationalization in the first place because great pressure was brought to bear by reformers and their civilian allies. But when the scope and intensity of the reaction to 417 became apparent, Colonel Peralta and many moderators hurriedly sought a compromise, fearing an irrevocable split of the political elite. The argument that nationalization would seal the defeat of the PID and pave the way to civil war by ensuring the victory of Ponciano was said by civilian and military members of the government to have had great influence with Colonel Peralta. Colonel Peralta's conversion tipped the balance of power to the compromisers from PID.

In the compromise announced by Decree 449, the reformers' position emerged predominant: in the final analysis, the coffee industry was placed under governmental control and the authority of ANACAFE was curtailed in the vital areas of national quota negotiation and domestic production controls. We might speculate that the reformers won as much as they did because they appeared the least concerned of the major forces with maintaining the existing mass-elite structure. Since both the moderators and the anti-417 forces were firmly committed to the status quo allocation of political power, significant leverage passed to the reformers in the form of their implied threat to destroy the existing officer-manager coalition unless their demands were satisfied.

IMPLICATIONS

This review of the political style of the Guatemalan political elite suggests a combination of traditional Latin American authoritarianism and constitutional democracy. Like the former, the *Gobierno Militar* was controlled by an elite drawing its power from institutionalized interests: the military, plantations, corporations. But the elite system was a coalition, not a caste; officers and economic notables were the products of different social strata rarely interconnected by blood, marriage, commerce or society. Only among the top military leadership—the Poncianos, Peraltas and Aguilars—did military families mingle with notables, and then not with the "old families."

But like the traditional Latin American dictatorships, the various elements of the elite exercised considerable autonomy within their spheres of interest: senior officers over the armed forces, planters over rural Guatemala, industrialists over labor. Control was effectuated through deference, suppression and a benevolent despotism in which the "legitimate" claims of the mass were defined by the elite rather than by autonomous vehicles and spokesmen of the middle and lower sectors.

Following the constitutional style of politics, the military government accepted the legitimacy of opposition within both the elite and the mass. There was a noteworthy absence of fraud, corruption and coercion in the elections conducted during Peralta's administration. And if voters were denied a wide range of alternatives to military candidates, they at least had one: the Revolutionary Party. Whether this alternative was sufficient to warrant the adjective "free" in regard to the elections is a matter for debate. It is clear, however, that the victory of PR and its subsequent taking of office on July 1, 1966, marked a transfer of authority to leaders not directly controlled by the 1963-66 political elite. In the background, however, the armed forces retained veto power over the actions of the PR government.[37]

The mixture of authoritarianism-constitutionalism that marked the style of the 1963-66 political elite seems to favor the former. In large measure this is the product of the prevalent mass-elite relationship. Key has pointed out that a crucial norm of an elite committed to constitutionalism is its willingness to hear and be guided by the constituency, to be responsible and responsive to the citizenry.[38] In one sense, the Guatemalan political elite was responsive to its constituency—but only a constituency defined in terms of the officer-manager coalition. Until the political elite define their constituency as the entire society, Guatemalan politics will not fit the constitutional type.

The two decades between the revolution of 1944 and the *Gobierno Militar* produced a growing potential for political eliteness on the part of the Guatemalan armed forces. The overthrow of dictator Ubico and the failure of several attempts against Arévalo indicate the dependency of the military on civilian support. By 1960, however, the armed forces had grown in relative strength to the point that even a partial military rebellion could come close to toppling the government. Three years later, Colonel Peralta and his colleagues were successful in overthrowing an established regime without demonstrable civilian support. There were no mass anti-Ydigoras demonstrations by civilians. Only after the successful *golpe* did the military actively seek civilian support. In effect, since 1944, a number of factors combined to increase the political power of the Guatemalan Armed Forces.

In the first place, between the end of World War II and 1960, the Guatemalan military underwent professionalization. North American advisers accompanied new hardware to Guatemala and Guatemalan officers were sent abroad for training. As a result of these experiences, the Guatemalan military reached new and higher levels of corporate loyalty as well as technical expertise. During the 1945-1960 period, Guatemala developed what Finer describes as "military syndicalism": a recognition of a particular identity and a feeling on the part of the officer corps that it alone is competent to determine such matters as size, organization, recruitment, disposition and equipment of the forces.[39] The emerging mystique of professionalism combined commitment to the traditional privileges of the armed forces with newer "professional" attitudes. Conspicuously absent from this mystique, however, was a dedication to the principle of civilian supremacy. Translated into political action, military professionalization meant sophisticated new means of violence to serve more effectively self-defined values.

While the armed forces were forging a sense of purpose and solidarity, the greater Guatemalan society was fragmenting. The social and economic elites, once a homogeneous tight-knit *Gemeinschaft*, became increasingly complex, differentiated and combative as the 1940s and 1950s brought an expanding membership with diverse experiences and interest. By the 1960s, conflict and separation had become basic conditions of intra-elite relations. There remained little if any basic commitment on which the social and economic elite could unify.

In the 1940s and 1950s, pre-revolution lethargy and submissiveness of the lower and middle sectors was in large measure replaced by new attitudes towards politics. This modification of the political culture approached a condition described by Almond and Verba as "Parochial-Participant Culture."[40] The traditional retainers of the civilian elite became ever less responsive to the demands and interests of the civilian elite. As new political socialization undermined established sociopolitical relations, similarly competition for power among diverse middle- and lower-sector interests made unified political action impossible.

Thus the armed forces were experiencing new heights of discipline, coordination and sense of purpose while civilian political power was fragmenting to a level approaching anarchy. The increased political power of the military grew less from the former factor than the latter: while traditional socio-political structures were losing effectiveness, no new structures were created that could effectively counter the power of the armed forces.

The technocrat is of central concern in the calculus of future Guatemalan politics. The technocrat is a force for change because he demands change. He is a force for change because he looks to the rewards of elite membership while attempting to create his power base in the middle and lower sectors. Perhaps the technocrat will drag the economic elite who need his expertise and pull the masses that need his leadership into an alliance aimed at establishing the supremacy of civilian authority. Or perhaps in Guatemala and similar small economically simple societies the limited demand for technical skill will restrict the growth of the new middle sector and consequently rob the nation of potentially progressive leadership. Or perhaps the military elite and their comrades will successfully coopt the technocrat by proffering wealth, status and limited influence as rewards for accepting the existing definition of politics. Indeed, the style of politics associated with the *Gobierno Militar* may continue indefinitely.

NOTES

1. This bloodless *golpe de estado* (coup d'etat) unfolded like a well-planned military exercise. The first step occurred on March 26, 1963, with the declaration by the president (at the insistence of the minister of defense) of a state of siege and suspension of constitutional protections. Three days later, Minister of Defense Peralta announced, via the mass media, the closing of the national airport, prohibition of all public meetings and pending "military maneuvers" in and around Guatemala City during the weekend of March 30-31. The officers sent to the palace found the president's luggage already packed. *El Imparcial, Prensa Libre* and other local papers carried detailed accounts of the overthrow of Ydigoras.

2. The events of 1944 are detailed in Kalman H. Silvert, *A Study in Government: Guatemala* (New Orleans: Tulane University, Middle America Research Institute Publication 21, 1954). For a discussion of the whole time period see Ronald M. Schneider, *Communism in Guatemala 1944-1954* (New York: Praeger, 1959), pp. 27-29. A review of many accounts of the period is found in Julio Adolfo Rey, "Revolution and Liberation: A Review of Recent Literature on the Guatemalan Situation," *Hispanic American Historical Review* 38 (1958): 239-55.

3. John J. Johnson, *The Military and Society in Latin America* (Stanford: Stanford University Press, 1964). Johnson argues the merits of the military as a vehicle for national development. An opposing, and critical analysis is offered by Edwin Lieuwen, *Arms and Politics in Latin America* (New York: Praeger, 1961).

4. Carl Beck and James M. Malloy, "Political Elites: A Mode of

Analysis," in *A Survey of Elite Studies*, ed. Carl Beck (Washington, D.C.: Special Operations Research Office, American University, 1965).

5. Robert A. Dahl, "A Critique of the Ruling Elite Model," *American Political Science Review* 52 (1958): 463-69.

6. Robert A. Dahl, *Who Governs? Democracy and Power in an American City* (New Haven: Yale University Press, 1961).

7. Older because post-1944 regulations forbid direct commissions from the ranks. And since appointment to the academy required formal education through the high school level, entrance was restricted to sons of middle-sector families who had received the level of education offered almost exclusively in urban schools. The writer is indebted to Jerrold Buttrey for making available his data on the Guatemalan officer corps.

8. Theodore Wycoff, "The Role of the Military in Contemporary Latin American Politics," *Western Political Quarterly* 13 (1960): 749.

9. Lauterbach's research in Guatemala uncovered similar attitude patterns. "A few interviewees said . . . that all they desired from the government was to be left alone." One industrial manager told Lauterbach, "I think tariffs are of no use here as long as consumers have no money. Low prices are much more important. For these views people call me a Communist." Albert Lauterbach, "Government and Development: Managerial Attitudes in Latin America," *Journal of Inter-American Studies* 7 (1965): 201-25. The writer found that attitudes concerning the role of the government and socioeconomic reforms varied with the type of enterprise (export or domestic oriented, industrial or agricultural) and to some extent with tenure as a political elite: individuals from established families tended to see government reform, as, at best, necessary evils, while post-1944 elites held a positive attitude toward the role of government and reform in the development of Guatemala.

10. Johnson, *The Military and Society*, p. 140.

11. *Prensa Libre*, July 18, 1963.

12. Arms were distributed to militiamen during the second week of June 1954. On June 18, Castillo Armas launched his "Liberation Army" against Guatemala from bases in Honduras. The Guatemalan armed forces offered practically no resistance and, on June 27, 1954, President Arbenz resigned and fled. In 1955, the Argentine armed forces rebelled against the Perón regime one week after

peronista labor leaders offered to establish a civil militia. William S. Stokes' summary of this situation applies also to Guatemala: "The Army preferred to maintain its monopoly of organized violence, and General Lucero (Minister of the Army) promptly rejected the offer . . ." *Latin American Politics* (New York: Thomas Y. Crowell Company, 1959), p. 116.

13. Johnson, *The Military and Society*, p. 143; Richard N. Adams, "Patterns of Development in Latin America," *The Annals of the American Academy of Political and Social Science* 360 (1965): 6.

14. For a discussion of the historical origins of the phenomenon, see Lyle N. McAlister, "The Military," in *Continuity and Change in Latin America*, ed. John J. Johnson (Stanford: Stanford University Press, 1964), pp. 153-54.

15. Richard N. Adams, "Social Change in Guatemala and U.S. Policy," in *Social Change in Latin America Today*, eds. Richard N. Adams et al., (New York: Vintage Books, 1960), pp. 243-48.

16. Samuel E. Finer, *The Man on Horseback: The Role of the Military in Politics* (New York: Praeger, 1962), p. 18.

17. Harold D. Lasswell, *Politics: Who Gets What, When, How* (New York: Meridian Books, 1958). p. 202.

18. The percentage of the national budget allocated to public health and low-cost housing fell from 33 percent in 1960 to 11 percent in 1965. The Peralta administration upped the share of the budget going to agricultural research from 15 percent to 21 percent, but in services designed for commercial producers not *campesinos* (peasants). Ten percent of budget funds went into electrification in 1965, an increase of 50 percent over 1962. In all, approximately 30 percent of total 1963-66 public spending was allocated to infrastructure projects—about the same percentage that went into all of the social service programs such as public health, education, welfare and so on.

19. For a discussion of the implications of the rise of the technocrat for Latin American politics, see John J. Johnson, *Political Change in Latin America: The Emergence of the Middle Sector* (Stanford: Stanford University Press 1958).

20. Carl Beck, "Bureaucracy and Political Development in Eastern Europe," in *Bureaucracy and Political Development* ed. Joseph La Palombara (Princeton: Princeton University Press, 1963), pp. 268-300.

21. On the sociopolitical structure of Guatemalan Indian

communities, see Ruth Bunzel, *Chichicastenango: A Guatemalan Village* (Locust Valley, N.Y.: Augustin, 1952); Oliver LaFarge, *Santa Eulala: The Religion of a Cuchumatan Indian Town* (Chicago: University of Chicago Press, 1947); Melvin M. Tumin, *Caste in a Peasant Society* (Princeton: Princeton University Press, 1952); Charles Wagely, "The Society and Religious Life of a Guatemalan Village," *American Anthropologist* 51 (1949); Charles Widsom, *The Chorti Indians of Guatemala* (Chicago: University of Chicago Press, 1940); and Roland H. Ebel, "Political Change in Guatemalan Indian Communities," *Journal of Inter-American Studies* 6 (1964).

22. Students of prerevolution Guatemalan politics have typically noted the role of the government as vehicle for elite interests. Whetten writes that: "Labor unions were virtually nonexistent; collective bargaining was unknown; and forced labor was an official government policy. Government was manipulated in the interests of the large landowners, the foreign corporations and the small upper class in Guatemala City." Nathan L. Whetten, *Guatemala: The Land and the People* (New Haven: Yale University Press, 1961), p. 332.

23. For a detailed discussion of sociopolitical ramifications of the revolution, see Richard N. Adams, "Changes in Power Relationships in the Guatemala National Social Structure: 1944 to 1966," paper presented to the Thirty-Seventh International Congress of Americanists, Mar del Plata, Argentina, 1966.

24. Stokes Newbold, "Receptivity to Communist Formented Agitation in Rural Guatemala," *Economic Development and Cultural Change* 5 (1957): 338-61.

25. Ydigoras' side of the story is presented in Miguel Ydigoras Fuentes, *My War With Communism* (Englewood Cliffs, N.J.: Prentice-Hall, 1963).

26. S. N. Eisenstadt, *The Political Systems of Empires* (New York: The Free Press of Glencoe, 1963).

27. *Decreto-Ley* 9 of 1963 established a registry of persons considered disloyal or "Communist" by the military government. Into this so-called "National Security Archive" went the names of union organizers, members of revolutionary parties, antigovernment activists as well as officers and leaders of cooperatives, agrarian-reform committees, unions and parties from the 1944-54 period. Denunciation of a *campesino* or laborer as "Communist" by a *comisionado militar*, local notable or any government supporter was sufficient cause for entry in the book.

28. Luis Armando Guerra of the Ministry of Labor reported in *El*

Imparcial, January 9, 1966. Not all the certified unions were viable. For the pre-1963 situation, see United States Department of Labor, *Labor Law and Practice in Guatemala* (Washington, D.C.: Government Printing Office, 1962).

29. Newbold, "Receptivity to Communist."

30. One-third of the organizations and one-half of the membership had been added in 1965. Data cited herein are based on the 1965 *memoria* (resume) prepared by the Cooperatives Section of the Ministry of Agriculture.

31. The forebear of the section, the Department of Cooperative Promotion, had been created in 1945 and maintained 21 regional officers to advise and promote cooperatives. By 1953, the department had received $878,128 in operating funds and had created a revolving loan fund from which $1,306,977 had been allocated. For a detailed analysis of the Guatemalan cooperative movement, see Augusto Melgar Rodriguez, *El Movimiento Cooperative de Guatemala* (Guatemala City: Faculty of Economics, University of San Carlos de Guatemala, 1963).

32. Ponciano was defeated and a moderately progressive civilian government succeeded Colonel Peralta. But, unhappily, this new regime was accompanied by a reemergence of a 1954-like terror. Various anti-insurgent, anti-communist organizations (of which Mano Blanca—White Hand—became the most ruthless) undertook a campaign of murder, torture and intimidation against real and fancied supporters of the insurgency and revolutionary politicians. Estimates of the number of murders committed by the right-wing terrorists vary, but 18 months after the inauguration of President Julio César Méndez Montenegro, terrorists of whatever political persuasion had accounted for 3,000 deaths. See *Visión*, December 22, 1967, p. 15.

33. This, of course, did not apply to insurgents who were the targets of military operations, summary justice and constant harassment. And "Moderate" only in the relative sense that the government neither murdered, tortured nor imprisoned on the scale of previous Guatemalan and other contemporary Latin American regimes.

34. John W. Durston, "Power Structure in a Rural Region of Guatemala: The Department of Jutiapa" (M.A. Thesis, University of Texas, 1966). Durston's research on the *comisionado* system is especially valuable.

35. V. O. Key, Jr., *Public Opinion and American Democracy* (New York: Alfred A. Knopf, 1961).

36. The discussion of associational interest groups relies heavily on the research conducted by Mavis Anne Bryant. See her "Agricultural Interest Groups in Guatemala" (M.A. Thesis, University of Texas, 1967).

37. Events in Guatemala since the accession of the civilian government as well as negotiations conducted after PR's popular victory in March 1966 suggest the validity of Johnson's proposition that the military is likely to function more as a veto group than as actual governmental rulers. John J. Johnson "The Latin-American Military as a Politically Competing Group in Transitional Society," in *The Role of the Military in Underdeveloped Countries* ed. John J. Johnson (Princeton: Princeton University Press, 1962), pp. 91-130.

38. Key, *Public Opinion.*

39. Finer, *The Man on Horseback*, pp. 26-27.

40. Gabriel A. Almond and Sidney Verba, *The Civic Culture* (Boston: Little, Brown and Company, 1965), pp. 11-26.

4
The New Latin American Military Coup

José Enrique Miguens

MILITARY INTERVENTION AS AN OBJECT OF STUDY

In 30 years, from 1935 to 1964, there were 56 changes of government by military coups in 20 Latin American countries. Since World War II, 31 incumbent presidents were ousted from office by the same means.[1] In a period of ten years from 1945 to 1955, seven Latin American countries had at least one military coup, four had two, four had three and one had four.

Argentina presents one of the most acute cases in the period after 1955. In this country from 1959 to 1966, there occurred 12 military coups of the *levantamiento* type.[2] The climax arrived in the presidency of Arturo Frondizi, who in less than four years of government suffered seven military uprisings, or *levantamientos*, the last of which ousted him, and 26 military *planteamientos*, leaving aside the numerous local and general strikes that further plagued his government.

At the present moment, in South America only, of 11 countries we find five civilian governments, five military governments established by coups and the lone intermediate type of General Alfredo Storessner in Paraguay.[3]

Social occurrences of this magnitude and importance, historical trends with this degree of persistence cannot be swept out as symptoms of political instability or disposed of as manifestations of the "Latin temperament."[4] They merit the most serious scientific study. That means a wide accumulation of refined empirical evidence, the clearest taxonomic conceptualizations and classifications and the use of a sophisticated methodology adequate to the object under study.

Unfortunately this has not been the case in the study of military interventions in Latin America. The amount of information is scarce and superficial and the concepts employed are vague and used in the most uncritical way.

One of the reasons may well be the propensity to secrecy on the part of the military all over the world and their reluctance to allow any filtering of information. But, in the case of Latin America, two more explicit reasons appear to the author as explanations of the weakness of military research there:

The first is the natural distrust military men have of intellectuals in general and in particular of university graduates who want to use them as objects of their studies. The distrust increases if these students happen to be foreigners and citizens of more powerful nations. The suspicion cannot be but reinforced by the disclosure in recent years about the origin of funds supporting American students' research in political and military fields in Latin America. These funds come in great part from military and intelligence organizations.[5]

The second reason for the weakness of this type of research is found not in the subjects, but in the observers. Political maneuvering, revolutions, use of violence and access to power by force involve the participants so deeply that it may be too much to expect from them candid expositions to foreigners. Furthermore, such activities are part of a complicated network of personal ties and loyalties that are very difficult for outsiders to grasp. This is truer when outsiders come from a different culture and are not provided with or prepared to employ the patient and laborious methodology of the cultural anthropologists. All this makes for misunderstandings and misinterpretations of ongoing events.[6]

DEFECTIVE METHODOLOGY

The central point in this chapter will be that the methodology employed to study the military interventions in Latin America has been inappropriate and that this inappropriate approach has operated to obscure the real meaning and characteristics of the more recent military coups.

The approaches to military intervention in Latin America up to the present moment can be ordered in two principal groups, each one with some subdivisions:

A. Evaluative or normative
   (a) Utilitarian
   (b) Naive or uncritical Marxist
B. Neo-positivistic
   (a) Atomistic
   (b) Aggregative
   (c) Conjunctural

The Evaluative or Normative Approach

In one of Harold Pinter's plays, *The Birthday Party,* one of the characters is an old-woman owner of a humble boardinghouse in a forgotten little town near an old-fashioned beach resort. Every morning when she appears in the kitchen, her husband, a coal miner, is reading his morning paper at the breakfast table. The dialogue monotonously goes the same way every morning:

(Wife)– "What are you reading?"
(Husband)–"The news."
(Wife)–"Is it good?"

Apparently she cannot understand any other categorization of the news other than good or bad.

This is precisely the attitude of the bulk of books dealing with the Latin American military. Their principal objective is to decide if they are good or bad, in an evaluative, moral type of approach.

The more superficial sector of this current of thought bases its moral judgments on subjective characteristics of the military in the most simplistic "good guy-bad guy" polarization. Military men

appear always as good guys in all the European and Latin American
reactionary nationalist literature of the thirties and forties or are
always bad guys (by principle) in the European and American
socialist and liberal literature up to World War II. The trend is now
being reversed, at least in the European socialist writings. The more
articulate and less openly ideological authors of the evaluative school
prefer to make their value judgments according to the consequences
of the military interventions for some historical goals that they
accept as valuable or desirable.

   The utilitarian writers: they all assume implicitly a mechanistic
theory of progress as a straight ascendant line that goes from the
most underdeveloped countries up to the political and economic
organization of the United States. In the best Stuart Mills tradition
they assume that this path to progress must be walked by every
nation under the exclusive guidance of the civilians, which means to
them exclusively the middle-class bourgeoisie of shop owners who
were the backbone of "industrial society," for the writers of the
time. In this pattern of thinking, as Lyle N. McAlister has nicely
shown, Latin American armies are "conceived of as a force external
to and interfering with 'normal' historical processes rather than an
integral element in them."[7] Military men are conceived as intruders
in a closed field reserved for civilians only.

   As Latin American societies seem not to reach the qualifications
of civilized societies, that is, civilian-ruled societies, the military can
be tolerated as part of the pathological and immature state of the
culture. But they will be judged according to the steps they take
when in government in relation to the desirable goal already
established and accepted by all. If the desired goal or end state of
the process is American democracy, the military will be excused for
their intervention when they help the "progress towards democracy"
or the "struggle towards democracy." They will be condemned if
they are labeled as "obstacles to the achievement of democracy."[8]

   If the accepted goal is progress or economic development
understood in Adam Smith's tradition as "the wealth of nations,"
they will be considered good if they help private investment, protect
free enterprise, organize sound taxation systems and reduce the
government bureaucracy. They will be labeled as bad if they act
differently.

The naive or uncritical Marxists: the mechanisms of thought of the dogmatic or uncritical Marxist writers on military interventions are not very different. The only difference lies in the assumptions.

They assume implicitly a dialectical theory of development superficially interpreted as a conflict between an entrenched oligarchy that wants to preserve the status quo and the forces of the proletariat that fight for their redemption.[9] In this context the military can only be what they call "the praetorian guards of the oligarchy," acting only to repress the popular movements and reestablish the balance of power in favor of the oligarchy every time the proletariat advances too much. Their assumption is that the armies belong to the parasitic superstructure and are "naturally" the watchdogs of the established capitalist order and their interests are tied with the ruling classes.[10]

In his excellent paper on the specificity of the Latin American military coup, sociologist José Nun makes a critique on Marxist grounds of these naive approaches to military interventions. Nun points out that even if these phenomena belong to the superstructural level they have a certain consistency of their own and that "in this case as in others, the ultimate determination by the class structure appears to be mediated and determined in turn by national traditions, by values that are acknowledged as theirs by the particular groups, etc." In the footnote he says that a simplistic class interest interpretation "has already entered the museum of vulgar interpretations of Marx."[11]

In conclusion: being presented with these two currents of thought, we cannot do less than adhere to the words of McAlister: "Lord Acton notwithstanding, it would be useful for research purposes to regard Latin American armed forces 'scientifically,' that is, as social phenomena rather than as disasters and their relationships to civil society as a problem properly belonging to history and the social sciences rather than to demonology," or, we will add, "to apologetics."[12]

The Neo-Positivistic or Empiricist Approach

While the approaches of the first type were normative, those of the second type, in their desire to be scientific, swing to the other side. Their concern is explanatory, their object to explain the emergence of military coups and, if possible, to forecast future coups.

In a neo-positivist frame of mind, they try to arrive at scientific propositions by searching for cause-and-effect relationships. But as the available information is scarce and unreliable, they try to solve the problem by hastily formulating propositions based on relationships of a very simple and superficial character.

Atomistic relationships: here the attempt to arrive at explanations is by way of searching for relationships of a monocausal or direct-linear deterministic type between simple and isolated elements connected between themselves in the void, outside of any social system. In my opinion their theoretical basis is atomistic.

One of the examples of this approach is found in a paper by Theodore Wyckoff.[13] He tries to explain the frequency of military action according to the differential impact of a given set of seven variables, some of them important, but none of them, not even the set taken together, relevant outside of a structural framework.

McAlister, in his critical paper on the methodology for studying civil-military relations in Latin America in which he suggests some very sound precautions, cannot himself avoid *en passant* to try his hand at a statistical association between two variables with two polar magnitudes each and the emergence of different types of military political control. The variables are: degree of social and political disorganization (high and low) and degree of professionalism in the armed forces (high and low).[14] In a later paper, McAlister frankly admits that he now finds "this scheme simplistic."[15]

Even Martin Needler, so perceptive in his case study of the Ecuadorian military coup in his last book, tries to relate the probability of emergence of a military coup with variations in economic conditions. His correlations of military coups with the ups and downs of the real per-capita income of the country shows that, of 15 coups, seven occurred when economic conditions were going up, seven when they were deteriorating and one with stable conditions.[16]

Others, such as Edwin Lieuwen, try to establish a direct relation between American military aid and the emergence of military coups.

"Military equipment and support from the U.S. was probably to some degree converted into political power. . . . U.S. military aid may have unwittingly tipped the balance in favor of the armed forces."[17] In a recent report prepared at the request of the Committee on Foreign Relations of the United States Senate, Lieuwen applies his theory, arriving at propositions like this: "To forestall future military take overs, it is recommended . . . the cutting of U.S. economic and military aid" and to use "the threat of cutting of military aid" in the case of military regimes in power.[18] The basic idea underlying the proposals is that United States military aid is the *Deus ex machina* behind everything and is the efficient cause that can produce direct effects per se.

These pretended causal relationships also fail when they are checked with empirical data. Charles Wolf tested statistically the relationships and concluded that the results "warrant a healthy dose of skepticism" and that "simple and easy assumptions about the political effects of military programs should be discouraged."[19]

Aggregative studies: in recent years an attempt has been made to try to explain military coups by the incidence of social origins of the officer corps. This has lead to a laborious search for family data of officers in each Latin American country, even in some cases data of families of wives, trying to locate their social class or the region of the country from which they come. As everybody realizes, military coups are not made by individuals, so the approach to the explanation of military coups tries to be aggregative, though not very refined.

To the author's knowledge, no one has succeeded in showing in systematic form the relationship between class or regional origins of the military corps taken as a whole and the emergence of military coups. On the contrary, it will seem that there is no relation at all in the corporate behavior of the armed forces, not even in the individual behavior of officers. Needler, in his study of the Ecuadorian military coup which had a conservative orientation, found that the families from which the leading officers of the coup came were predominantly middle class and lower middle class. He concluded that "social origins seemed not to stand in any systematic relation to the political orientations assumed by high military officers." He also found that the army officers came overwhelmingly from the *sierra* (mountainous area), while naval officers came from the coastal provinces, and concluded: "This divergence in regional origins, however, seemed not to give rise to systematic differences in political orientation."[20]

There are two errors in this approach:

1. The writers, being intellectuals, tend to think that the officers who join a coup are motivated by political ideologies or affiliations. The real situation is very different. Officers, when they are not ordered by their superiors, join coups motivated by a wide range of personal loyalties and ascriptive personal ties. In a case study the author made of two coups in Argentina, the answers of the responding officers about the reasons why they joined the coup nearly all ranged from: admiration for the leading figures of the coup, comradeship with other officers already enlisted in it, desire to follow their regiment, affiliation to functional subgroups such as the artillery, the military engineers, the major staff officers or to informal subgroups such as cliaques, lodges and the like. The same was found in the only other case study the author has knowledge of, the one of Needler on the Ecuadorian coup of 1963. His conclusion was that personal loyalties and allegiances of the officers were decisive: "investigation revealed that ... groups and cliques clustered around particular individuals, of quite diverse political orientation and dominant motives. The reader may feel, as the author did, that this stress on individual motives and personal connections (is mistaken).... nevertheless, one must accept facts as they are."[21]

2. Leaving aside the theoretical weakness of this intent to relate personal ideologies with individual social origins, in the case of military officers it forgets four aspects that the author can only enumerate: the strong processes of socialization that officers receive, not only in the military academies but also during their careers, their garrison years and in their later high-level studies at home and abroad; the lack of class

consciousness and the distorted political ideologies of social classes in Latin America;[22] the strong value commitments that are more important than any other factor in the regulation of their interaction with other members of the society or of their organizational behavior;[23] finally, the acceptance by all professionally trained military personnel throughout Latin America of the primacy of the interests of "the Institution" over any other interest, be it personal or political, at least at the conscious level and in the acknowledged meanings and common understandings of this norm.

Conjunctural: other authors in the same wide current of neo-positivistic thinking try to plot through time the number and frequency of military dictatorships and military coups in Latin America to draw graphs and charts and to deduce statistical trends. With these charts only, they discuss short-term cyclical movements, long-term secular trends, cycles, waves and lines of evolution and regression.

Writing in 1961 and looking back, Lieuwen concludes: "The long-term secular trend is away from the former (military governments) and is moving towards civilian government."[24] "The rapid disappearance of military rulers from the Latin American scene over the past five years suggests that the armed forces involvement in the Latin American social crises may be waning."[25]

A simple statistical graph that shows the trends in military dictatorships from 1935 to 1964 was made by Needler. Analyzing the chart, Needler says: "Conclusions of great interest can be drawn. Clearly the factors that produce military dictatorships seem in part cyclical. At the same time, the cyclical pattern reproduces itself around a clearly descending trend line, so that each successive peak in the number of dictatorships existing contemporaneously is lower than the last. . . . Similarly, successively lower levels of dictatorship are reached at each low point in the cycle. . . . The oscillation between practices based on democratic and authoritarian norms is clear—'permanent instability.' Yet the evolutionary tendency at work is equally clear."[26]

The graph line drops off in 1961 and then begins an upward trend up to 1964, the last date shown in Needler's graph. Using the methods of the neo-positivists, we reduced the points in the graph to a straight-line trend to control the small cyclical fluctuations and then projected the trend. Taking 1961 as the final point and projecting the line trend, the forecasting in 1961 would be clear: There will not be a single military government in Latin America by 1964! Even taking 1964 as the final point, the projection for the future will lead to the conclusion that there will not be a military government in Latin America by 1968!

As we will try to show, 1964 and 1968 are precisely the two starting points of a new type of military coup. No deterministic theory could have forecast this change of trends.

These coups are very similar among themselves and completely different from the others. These similar coups have appeared in different countries of Latin America with different degrees of development and complexity and with different degrees of dependency. No deterministic theory can account for this similarity and for this qualitative change.

QUALITATIVE CHANGES IN MILITARY COUPS

Between 1961 and 1965, ten military coups occurred in Latin America. In June 1962, the Peruvian army did not allow the winning candidate, Victor Raúl Haya de la Torre, to become president of the country but instead installed a junta headed by General Perez Godoy. In March 1963, the Guatemalan army took power, followed in July 1963 by the Ecuadorian military junta with representatives of the three services taking control.[27] In October 1963, General Osvaldo López Arellano seized power in Honduras.

Brazil followed this path with the military uprising of March 1964 headed by Marshal Humberto de Alencar Castelo Branco and, in November of the same year Army General Alfredo Ovando Candia and Air Force General R. Barrientos Ortuno formed the double-headed government of Bolivia.

Parallel to this military unrest in the continent run the two military incidents—of September 1963 and April 1965 in the Dominican Republic and the ones of September 1962 and April 1963 in Argentina—with violent confrontation of two rival military groups.

For many reasons, which for lack of space will not be elaborated on, we consider all these military interventions in the period 1961-65 as belonging to a transitional or intermediate category between the classical military coup from 1920 to 1961 and the new professional military coup from 1966 on.[28]

A new type of military coup has begun to emerge since 1966. Its rationale can be found in such actions as the speech of the commander in chief of the Argentine Army, Lietuenant General Juan Carlos Onganía, at West Point Military Academy about the position of the modern armies in Latin American societies, the first Pan American meeting of major military staffs and the failure of the first stage of the military intervention in Brazil.

The coups under this category are the following: the *levantamiento* of June 1966 in Argentina that put Lieutenant General Onganía in power; the coup d'état led by General Barrientos in Bolivia; the *levantamiento* of the Peruvian Army in October 1968 that put General Juan Velasco Alvarado in power; the *levantamiento* of the National Guard of Panama under the leadership of Brigadier General Omar Torrijos, in 1968, which installed the military junta of Colonel José M. Pinilla and Colonel Bolívar Urrutia; and finally the palace coup of December 1968 in Brazil by the "hard line" officers that forced General da Costa e Silva to institute a declared and total military rule.[29]

The sequence is impressive: one coup in 1966 and four coups in 1968. It is my opinion that these five coups have different characteristics from all the other previous Latin American military coups.

If we take as the unit of analysis the armed forces or what the military themselves call "the Institution" and treat it as an antagonist in the Parsonian sense, the differences between the older or classical military coup of 1920 to 1961 and the modern or professional military coup of 1966 to the present, by contrast, appear very clear:

The Process of the Coup

In the old-fashioned military coup the process followed a typical path:

1. Political discussions began in the officers' mess of the regiments and the military clubs in the cities by officers on active service from the rank of major up, retired generals and civilian politicians of the opposition parties who were, in the Latin American political jargon, "knocking at the doors of the barracks" asking for a military coup.

2. Coalitions were made between chiefs of regiments with their equals, not according to their their political ideologies, but in accord with personal ties, loyalties and allegiances.

3. The strength of the rebel and loyal forces was evaluated according to the number of regiments recruited by each.

4. A prestigious military figure was appointed as the head of the revolution. No convictions were required, not even on the need for a revolution, but only prestige, seniority and followers. Very often the person picked was the most undecided about the desirability of a coup; by selecting him, the balance of forces would be swung over towards the revolutionary side. Logically he would consider the objectives accomplished with the overthrow of the president and he would begin to make preparations for returning the country to institutional "normalcy" and to "democratic" elections.[30]

5. A coalition cabinet was appointed which was composed of different political parties with the exception of the one that was in power and the populist parties considered dangerous or unreliable. This means that only bourgeois parties were admitted and that the parties in the cabinet considered themselves as the possible and future heirs of the revolutions, regardless of the popular support which they enjoyed from the voters. The roots for conflict, internal strife and indecision in government were thus established.

6. The political party with better contacts with the military or the one with better voting chances would begin to exert pressure for elections, profiting from the already existing

pressures from the local American embassy and the declarations of American newspapers and congressmen.

7. Elections would be held with the participation of only the "acceptable" political parties.

8. The loser parties would protest the results of the elections, charge fraud and begin to conspire with their military friends for the next revolution against the winners. The circle closes on itself.

9. The prospect of a future military coup would be in the minds of everybody and all (government, political parties, businessmen and military) would behave accordingly.

The process is different in the coups of the most recent period:

1. The decision to make the coup is made by the commander in chief of one of the three services with the advice and technical help of his major staff. The rank of the officers involved in the decision-making does not drop below the commanders of the military regions of the country (four or five top-level officers).

2. No civilians are admitted in the preparation and decisions except some technicians employed as advisers; politicans are completely excluded and considered dangerous.

3. There is no coalition cabinet; government posts are filled with the military or civilians not affiliated with political parties. All political parties are carefully restricted and maintained outside the governmental circles.

4. No promise of immediate elections is made. On the contrary, the military government makes known clearly that it intends to stay and has no intention of returning to the barracks.

The Objectives of the Coup

The classical coup had no clear objectives nor defined goals.
The *proclamas*, or manifestos, were full of grandiloquent appeals
to reestablish morality, defend the values of nationality, stop
communist infiltration, restore order and hierarchy, fight against
tyranny or against demagoguery or both at the same time,[31] install
real democracy, follow the national will of the people, restore the
sacred values of the household, the fatherland and so on.

A classic in the field is the Manifesto of the Military Junta of
Ecuador of 1963: "A gigantic clamor has been born of the most
healthy popular emotion, which demands the reestablishment of
moral values in a country which stands in risk of being precipitated
into the abyss of dissolution and anarchy through the corruption of
an irresponsible government which does not represent the National
Will and which has transformed itself into an instrument of
Communist infiltration." It can only be matched by the statement
of support of the Conservative party: "The (unseated) Government
has provided favorable ground for the operation of Communism,
which threatened to destroy the imminent and eternal values which
form the essence of Ecuadorean life, founded in the democratic
principles of Western Christian civilization."[32]

Some authors believed that the vagueness of the manifestos was a
clever trick for hiding the real and deep motives of the coups. In the
author's opinion, the vagueness and grandiloquence were very often
a device for obscuring the real fact that the coup had no policy goals
outside of some very small objectives. Very little remained to be
done except to wait for the politicians to return to power after these
small objectives were obtained, that is, the firing of some small
bureaucrats who had received bribes, the cancellation of some
governmental contracts seen as the result of undue influences, the
return to work of some strikers or the creation of a censorship office
to stop pornography and in some cases, as the 1943 coup in
Argentina, to control the use of slang words in popular music.

*In the modern professional military coup the situation is
completely different.* The officers, through the cumulative effects of
action in previous military governments, have acquired experience

and political skills and have learned the ropes of the administration. Each one of the recent coups was backed by a specific military political ideology elaborated by prominent military figures and in the higher academies of the services. This ideology in military terms is known as "doctrine."

The doctrine of the Brazilian coup was elaborated in the Superior School of War, which they call "the Sorbonne," by Marshal Castelo Branco and a group of well-trained colonels. The objectives for the Argentine revolution were drawn up officially by the major staff of the army upon directives of the commander in chief and organized in what it called "the 16 file holders" which constitute an agreement on policy dealing with the principal social and economic problems. A large number of military writings have defined the role of the army in the promotion of the Argentine society, among which we consider the most important the ones by General Rattembach, General Guglialmelli, General Villegas and Lieutenant Colonel Orsolini. In Peru, the doctrine was elaborated in the Centro de Altos Estudios Militares under the direction of General José del Carmen Marín, and the revolutionary government is following the plan step by step. An analysis made of the issues of the *Revista Militar*, the official journal of the Peruvian Army, shows the change in its contents after 1962. In this latter period, a high proportion of articles began to appear dealing with the role of the army in relation to national development and modernization and its relation to the society.[33]

The political aims of the military governments are rationally defined in what are called "national objectives" classified in a set of basic principles under a general common objective: "integration" in Argentina and "national strength" in Brazil. The general idea of policy implementation for these rationally defined principles is that they can be obtained by coercion and the maintenance of "order," understood approximately as would be "law and order" by a small-town, middle-class Republican voter in the United States.

The social discipline and cultural stability that are obtained may lead to a decrease in tensions but may also lead to a loss of dynamism.

The Position and Role of the
Armed Forces in the Society

*For the classical coup, the army was a provisional instrument for
reestablishing order in the country but was not considered qualified
to govern it.* The majority of officers inwardly felt that governing
was a task for politicians and that they were at the service of the
political parties. The stereotype of the Latin American Left was that
these officers were the "praetorian guards of the oligarchy,"
referring to their praetorian or police role as supporters of the status
quo.[34]

Continuing this loose figure of speech only for the sake of
explaining the difference, we will call the new coup officers in Latin
America the "centurions" or "legion commanders." The Latin word
for the commander in chief of the legions was *imperator*
("emperor"). The way the legions enthroned their emperors in the
last period of the Roman Empire and their relations to their
weakened society render a better comparison to the present position
of the armies in Latin American societies than the rather modest
police functions of the praetorian guards at the time of the
Republic, be it in Rome or in Latin America.[35]

Confronted with the confused and conflicting political situation
and the ambivalent line of policy that the civilian governments must
follow due to their structural limitations, the army corps, as a
practice, considers itself the only pure and patriotic group and the
only one able the manipulate the situation and lead the country to
progress.[36]

Its main concern is to maintain the unity of the army, preserving
the doctrine and getting rid of heterodox or heretic officers. Its
principal function will be to foster the dynamics of economic
development, to control the purity of the doctrine and the
achievement of the established objectives. These self-envisaged roles
are surprisingly similar to the function of "the movement" in fascist
and socialist countries, to the "vanguard function" of the
Communist party according to Lenin and to the "purity keeping
functions" of the *Sierra Maestra* combatants in Castroist Cuba.[37]

Organization versus Political Elites

For the new Latin American rulers, to govern is to administrate. All developmental problems can be solved technocratically with the advice of theoretical economists, organizational experts, simulation and computer techniques following the way of approach to the logistic problems of war by the contemporary technical armies all around the world.

Politics and professional politicians are out of the picture. The ministries of government or of the interior that are in charge of politics in Latin America are now reduced to the control of the police force and preparation of laws and decrees. Parliaments that were the arena for political life are closed—in Argentina on the grounds of being inefficient and in Brazil for not being sufficiently docile. The basic orientation seems to be the creation of a new social group of administrators and technicians to consolidate a bureaucracy in the Weberian sense that will take the place and the functions of the political elite. Detailed blueprints for the reorganization of public offices, elaborate delimitation of jurisdiction and power, careful enumeration of the steps for short-range and long-range planning are the stuff with which policies are made.

The situation is up to now very fluid and the processes are not yet established. They defy classification and comparison with other known political systems, even if some of the trends are similar to the European bourgeois and fascist movements. The regimes of Marshal Henri Pétain in France and General Francisco Franco in Spain are perhaps the most similar.

A very similar ideology of a nonpolitical, technological approach appeared in a little-known secret movement behind the Vichy government in France called *sinarquisme*, and is also a typical feature of the present military governments all over the world. Also it was a constant objective in fascist Italy, but in a very different societal context and emotional "pathos."

The possibility of obtaining economic development without social and political development, which means participation and equality, seems to be doubtful in the long run even if some short-term economic gains can be obtained.

The lack of flexibility of these types of political organizations will probably create very difficult problems in transitional and rapidly changing societies. But only experience can say the last word.[38]

SUGGESTED METHODOLOGY

The object of this chapter was not to comment on or even to evaluate the new military regimes of Latin America, but to show how the defective methodology employed up until now has prevented us from seeing the qualitative changes in the coups.

It is not unfair to say that, in spite of many valuable contributions to the increase of information on military interventions, the methodology applied until now in the study of Latin American coups has failed to forecast the emergence and to grasp the importance and characteristics of the new type of coup.

No knowledge can be obtained with dogmatic judgments of value, but also no understanding can be obtained with positivist procedures. The basic methodological error in both approaches was to treat the armed forces in Latin America as passive objects responding mechanically to outside stimuli and as having constant properties through time. We will suggest, as more adequate to the object under study, a more voluntaristic type of approach.

The unit of analysis must be the armed forces, "the Institution" as a specific collectivity inside a global society, with a subculture of its own and a certain level of organization. This collectivity can be studied in accordance with Parsonian theory, as an antagonist in a situation. In the situation we can distinguish aspects of the social structure and aspects of the cultural system, or what Germani in his theoretical framework for the modernization process calls "contextual conditions."[39] Germani and Silvert make a valid starting point in that military intervention in any country and in any cultural situation "generally implies a weakened and sick system," a disorganized social system.[40]

Turning to the other side of the action unit, the antagonist, a detailed study will be needed of the collective motivations, the institutional interests and the value commitments of the armed forces as a collectivity.[41] Nobody will deny that in the coups of recent years a fundamental interest at stake was the protection of the unity of the army, and one of the principal motivations was fear that the maneuvering of the civilian governments in their search for control of the army would endanger its unity and its established universalistic norms for promotions. This motivation appeared very clearly in the case of President João Goulart in the Brazilian uprising of 1964 and in the case of President Arturo Umberto Illía in the Argentine uprising of 1966. The internalized values of loyalty, honor and discipline help to explain the distrust by the military of civilian politicians and a knowledge of the value commitments of the armed collectivity helps to make understandable their behavior when in power.

The techniques of interactional and process analysis can be employed to study how tension develops and conflict arises between the armed forces and civilian governments. One of the principal negative influences is the erratic policies of the incumbent civilian government, its weaknesses and uncertainty in dealing with the problems of the country and also the cumulative effects of its policy towards the military, that is, increasing the opposition for forcing the retirement of high-level officers, creating resentment by altering the legitimate promotions or degrading the image of the armed forces among the public by ordering them, for example, to intervene in strikes and civilian disorders. On the other side of the interactive relations, the cat-and-mouse play done by the powerful armed forces creates difficulties for the civilian government, denying collaboration to curb civilian disorders or trying to impose their point of view in difficult political decisions.

The time element cannot be left out of any scientific study of military interventions, not by way of attempting to detect cycles in the void, but by analyzing the cumulative effects of past decisions and experiences over subsequent behavior. Any social process has a cumulative load that establishes the possibility of certain alternatives while eliminating others. In a previous essay, we coined the concept "successive totalities analysis" for this type of study.[42] The phrase is meant to suggest that each present situation is in some ways defined and limited by past situations. Two examples of this analysis are: (1) the importance of government experience acquired by the military through successive coups should make it easier for them to rule now and (2) the continuing experience with coups over time increases the expectation of new coups on the part of all and makes them behave accordingly.

The specific differences in the processes of development of coups in the several different countries must also be taken into consideration. Germani has called attention to the importance of understanding what he calls the "historical starting point."[43]

Finally, the techniques of organizational analysis and of decision-making processes in these organized and hierarchical groups cannot be excluded. The same can be said of the usefulness of the techniques of systems analysis for increasing our knowledge of the military subsystem of the Latin American societies and its transactions with other subsystems of the society.

In Summary:

1. The qualitative changes that appeared in the Latin American military coups have shown the inadequacy of the methods employed to analyze them.

2. At the same time, the constancy with which these coups appear in their societies and the importance they are acquiring make them as object for study that must be dealt with scientifically.

3. This specific type of reality calls for methodologies based on the Parsonian theory of action due to the fact that armies in Latin America are not passive objects but are originators of their own behavior.

4. These collectives can be considered as participants in a social, economic and cultural situation who realize their goals, moved by specific interests and motivations and according to certain value commitments.

5. Their interaction with other participants at their same level makes for the development of a process that follows typical sequences according to the historical starting point and to the cumulative effects of the successive previous total situations.

6. The decision to take control of the government and the modes and ways of governing results from the structural aspects of the organization and its internal processes.

7. At the same time, as the military sector is not isolated but is a part of the total system of the society, not only does it have permanent transactions with the other subsystems but any change in one of the subsystems will modify the others and the functioning of the whole society.

NOTES

1. Martin Needler, *Political Development in Latin America: Instability, Violence and Evolutionary Change* (New York: Random House, 1968), p. 60.

2. For the sake of conceptual clarification I will try to define accurately the Latin American political jargon on military interventions: *levantamientos*, or uprisings, are called military coups when armed troops in war equipment leave their barracks illegally and occupy the strategic points in the cities and patrol the streets with or without opposition of other military forces. *Pronunciamientos* are generally uprisings made by way of a declaration of an army commander of high rank that he and his men are against the legal order, with the troops ready to act but remaining inside the barracks or occupying defensive positions, but with no occupation of the capital city or the seat of government. *Planteamientos* are formal presentations of the commander in chief of one or all of the three services in the name of the armed forces and with the implicit menace of force to extract some measure from the legal government. *Cuarteladas* are isolated uprisings in one or some regiments in which the subordinate officers take the power from the chief with or without the aid of outsiders and declare themselves in favor of one or another party, policy or person. When civilians collaborate in the *coup de main*, it is called *asonada*. When it is of very little relevance or without political importance, it is called, scornfully at least in Argentina, *chirinada*, in memory of a police sergeant by the name of Chirino who produced one of these alterations of the legal order.

When the military coup happens inside the military government, it can be made by the executive head of government with the aid of a group of loyal officers, or can be made by a dissenting group of officers to impose some changes. In both cases force or the threat of force is involved, and in both cases the result is a drastic and unexpected change of policy. I will call the first *golpe de estado* (*coup d'etat*) and the second *golpe de palacio* (palace coup). They correspond approximately to the two different meanings of the second definition of the term "coup d'etat" given in *Webster's Dictionary*.

3. Civilian: Colombia, Ecuador, Guyana, Uruguay and Venezuela. Military: Argentina, Bolivia, Brazil, Chile and Peru. Intermediate: Paraguay.

4. Gino Germani and Kalman Silvert, "Politics, Social Structure and Military Intervention in Latin America," *Archives Européennes de Sociologie* 2 (1961): 62-81.

5. In the abundant literature about the Camelot Project, the author could not find any comment on the negative repercussion it had on the Latin American military. Everybody seems to take for granted and work on the assumption that they were partners in the project or at least passively resigned to have their countries scrutinized on one of its most touchy fields. This unconscious starting point that treats them as a passive object responding only to outside stimuli distorts most of the studies made on the Latin American military, vitiates the validity of their conclusions and deprives them of any forecasting power, as we will see later.

6. One recent example is the misguided interpretation that Kenneth F. Johnson gives to the famous peronist (not irgoyenist as he wrongly states) mob's slogan *alpargatas si, libros no*, which for all informed analysts is the clue to the meaning of the movement and to the ambivalent attitudes of the armed forces towards it, as signifying "footwear first, books later." See Kenneth F. Johnson, *Argentina's Mosaic of Discord: 1966-1968* (Washington: Institute for the Comparative Study of Political Systems, 1969), p. 58.

7. Lyle N. McAlister, "Civil and Military Relations in Latin America," *Journal of Inter-American Studies* 3 (1961): 343.

8. Hegel, in the Jena version of his *Philosophy of History*, speaks about what he calls the the *Namengabende Kraft*, which we will translate freely as "the power that holds the one that can put a label on others." See Ibid., p. 344.

9. It is interesting to point out how the concept of redemption of the proletariat has disappeared from Latin American Marxist

literature. "Redemption" has been changed to "world revolution of today" after the Reunification Congress of the Fourth International in Italy (1963) and "proletariat" has been changed to "popular forces" to widen its meaning and increase its content.

10. This dogmatic position helps to explain the position of the Communist and Socialist parties and all the intellectual Left against the populist government of Perón in Argentina. Today the young intellectuals of the Left deplore this position of their elders as a historical error. For them, following the same line of thought, the military-supported regime was good.

11. José Nun, "A Latin American Phenomenon: The Middle Class Military Coup," in *Latin America: Reform or Revolution?* eds. James Petras and Maurice Zeitlin (New York: Fawcett, 1968).

12. McAlister, "Civil and Military Relations," p. 347.

13. Theodore Wyckoff, "The Role of the Military in Latin American Politics," *Western Political Quarterly* 13 (1960).

14. McAlister, "Civil and Military Relations," p. 344.

15. Lyle N. McAlister, "Recent Research and writings on the Role of the Military in Latin America," *Latin American Research Review* 2 (1966): 13.

16. Needler, *Political Development in Latin America*, pp. 61-62.

17. Edwin Lieuwen, "The Military: A Revolutionary Force," *Annals of the American Academy of Political and Social Science* 334 (1967).

18. Edwin Lieuwen, *The Latin American Military. A study prepared at the request of the Subcommittee on American Republic Affairs of the Committee on Foreign Relations, United States Senate* (Washington, D.C.: Government Printing Office, 1967), p. 31.

19. Charles Wolf, *Orbis* 8 (1965): 890-93.

20. Martin Needler, *Anatomy of a Coup d'Etat: Ecuador 1963* (Washington: Institute for the Comparative Study of Political Systems, 1964), p. 37.

21. Ibid., pp. 38-39.

22. Alain Touraine, "Industrialization et Conscience Ouvriere a Sao Paulo," *Sociologie de Travail* 4 (1961).

23. We employ the term "value commitments" in the rigorous Parsonian sense. See Talcott Parsons, "On the Concept of Value Commitments," *Sociological Inquiry* (1968).

24. Edwin Lieuwen, *Arms and Politics in Latin America* (New York: Praeger, 1961), p. 171.

25. Lieuwen, "The Military: A Revolutionary Force," p. 293.

26. Needler, *Political Development in Latin America*, p. 42.

27. Naval Captain Ramón Castro Jijon, Colonel Cabrera Sevilla and Colonel Gandara Enriquez of the army and Aviation Lieutenant Colonel Freile Posso.

28. We leave out of consideration the premodern military interventions in Latin America from independence days to World War I.

29. See note 2 for the definition of all these terms.

30. Needler uses the term "swing man" for this role. He goes on to say: "During the recent period the basic situation described above has been most faithfully reproduced in reality in Argentina, Brazil and Peru and with local variations in Guatemala, Ecuador, the Dominican Republic and Honduras. See Needler, *Political Development in Latin America*, p. 70. We will only add—up to 1966.

31. A contradictory objective such as this was given in the Argentine coup of 1962 against President Frondizi who was at the same time accused of being a Communist agent and of having sold out to American imperialism.

32. Needler, *Anatomy of a Coup d'Etat*, p. 28.

33. L. North, *Civil-Military Relations in Argentina, Chile and Peru* (Berkeley: Institute of International Studies, University of California, 1966), pp.52-57. See the figures and the more detailed comment.

34. See Samuel P. Huntington, *Political Order in Changing Societies* (New Haven: Yale University Press, 1968).

35. We are using the term in its bare historical meaning, not referring to the very refined and interesting scientific concept recently developed by political analysts such as Lasswell, Huntington and Rapaport.

36. See the structural limitations of the three political models for development in Latin America in Charles Anderson, *Politics and Economic Change in Latin America* (New York: Van Nostrand, 1967), chs. 4 and 5.

37. We are indebted to Professor Amos Perlmutter of Harvard University for an exciting discussion and the then unpublished manuscript of his excellent paper that enlightened us on the similarities and differences of the modern military coups in the Middle East.

38. For a critique of the ideologies and an appraisal of the possibilities for new Latin American military governments we recommend the studies of Celso Furtado and H. Jaguaribe in *Les Temps Modernes* 23 (1967) on the Brazilian military regime; for the

possibilities of military government in general see Perlmutter's work; and for the basic and stimulating concepts of "elite manipulation from above" in opposition to the more promising for Latin America "revolution from below," see Irving L. Horowitz, "The Military Elite," in *Elites in Latin America*, eds. Seymour M. Lipset and Aldo Solari (New York: Oxford University Press, 1967).

39. Gino Germani, "Stages of Modernization in Latin America," *Studies in Comparative International Development* 5 (1970): 155-75.

40. Gino Germani and Kalman Silvert, *Estructura Social e Intervención Militar* (Buenos Aires: sociedad de masas, 1966): p. 228.

41. Parsons, "On the Concept of Value Commitments."

42. José Miguens, "Acontecimiento y actuación en el estudio de la realidad social." *El conocimiento do lo social y otros ensayos* (Buenos Aires: Perrot, 1953).

43. Germani, "Stages of Modernization in Latin America."

5
The Development of the Guatemalan Military

Richard N. Adams

There is implanted in the Western scholarly and political communities the idea that Latin American nations have been intermittently under military governments since the time of independence. This is unfortunate because, first, it is of dubious truth, and second, it has obscured the fact that the military has grown in strength over most of the area in recent years. An examination of the comparative power structure of Guatemala since the Ubico period makes it quite clear that just because there was a dictatorship during the 1930s this was not necessarily a military government. Furthermore, the military since that period has had its own very significant history, which relates Guatemala to the United States as well as to other countries and which has enabled it to emerge in a national role which it could not have performed before.[1]

Three processes are currently taking place in the activities of the military: (1) professionalization; (2) incorporation; (3) an assumption of regnancy. In a study of this scope, it is impossible to explore the historical roots of these processes. The current performance, however, can be seen in the light of concomitant structural changes. The underlying trend is an increasing assumption of power and exercise of control for various purposes. Each of the three processes listed above reflect an aspect of this increasing control.

PROFESSIONALIZATION

The military was first seriously professionalized under Garcia Granados and Justo Rufino Barrios in the nineteenth century. In addition to initiating the *Escuela Politécnica* in 1873, a reform of the armed forces was undertaken. Earlier in the century it was possible for officers of garrisons to ignore orders from the central government with impunity. Zamora Castellanos cites two cases in which commandants who were to be replaced simply took over the garrisons and refused. One, Rafael Ariza y Torres, bestowed a colonelcy upon himself and declared himself *commandante General de las Armas;* the government finally recognized both. The *Escuela Politécnica* was originally set up and run by Spanish officers and, by the turn of the century, had developed a strong *esprit de corps.* Presumably, some were finding it possible to make a career in the military service.

The identification of the military with the nation and the creation of a career for officers have produced an increasingly professional officer. Professionalization, in this sense, refers to the coincidence between primary interest and occupation. It means devoting most of one's efforts and attention to the chosen line of work and a motivation to maintain or improve one's status among professional colleagues. There is no question that being an officer in the Guatemalan army or air force may constitute a career; furthermore, it is increasingly being perceived as a profession. Professionalization in this sense should not be confused with "apolitical." The tendency of some contemporary writers on the military in Latin America to equate professionalism with nonpolitical concerns is misleading in the case of Guatemala. Were we to have followed this line of thought, the most "professional" army in recent years would have been that of Ubico. The position taken here is that men of any profession may well also be political; their political action may or may not interfere with, obstruct, or enhance their professional work.

The major obstacle to professional identification in the Guatemalan military is not politics but economic support. The economic organization of the armed forces makes it difficult, if not impossible, for an officer to be entirely professional. While emphasis is placed on advanced training, the salary system makes it almost impossible for an officer to be satisfied with the income he receives, and forces the more ambitious individuals to spend a great deal of time trying to attain a better position.

The salary issue was a major obstacle to professional development within the army. The new second lieutenant received a basic pay of some $75 a month, with a $50 mess allowance, $25 for a wife, and $5 for each child. Each increase in rank brought a $25 per month increase in salary and regular promotions were scaled to occur about once every three years. No one in the army viewed these salaries as sufficient. It was expected that an officer seek additional income. The question then became one of how it was obtained and what effect that had on the professional role of the officer.

There are two principal avenues for an officer to obtain extra income. One is to obtain within the government a military position that has a *sobresueldo*, an additional stipend that accompanies certain posts. Most major positions have such salary additives, and they vary from one post to another. The fact that the major official fund sources are attached to the limited number of such positions means that a high value is placed on obtaining them. This is the specific economic mechanism that promotes power-seeking within the army. Merely to survive on the official income, one must strive to obtain and keep the higher-paying posts.[3]

The other source of income is private enterprise outside the army. Officers are allowed to initiate and carry on almost any kind of private venture they wish, with certain exceptions. They are not allowed to own liquor factories or to run cabarets. As is the case generally in the cultural traditions of the Guatemalan upper sector, however, ownership of land is given a particularly high priority. Officers who can obtain estates through one means or another will almost inevitably do so. Among the complaints of the peasantry in colonization areas have been those about the high number of officers who have been granted land.[4] A very few work it themselves, usually with the help of laborers, but most of the time they simply collect rent on it. There are fairly well-known cases, such as that of the former national estate of Santo Tomás in Escuintla, which was repartitioned among some sixteen officers, including some of the leading colonels, with each receiving sixty-four manzanes or more of land.

The problem of income is a serious one for officers. Training in the *Escuela Politécnica*, together with upper-sector aspirations and tastes, gives the young officer graduate a view into the perquisites of good living but almost no means of access to them. The two channels available to him have inevitable consequences. If he opts for seeking positions with *sobresueldos*, he must inevitably become involved in political action, usually both within and outside of the military service. If he opts for private ventures, it means he must obtain capital, and the most readily available sources are those which are open to him by virtue of his military position. Of course, the higher the position, the easier it is to obtain capital, and vice versa.

Both avenues (and they are often used together rather than separately) may lead to conflicts with professionalism. The individual seeking politically powerful positions must inevitably compromise his professional attitudes; and the individual engaging in private enterprise obviously will have demands on his time and privileges that conflict with military responsibilities.

Although low salaries pose serious problems to professional development, there are other factors that build a more professional situation within the army. The most important of these is the postgraduate training that the officer is expected to undergo. Although it was not possible to obtain data on the amount of additional military training that officers have had available to them., Table I shows that following the 1944 revolution, there was a severe de-emphasis on the officer graduate taking additonal courses outside the military service. While it was previously customary for a small proportion of the officers to seek such additional education, the post-1944 military establishment discouraged an officer from seeking additional extra-military education and provided neither effective opportunity nor any regular program for him to do work at the nation's universities. The emphasis was placed, instead, on additional professional training. It is fairly obvious to the younger officer that training, especially in foreign countries and currently in the United States, provides the individual with both skills and social contacts that are to his benefit, as well as contributing positively towards his possibilities for advancement and better positions. This training, which dates back well into the pre-revolutionary era, has become increasingly one of the features that serves to distinguish the new younger officers from the older members of the service, separating them both in experience and their sympathies.

In recent years, the most important army elite training has been that related to ranger and counter-insurgency work. The appearance of guerillas has provided the Guatemalan army with a real enemy for possibly the first time since Justo Rufino Barrios led Guatemalan forces to Salvador in the name of central American union. Traditional military training is obviously entirely inept for this kind of a war, and the protracted war in Vietnam made some Central Americans aware of the potentials of guerrilla warfare.[5]

With the initiation of guerrilla activities following the failure of the November 13 revolt in 1960, the importance of counter-insurgency training became increasingly evident.

Counter-insurgency training has been provided by the United States. Fearing a Latin American insurgency movement comparable to that of Vietnam, the military establishment had initiated a few years before a program for training Latin American officers in methods of warfare appropriate to guerrilla activity. Among their students were some young Guatemalan officers who were involved in the November 13 Movement. Upon the failure of this coup, a few of these fled to the interior and began what was to erupt a few years later as a full-scale guerrilla operation. In a very real way, guerrilla activity in Guatemala, while ideologically aided by Fidel Castro's success, has been directly helped technically by the United States. In its enthusiasm for developing counter-insurgency skills in the Latin American armies, the United States provided the basic training of the leaders of the first years of the movement. These leaders, in turn, were at that time reacting in part to United States dominance in the military and other affairs of Guatemala, especially those related to the training of anti-Castro (Bay of Pigs) forces in the *Finca Helvetia* on the Pacific Coast. While there may be dissension within the army itself over the role of guerrillas in the country, the presence of an active enemy and the opportunity for counter-insurgency training have played a positive role toward professionalization of the service.

One final suggestion concerning this issue is the relatively minor role played by family in the overall military establishment. In estimating the relative importance of criteria in selecting individuals as colleagues within the service, one observer felt that both political considerations and the individual's ability came before family. While there are sets of siblings and obvious cases of relationships among officers, there seem to be no "old military families" in Guatemala. Furthermore, while the sons of some officers do follow their fathers' careers and admission to the *Escuela Politécnica* encourages this by providing preference for such candidates, informants generally agreed that the much more common pattern was for the children of officers to go to the university.

Familialism in Guatemala could work both for and against professionalization. It could enhance professionalization were various generations to consistently go into the service, thereby passing down through the home the traditions of the service. But in many Latin American situations, obligations pertaining to familial relationships frequently come into direct conflict with professional duties and requirements. The apparent lack of traditional military families in Guatemala is probably indicative of high professionalization, rather than the reverse. The relative absence of the influence of family relationships is not necessarily due to any conscious effort to achieve a more professional service. It may be that the low salaries paid most officers discourage young men, and the sheer antagonism manifest among young people in secondary schools regarding cadets and militarism is probably enough to discourage the sons of some officers from pursuing their fathers' careers. If the father has been especially successful, then the child probably has enough advantages so that the special privileges of the service mean relatively little. He can do better outside. If the father has been unsuccessful, then the life experienced by the son probably affords little that is attractive enough to recommend itself. Whatever the reasons may be, the attrition among students entering the *Politécnica* is extraordinarily high and suggests that a serious career is not yet the fully attractive thing it might be.

INCORPORATION

The officers' corps of the Guatemalan military has developed into a corporate group. The establishment of the *Escuela Politécnica* in 1873 laid a necessary basis for this, but it was not until the post-1944 revolutionary period that the protective devices and perquisites became so evident that there were positive advantages to staying in the military.

To say that the military protects its own does not mean that there are no factions, that officers will not oppose or even, under certain circumstances, kill one of their own. The comparison may be made with any other profession in Guatemala. To be a physician or dentist does not obligate the individual to make special allowances for his fellow professionals. Professional associations exist for various purposes, but there is no effort to live in a society of physicians or dentists. In contrast, the corporate quality of the military establishment is such that it encourages its members to seek their rewards almost entirely from within the establishment.

One of the most important characteristics of the military is that, except in extraordinary circumstances, it is most reluctant to ostracize or seriously punish one of its members for misconduct. The most outstanding example of this was the absence of penalties to the perpetrators of the November 13 Movement. While many officers were involved in this, almost none were punished. The most common way to take care of an officer who has proved himself to be inconvenient is to retire him or to send him off on a diplomatic mission, usually as military attaché in a foreign embassy. Retirement, however, is heavier punishment than assignment abroad, because it does remove the individual from some of the privileges available to those on active duty.

The circumstances under which an officer may be more severely punished most commonly stem from outside the military. A major example here is what happened to Arbenz and the few officers most closely associated with the excesses of the Arbenz regime—Rosenberg, Cruz Wer, Alfonso Martinez, and Wayman Guzmán. All of these officers fled the country when Arbenz went into exile. They did so, however, less because their fellow officers were against them than because they had achieved a public notoriety such that they might have been subject to severe treatment in the months immediately to follow the fall of their government. Another circumstance in which individuals are punished is when they have become the object of concern of a particular chief of state. This was the case under Ydígoras, for example, when imprisonment and even torture were inflicted on an officer whom Ydígoras particularly disliked. Here again, however, it was not the military establishment that was involved, but rather the police used against individual members of the military.

In recent years, the military has taken positive steps to provide means of support for its retired officers, above and beyond that which individuals may have from their own private business or farming ventures. Among the training courses available to officers are some in public administration. It was argued by one informant that these were especially felt to be important, since officers, upon retiring, could then take up positions as departmental governors or in the various state ministries. This provided both for the individual's future and also helped supply the nation with trained public administrators, which it clearly is lacking.

Perhaps the most important innovation in recent years to contribute to the corporate quality of the military officers' establishment has been the increased perquisites made available to the officers and requiring *Escuela Politécnica* training. The military commissary was established after the 1944 revolution so that officers could buy food, appliances, and items generally available at department stores at reduced prices. This was of particular importance for items such as imported liquors, which could be sold tax free. The commissary provided not only the officers themselves with needed items at reduced prices, but was used by some to obtain goods for resale, thus providing the individuals concerned with extra income.

The military hospital provided free service for active-duty officers and their entire families, including parents. In a society where responsibility for one's family extends both upward and downward, this extended family care is an important service. In recent years, the army has purchased lands in and around Guatemala City and undertaken the expense of subdividing them into housing lots. These have been made available to officers at a cost proportional to the original purchase price and at low rates of interest, thereby reducing materially the investment necessary by the individual officer. Here again, the opportunity presents itself for the officer to rent out the lot or house, therby turning the matter to direct financial advantage. Finally, the *Fondo de Prevision Militar* acts as a credit union for the military, a credit facility still relatively unavailable to other segments of the population.

Unquestionably one of the central mechanisms conducive to the corporate quality of the army has been the *Escuela Politécnica*. Since the school picks up youths shortly after they have finished primary school, they are still highly impressionable. Free matriculation at the *Politécnica* involves a commitment to remain in the service for six years thereafter. This means that the day-to-day associations of the individual are severely restricted to his colleagues in the service from the middle teens to the middle twenties—the entire early adult life. This period, during which the individual in Guatemala generally becomes politicized, is spent in a restricted military society. From the point of view of creating a cohesive corps, this could hardly be bettered.

As may be expected, however, an inevitable characteristic of large corporate organizations is internal factionalism. Within the military, the major rewards of power and income are limited and there is necessarily a significant amount of internal competition. Furthermore, although the organization may be corporate, it is completely Guatemalan, and its members of necessity are concerned with the state of the national society as well as their own microcosm.

The social cleavages in the military organization are of two types: those distinguishing officers from enlisted men; and those defining factions or differentiation within the officer corps. The present study unfortunately touched only in passing on the situation of the enlisted man and the noncommissioned officer in the army. It is a subject that needs real study and an adequate understanding of the full role of the army in the country at large will not be had until such a study is made.[6] An indication of the gulf that separates the officers from their enlisted troops may be had by figures made available on the language and literacy situation. One report states that "... of the total of individuals who enter the Service (Permanent Force and Military Reserves), 62.50 percent are illiterate and 57.13 percent belong to the Indian race, and of these, 13.71 percent speak no Spanish when entering and only 30.63 percent have Spanish as their maternal tongue."[7] The quality of the differentiation between an officer's corps, all the members of which have at least secondary school education, and an enlisted population, in which less than a third even have Spanish as a native language, is patent.

It has always been the practice, and continues so today, to recruit or conscript men from the ranks of the Indian and rural Ladino population. To be liable for conscription is a good index of one's lack of power to avoid it. The Ladino town dwellers of the western Indian region are generally not subject to recruitment, although the poorer may be enlisted in the local reserve units and be subject to training on a weekly basis. The distinction between officers and enlisted men follows a thoroughgoing caste line. It is more than just similar to the national scene: it is a caricature of it. One officer distinguished the Indian from the eastern Ladino conscript by indicating a preference for the former. Once you broke his customs, he explained, the Indian was much easier to change and discipline than was the Ladino.

That the Indians also receive somewhat different treatment was illustrated by one of our informants. He held that there was some sort of difference between the military who worked in the eastern and western parts of the country. In trying to clarify what this difference might be, another informant explained that officers who, upon leaving the *Escuela Politécnica*, were sent to the western region for their first tour of duty, dealt entirely with Indian soldiers. The pattern of treatment of the Indian soldiers was rather harsh; many understood little Spanish when they were conscripted and they tended to accept some degree of humiliation without reacting. Young officers who, in a sense, learned how to treat soldiers in the Indian areas would, upon occasion, be transferred to the *oriente* (east). There, the patterns of behavior learned in the west not only did not work, but caused violent reactions. The oriental Ladinos, regarding themselves as individualistically as young officers, refused to carry out orders under humiliating terms and, in a few instances, physically attacked the officers.

While no study has been made, nor does it appear likely that an objective one may be made in the near future, there is little evidence that what may be described for the officers also holds true for the Indians. The degree of professionalization among noncommissioned personnel is so slight that it is reported that there is almost a 50-percent turnover of enlisted men every two years. There are few benefits that make it attractive for them to identify strongly with the institution. The only areas in which they may be said to gain something are language, literacy and a mild degree of politicization. The army has, with some consistency, supported a program of literacy for its recruits, as well as produced materials for civilian programs. Similarly, the participation in anti-guerilla campaigns must have some side effects upon those soldiers who are curious as to what they are doing. Finally, conscripted monolingual Indians are taught Spanish during their two-year period. Taken together, these, and possibly other less evident features, serve to Ladinize. Since most recruits are either kept in the region in which they are recruited or sent to Guatemala City, they generally have little opportunity to become familiar with the country at large. Taken as a whole, there are few areas of Guatemalan life that are less known than the life of the enlisted man. What the army does to him and what he contributes to the army have never been systematically studied.

Aside from the officer/enlisted man differentiation, major factional lines within the military have formed around the following differences: army/air force; line officer/*Politécnica* graduate; young/old; liberal/conservative; and vertical divisions of loyalty, coupled with specific ties of common graduating class and the *centenario* (centenary) relation.

The army/air force split is unquestionably the most recent of these. Originally the flyers were army officers with flight training. After the Second World War, however, when the air force received some planes and clearly had their own barracks and bases, the differentiation between the two became increasingly evident. Among the gifts showered by the United States after the fall of Arbenz were a set of World War II Mustang fighters. The final turning point can probably be dated from the November 13 Movement. Ydígoras, in order to keep the air force loyal at that time, promised them new equipment, distinctive blue uniforms, better flight pay and license to earn money on the side by flying. Since that time, the split between the army and the air force has widened appreciably. The position of unique power held formerly by the army has been sharply disturbed by this division and Guatemala has now entered the ranks of those countries in which different branches of the armed forces may take different sides in the national political scene.

The distinction between the line officer and the *Escuela*

Politécnica graduate is one of the oldest of the cleavages, but one that is gradually becoming less important. The most famous relation in which it played a role in recent history was the fact that Arana was a line officer and Arbenz was a school graduate. The general history of this affair is fairly well known, and the details are not relevant to the present analysis. It was a case, however, in which the distinction contributed directly to the entire national political process.

We earlier described the castelike distance that separates officers from conscripts. In past years, there were many line officers who never went to the *Escuela Politécnica*. Of these, some were named out of the ranks and during the nineteenth and early part of the current century, there were cases of individuals of humble origin who reached positions of extraordinary power. The most famous of these in recent years was Ubico's secretary of war, General Jose Reyes. Today it would be almost impossible for a person to reach such a position in the service without a *Politécnica* background.

One of the devices used to strengthen the officer corps following the 1944 Revolution was to pressure line officers to go to the *Escula Politécnica* and take a degree. Table 1 shows the beginning of matriculation of such line-officer students in 1945. There are a number of interesting features to be noted here. In the first place, if one compares the attrition of line officers in the 1945-54 decade with that of the newly matriculating students, it is clear that the line officers were committed to the military profession to a much greater degree than were new candidates. It will also be noted, however, that all of the colonelships given after the 1944 revolution were to line officers; none were given (as of the cut-off date of these data, 1963) to any newly matriculating candidates who entered the *Politécnica* after 1944. White the government tended to follow the policy of naming no more line officers directly from civilian life after the 1944 revolution (except special instances, such as medical officers), it seems to be the case that the officers who had been in the service prior to 1944 were able to obtain the army's highest rank by 1965. Whether matriculation at the *Politécnica* was an effective prerequisite to this rank or not is not clear, but the data in Table I indicate that 73 percent of the line officers who did matriculate achieved the rank of colonel.[8] The line officers who attended the

Politécnica did not necessarily regard it as a privilege, nor did it make them feel closer to the society of regular *Politécnica* graduates. Many of them refused to wear the special insignia allowed only to graduates of the school.

The features that characterized the line/*Politécnica* distinction are, today, increasingly characteristic of the distinction between older and younger officers. "Young" here refers primarily to the post-1944 graduates. With the advent of the revolution and the role played by the *Escuela Politécnica* in it, greater emphasis has been placed on equipping the officer candidate for participation in national political life. The process of politicization, to be described shortly, is specifically relevant in the younger officers. Under Ubico, officers were supposed to be strictly military men and answerable to the military. Ubico allowed no politicking among his officers.

Older officers today criticize their younger colleagues for being too concerned with a comfortable life and perquisites than with the real responsibilities of military service. Younger officers, however, have tended more to participation in foreign training, especially counter-insurgency. The older accuse the younger of being "Leftists" or "Communists," whereas the younger regard the older as conservative and old-fashioned. In 1950, Monteforte Toledo submitted a questionnaire to 30 students of the *Escuela Politécnica* and 30 graduates aged 29 and 30. While there is no evidence that the selection of persons interviewed was in any sense random, the reported differences do not seem to show a consistent conservative bias by the older officers. For example, responses that could be interpreted as showing a conservative bias for the graduates are seen in Table 2.[9] On the other hand, there were a number of questions that could have shown such conservatism but did not do so, as seen in Table 3.[10]

Although technically defective and outdated, these data are reproduced here because they are the only actual questionnaire materials available on the military-officer population. The *Escuela Politécnica* now generally refuses to allow any sociological inquiry to be carried on and it has proved equally impossible to obtain permission of the officers in charge to allow such questions and interviews of soldiers or officers on active duty. Of greatest interest here, if these data are at all valid, is that the old/young distinction at that time did not conform to a simplistic political dichotomy. The features of the older graduates do, however, seem to conform to what one might predict if he were to relate them to the Ubico period: strong friendship with the United States, a civil government with no political parties, a somewhat directed economy with no labor unions, a general disinterest in the Church and a strong hand with the Indians.

This brings us to the fourth of the dichotomies within the corporate officer groups, that based on political predilections. The author is not convinced that a clear dichotomy really exists, but there are various references to it in literature, especially during the Arbenz regime. Ronald Schneider refers to "a new force . . . coming into control of Guatemala, an alliance of the young 'school' officers of the army with the extremist leaders of organized labor."[11] Although Schneider reports this as established fact, there is serious doubt that any such alliance ever existed. R. Baker holds that, "It must be stressed that Arbenz's favoritism created serious conflict within the armed forces. He had created a privileged class of junior officers who received rapid promotion, special favors, and choice assignments." This, however, merely states that there was an intentional effort to split young from old, a factionalism already noted. Moreover, Baker notes that "The Communists [sic] had not launched a major organizing campaign in the armed forces. (Nonetheless, they had attracted a few converts among junior officers and cadets.) Instead, they chose to infiltrate the ranks of the judicial and civil guards—the national police forces of Guatemala."[12] Although Baker refers to the younger group as if they were politically loyal to Arbenz, he mentions only two by name and fails to explain the lack of support from the alleged "group" when the army abandoned Arbenz in 1954. Baker does note, however, that "most officers were probably neutral or undecided."

Indeed, while there were certainly officers loyal to Arbenz, that some kind of "alliance" existed was probably more a figment of anti-Arbenz or anti-Communist paranoia than of systematic connivance between the two sectors. It is not clear at present that there is any real political split within the officer corps, although there are surely various shades of political interests and commitments. While there is little question but that the military is generally predisposed to find its interests closely allied to those of landholders and the upper sector generally, individual members are perfectly capable of learning alternative philosophies or identifying their interests with elements of the lower sector or with international interests antagonistic to that group. Since the first guerrilla bands were led by *Politécnica* graduates, there is ample evidence of this.

The internal organization of the officer corps is not easy to delineate, except by hearsay. There are two features that were mentioned by many informants as being of particular importance: the bond of belonging to the same graduating class, or *promoción*, and the *centenario* relation. As is the case in most western educational institutions, students entering at the same time and living through the years of training together form an especially important bond. Within the corporate life of the officer corps, graduates of the same class continue through their professional lives to recognize a special loyalty to each other and to make allowances that would not occur otherwise. An officer who finds himself in a position of particular power tends to seek at least some of his supporters from among those of his same class.

The *centenario* (centenary) relation is similar, except that it exists between two individuals rather than a group. Upon entering the *Politécnica*, each new candidate is given a consecutive number. The special relationship occurs between individuals with the same last two digits in their numbers. An individual who has (picking a number at random) number 421 will have a special responsibility for number 521 when he enters. The elder is particularly responsible for the welfare of his younger *centenario* during his years at school and through the rest of his military career. If an individual achieves power, then his *centenario* will generally be on the scene too.

Graduating class and *centenario* relations are of importance because they obviously serve to crosscut certain faction lines that have already been described. Older men thus have special responsibility for certain younger men, and political preferences can often be laid aside through the necessity of recognizing the loyalty expected of the members of one's own class year. There is a story to the effect that an evening party was held a few years ago by members of a particular class and in attendance was Yon Sosa, the guerrilla leader. The fact that in the regular line of duty he was the official enemy of the officers present was put aside for an evening in recognition of the fact that he was also of the same graduating class. While I cannot vouch for the story, the mere fact that it has been rumored is suggestive of the importance generally attached to the relationship involved.

Even with the internal organization, loyalty within the service also varies with political affiliation outside. One informant specified that the politics of the individual was the prime consideration determining who would be a loyal follower. This means that loyalty and politics within the service are intrinsic parts of the politics on the national and international scene. While this has obvious consequences for the professional quality of work, it also means that the power structure of the military is not only similar to that of the upper sector as a whole, but an intrinsic part of it. Since major benefits are derived from appointments to posts and these are granted by individuals in power, the vertical structure of military appointments is conducive to an apparent "personalism"—which is perhaps better seen as a mobility device.

The officer ambitious for success in the service must seek certain kinds of positions; to do so, he must profess a politics that will enable him to be granted the desired appointment. Which politics are most indicated depends upon who happens to be in control at the moment. Politics and personal loyalties are a latticework woven against the framework of the general power structure.

The officer corps, while clearly part of the upper sector, has developed specific relations with certain other elements of that sector. Of particular importance are relations with the landholders, the Church, the United States and university students.

The general political position of the military is indicated by the kinds of relations that hold with certain other sectors of the population. Until the Second World War, the military and the landholders had a running feud over the allocation of labor. The army wanted to conscript men and these men could be most readily obtained from the rural labor force. Until that time, however, labor was generally short, and the landholders tried to protect their own laborers from military service so that they would be available for agricultural work. The landholders saw the military as a parasite. The army, for its part, complained publicly during the 1920s that the landholders were hiding their laborers. This antagonistic relation was vitiated by two things. The general increase in the laboring population permitted the landholders, by 1950, to be less sensitive to the loss of labor and, in some instances, to be glad of it. And events in the world-power structure were making nations like Guatemala the scene of cold-war conflict. Since the shortage of manpower for cannons and coffee as an issue has been replaced by the common threat of world-wide socialism, the landholders and military have grown together. One still hears complaints by landholders that the military are parasites; and by the more liberal military that the large landholders are rapacious. But of much greater importance is that politically inclined landholders have no hesitation in seeking military action and military controls increasingly in order to defend themselves against what they see to be a communist threat.

A similar change has occurred between the military and the Church. With the installation of a liberal regime in 1871, Guatemala's official and emotional position was extreme anticlericism under the liberal political banner. This continued through the revolutionary period of 1944-54. The same concern that brought landholders and military together, however, also brought the Church increasingly to the side of the army. Although it was given no public promotion, the Jesuits under Ubico were encouraged to start schools in Guatemala City. When the public issue became communism in the early 1950s, the military found in the Church an ally it needed for closer contact and control over the rural population. First Castillo Armas, then Ydígoras, opened the society again to active Church work. Both regarded themselves as military men of liberal persuasion, and believed that such cooperation was necessary to keep socialism out.

A final and crucial ally of the military is the United States, specifically its military, diplomatic, and commercial communities. The relationship has long been an active one, but it has seen some problems in recent years. Prior to the "Good Neighbor" era, the role of the United States in Guatemala was not unlike that elsewhere in Central America. The United States operated semiopenly in governmental affairs, helped keep Cabrera in power, and by the early 1930s the *Politécnica* was under the directorship of an American military officer. American marines were accused of funnelling arms to the anti-Unionist party in the early 1920s.[13] During the Second World War, the U.S. military had a large contingent in Guatemala for purposes of Panama Canal defense. Since that time, including the entire revolutionary decade, there have usually been U.S. military attaché and mission officers in the country.

Beginning particularly with the United States' role in the fall of Arbenz, there has been an increasing ambivalence on the part of the Guatemalan military toward the United States. On the one hand—militarily—there is heavy dependence on the United States for a continuing supply of arms and training. Specifically in counter-insurgency work, U.S. sources have been of primary importance. While the Guatemalan military will not publicly take a political position against the United States, the dependence is a constant source of irritation to the nationalistic pride of Guatemalan officers.

The specific set of events that flamed this antagonism had to do with the succession of Castillo Armas. Because the military's refusal to take to the field in defense of Arbenz played a major role in the collapse of his regime, many officers felt that they had a right to determine the succession to the presidency. The United States, however, succeeded through diplomatic moves in gaining the position for Castillo Armas. Military feeling against the Liberation Army was particularly strong, and when Castillo demanded that they receive special recognition by leading in the victory parade, the military was enraged. One result was an attack by the cadets of the *Escuela Politécnica* on a small contingent of liberation forces billeted in the Roosevelt Hospital. The cadets were relatively successful and had to be called off with guarantees that they would not be punished. Castillo then sent some students home and others abroad on scholarships. With no students left, he then closed down the *Escuela Politécnica* for two years. Since most of the military officers were *Politécnica* graduates and looked at the cadets' action as little less than heroic, they saw the United States looming behind Castillo as the real cause of what was interpreted as an insult to their alma mater.

When Ydígoras arranged that Cuban anti-Castro forces should be trained at a private estate on the south coast, the military again saw the United States acting as a foreign power, using Guatemalan soil for foreign forces without the national military's consent. This was regarded as being of dubious value to Guatemala, and whatever payoff was to be had was clearly being received solely by Ydígoras and the owner of the estate, Alejos. The Guatemalan military was not benefiting from it. This issue was a principal rationale behind the November 13 military revolt, and when that uprising failed the government was accused of using planes flown by foreign pilots from the training camp against Guatemalan military units. It has been suggested that Ydígoras's flight to Quezaltenango during the revolt was due in part to the fact that he felt he could rely on the foreign forces at Helvetia to protect him should the revolt prove difficult to contain.[14]

The consequence of all this is that while the military rely and depend upon the United States as a source, anti-United States feeling is not limited to some alleged "left-wing" segment of the Guatemalan military establishment. It was manifest through much of the Peralta administration, when the top positions in the Guatemalan government were manned almost entirely by military men and they refused to accept most efforts to provide U.S. aid in economic development. It seems to be the case that it was not only the younger contingent of the military who were mainly active in this; many of the older and more conservative members were delighted to see the frustration of U.S. officials.

This relationship also reflects the increased incorporation of the Guatemalan military. While the United States provides materials and training, Guatemalan officers are careful not to reveal specific statistics and figures about their own condition. They feel that the integrity of their own service is threatened by the larger power and bring their corporate quality into play as protection. Even strongly conservative officers in the Guatemalan military go to considerable lengths to make it clear that the United States is not supposed to be running the Guatemalan army.

In contrast to the three relationships so far described, that which holds between the military and the university students has been consistently antagonistic. Students have a long tradition of categorical opposition to the military. They fought the army in 1870 and did so against Ponce in 1944. The military has always been a principal target in the annual *Huelga de Dolores*, the burlesque spoof that the students (when permitted) stage annually to criticize current events. Until 1950 or 1951, an open fight between students and cadets was a regular part of this annual affair; at that time, the cadets were sent out of the city on maneuvers so that there would be no contact.

The reason today for this antagonism is, if anything, greater than in the past. As will be explored in the next section, the interest of the military in government now makes them a greater threat than ever before to the civilian students. The corporate quality of the army, discouraging its officers from even taking university work, helps promote the separation. Since students do not constitute a corporate entity themselves, the conflict between the two is a peculiar one. It will presumably continue so long as the military manifest any continuing interest in governing.

AN ASSUMPTION OF REGNANCY

The "assumption of regnancy" refers to what appears to be an increasing trend in the Guatemalan military for which there is no ready term in English. There is evidence from various events that the military, as part of its increasing corporateness and continuing politicization, has been moving toward a regulating position in governmental affairs. It is, in a sense, taking over the ruling of the country.

In the first place, in recent years the elements of the military have been regularly involved in governing Guatemala one way or another. Between 1900 and 1966, the Guatemalan chief of state was a military man for 37 years.[15] Three of the last five took power by other than constitutional means. Also, the armed forces themselves have been used almost exclusively for purposes of internal control. Even José Rufino Barrios's attempt to recreate a united Central American union was aimed at creating a larger domestic scene. As other observers have noted,[16] this is characteristic of Latin America in general. In Guatemala, both in terms of the general orders and in actual practice, the army has been used to supplement the policing activities of other agencies and sometimes to substitute for them.

It can be argued that the responsibility of the military for fighting external wars has, for practical purposes, atrophied. One of the structural consequences of the establishment of the United Nations and the Organization of American States, each under the domination of one or more of the major world powers, is that the possibility for small and underdeveloped nations to carry on small wars is very much reduced. When Peru and Ecuador, or Costa Rica and Nicaragua, or another set of lesser powers get close to armed conflict, the peacemaking mechanisms of the large powers go to work to put a stop to it. War has increasingly become a prerogative of major powers and insurgents, and the government of Guatemala has lost any initiative it may have had. The obvious consequence of this is that while Guatemala has waged no real outside wars since the last century, it probably will find now that it cannot have any. It does not follow from this, however, that the military has no function. It is not that wars have disappeared, merely that the right to initiate them has changed hands.

It is clear that the Guatemalan military has played an important role in ruling in the recent past and that the scope of its interest in this activity has expanded since 1944. The overt rationale for this has been the internal threats of armed insurgents and "communism." There are two conditions, however, that lie behind this increase: the technical and material aid from the United States military; and the gradual increase in power of the central government.

During the Second World War and years preceding the fall of Arbenz in 1954, the United States contributed relatively little to the Guatemalan military establishment. Beginning in 1956, the United States Department of Defense cites the following as the annual deliveries of the Grant Aid Program, chargeable to appropriations:[17]

(in millions of dollars)

1956	.3	1960	.2
1957	.3	1961	.4
1958	.1	1962	1.3
1959	.05	1963	2.6
		1964	1.4

In comparison with the rest of the Middle American countries,

Guatemala received more than any except the Dominican Republic. These figures show that the input of U.S. aid began in 1956, but that it remained relatively low until fiscal year 1962, at which time it tripled in one year, then doubled again the next.

No matter what other factors may have been involved, it can hardly be a coincidence that the first time in recent Guatemalan history that a military government has taken over the entire control of the country occurred after it had received some millions of dollars worth of equipment from the United States. "As if" history is unsatisfactory for facts; one must certainly speculate whether the military would have been equipped to undertake so vast a job a few years before.[18]

The other, and more profound, factor that contributed to the movement towards military regnancy has been the gradual increase in power and controls of the central government through the continuing nationalization of the country as a whole. In the early days of the republic, the military could not have played such a role because it was not sufficiently cohesive. At the end of the nineteenth century it still could not have done it because the country was still essentially regionally separated and sheer military force could not have assured continuing government over such a long period of time. By 1960 15 years of politicization had followed the revolution. Landholders no longer expected to treat their estates as isolated domains. For the most part, they wanted improved communication and transportation facilities, thereby marking the emergence of Guatemala from the era when a region ccould even consider political succession. The kind of power exercised by Ubico relied on a scattered population, lack of communications and ignorance regarding political activities. The Guatemala that the Peralta government took over in 1963 had tasted of political power: the population was increasingly concentrating in Guatemala City and the country had shrunk under extending telegraph, telephone, radio and roads. With this shrinkage, the government had grown to exercise much more control than had been the case under Ubico, although the manner of that control was not so subject to the whims and tastes of a single individual.

This expansion of power by the central government cannot be explained here except in most general terms. Similarly its style of expression, at once a matter of Guatemalan cultural history and response to outside pressures, is a complexly interwoven product that requires an inquiry far beyond the scope of the present one. Given this expansion in power, however, it became possible for whoever took control of Guatemala to exercise that control more broadly than had previously been the case. This involved a change in the basic power structure and the emergence of more complex governing arrangements than had obtained before. When the military reached the position that it could handle such a complex situation, it could, and did, undertake to establish such a rule.

Besides these two general changes in basic conditions, there were two specific threats that caused the military to react as a corporate entity to defend itself. The first of these were the periodic attempts, both successful and unsuccessful, to arm other sectors of the population in order to bring a counter force to bear on the military's power. The second was the emergence of guerrilla forces following the November 13 Movement.

Prior to the revolution of 1944, it was standard practice for upper-sector citizens, especially in rural areas, to keep arms in their homes. These were used both for hunting and for personal protection. Among the lower sector, the possession of arms was more sporadic, yet especially among Ladinos, it was usually desirable to have them around for the latter reason. Beginning in 1944, there occurred a set of national events that served to spread the possession of arms. The first was the abortive Caribbean Legion, established to promote democracy elsewhere in the Caribbean. While this effort never proved conclusive in its original design, it did serve to introduce arms to its adherents in the country.

In 1954, a much more famous case occurred. Prior to the liberation, and surely one of the triggers of that event, a shipment of arms from eastern Europe arrived at Puerto Barrios on the *Alfhelm*. These had been contracted for by Arbenz with the goal of arming the agrarian committees, those rural cadres entrusted with the process of agrarian reform in the provincial areas. Arbenz, aware that the army was becoming increasingly suspicious of the political flavor of his government, sought to circumvent its power by this means. The army intercepted the shipment at the dock, however, and did not allow it to diffuse into the country. In spite of this, the political parties and mass organizations of the period facilitated the irregular spread of arms to leaders and members, so that while there was neither a consistent concentration nor an orderly distribution, the possession of arms became more widespread. Finally, the 1954 liberation movement itself was an entirely new source of arms, both in the urban areas and in certain parts of the rural area. Much of the U.S.-supplied funds for that movement went into the purchase of weapons that are still abroad in the hands of politically conservative and reactionary elements.

The most recent formal distribution reported to the research team occurred under Ydígoras Fuentes. In 1959 his supporters organized, particularly in the *oriente*, a series of vigilante groups whose principal function was to intimidate those peasants who would not support him. They distributed arms, including machine guns. With the fall of Ydígoras these groups quickly evaporated, but the arms they received presumably have remained in the rural areas. The military has been increasingly aware of the buildup in civilian armament and it certainly must weigh in their concern with the balance of power in the country at large.

The other threat, the appearance of guerrillas, has naturally been of much greater recent concern. The first two years of guerrila activity, during the Ydígoras administration, saw little effective counteraction. It was a period during which Yon Sosa, Turcios and other November 13 escapees were formulating and developing their philosophies and plans of action. At this time they were not taken entirely seriously and spent some of their time outside the country. According to Yon Sosa's description of his conversion into a guerrilla leader, he had not been aware of the real discontent that was latent among the peasant population. Upon discovering this in his attempt to formulate a successful coup at the time of the November 13 Movement, he then turned to the peasant population entirely and withdrew from any further attempt to steer the military into a significant revolt.

Following the assumption of power by Peralta Azurdia, the guerrilla forces became clearly differentiated. Both leaders spent time outside of the country, reportedly in Mexico and Cuba. Yon Sosa, operating primarily in Izabal and Alta Verapaz, carried on sporadic attacks both in that area and occasionally in the capital city. Turcios developed his work in the Sierra de las Minas on a somewhat different, and probably sounder, operational philosophy. He spent more time in the indoctrination of peasants and, assuring himself of a firm peasant base in the mountains, venturing forth somewhat less and showing himself to be less flamboyant than Yon Sosa. Both were for an immediate socialist revolution, but Turcios became much more closely allied with the Guatemalan communist party, the *Partido Guatemalteco de Trabajo*. The party, at that time, regarded Yon Sosa as somewhat unreliable, both militarily and ideologically. During the period of the study in 1965, the Yon Sosa band was losing its effectiveness, apparently from the failure to secure a peasant base. Turcios' group, on the other hand, had made it public that they were working on a strategy that allowed for 15 or 20 years of conflict.

Although both groups had succeeded in issuing mimeographed newspapers and newspapermen and even American TV reporters carried out extensive interviews with the leaders, the government under Peralta publicly regarded the guerrilla forces as bandits. In the course of informal conversations during the summer of 1965, we found that urban government and private individuals alike spoke of the guerrillas as being more of a bother than a menace. In subsequent months, however, this attitude began to change. Through kidnapping of wealthy individuals for ransom in 1965-66, they built up what conservatively can be estimated to be some $500,000 in cash. They continued to obtain most of their arms from the military, usually through raids or by killing individuals. They began more systematically to kill private citizens whom they felt were harmful to their safety. Even though the Peralta government kept almost all information of guerrilla activities out of the newspapers, the military presumably became increasingly aware of their danger. The government also began to receive increasing kinds and amounts of United States military aid. When the government was taken over by Julio César Mendes Montenegro in 1966, it was with the reported understanding that the military would be free of civilian government controls insofar as the pursuit of guerillas was concerned.

It is neither possible nor appropriate here to attempt to outline the recent history of guerrilla activities. They have received amazingly, although episodic, wide coverage in the press, both in

Mexico and the United States, although presumably information of immediate tactical value is missing from most accounts.[19] Of importance from the point of view of understanding the military, however, are the following points: (1) The guerrilla leaders in the earlier phases were *Escuela Politécnica* graduates who claimed they were rebelling against those elements of Guatemalan society that were inhibiting the national destiny. By virtue of these two facts, they had wide-ranging relationships within the Guatemalan military and this surely made it difficult for some officers to seek them out to kill them at the outset. Their challenge to the United States was subtly appreciated in military circles, and the corporate quality of the military gave them an initial degree of protection. (2) The early guerrilla leaders were trained to counter-insurgency by the United States and thus were more than mere amateurs, even though they varied in their strategic skill in applying their learning. (3) They had adopted a political position in favor of extreme socialist revolution and refused to be involved in any democratic processes of elections or compromises with the government. They thereby placed themselves in direct opposition to the entire established regime. (4) They called upon and received a continuous, although quantitatively unknown, support in men and materials from urban dwellers. especially from sympathetic university students. Their operation was by no means a rural one, but was geared to the urban-rural axis upon which the country as a whole was based. They also, at least in the early period, had irregular contacts and temporary understandings with some national political figures. (5) And finally, at least one of the organizations was operating on a long-term plan that involved a strategy of placing the Guatemalan military in such an awkward position that it would be necessary to bring in the United States Marines. Reflecting possibly on the fact that Sandino in Nicaragua was never beaten by the Marines and that the position of the U.S. forces in the Dominican Republic at that time was becoming increasingly embarrassing they felt that the United States' presence would effectively neutralize the Guatemalan army, help to shatter its corporate quality and prove it to be so ineffectual that its more revolutionarily inclined officers would abandon it.

Given that the military was faced with these threats within the nation, the final question leads us to explore just what some of the processes have been whereby the military has gradually moved towards regnancy. These have consisted of two major paths: (1) the increasing spread of a network of contact with the general population; and (2) an experiment in government.

The network of contacts has been of two kinds. The first has already been alluded to and consisted of the identification of interests with certain other sectors of the population. The landowners and the Church have both become specific allies, and the older conflicts with these sectors have in the main disappeared. The second kind of contact has been an attempt by the military to extend controls more directly over the peasantry and provincial population. The prerevolutionary military consisted of a few officers and small garrisons, with the officers keeping rather more to themselves and treating peasants as the inferiors they were thought to be. The only contact that the peasants had with soldiers, aside from being conscripted, was to be rounded up to be taken to vote, or to see the army in its police role. Because of this general picture, the military had neither any idea of what was going on among the rural population, nor was it appreciated by that population.

In the years following the November 13 Movement, two steps were taken to rectify this situation. In order to gain more knowledge about political and other affairs of interest, the army revised the role of the military commissioner, and civic-action programs were initiated. Until this time, the commissioner was an army reserve appointee in each municipality and large estate, whose principal responsibility was to round up the conscripts and deliver them to the army and occasionally report matters of interest to the military. They had aides in the smaller settlements. They were usually ex-soldiers, often noncommissioned officers, and were responsible to the chief of reserves, an officer located in the capital city of the province. The chief of reserves, in turn, was responsible to the chief of the military zone.[20]

During the revolutionary period, the commissioners were already perceived by the emerging peasant organizations as real or potential threats. Baker reports that the "Communists" tried ". . . to effect changes in the military commissioners, the local military auxiliary units stationed in the rural areas which came under the ultimate control of the chief of the armed forces. Officers of the local branches of the CNGG (National Confederation of Guatemalan Peasants) flooded the offices of armed forces chief Diaz with requests for the transfer of commissioners who opposed agrarian reform or resisted CNGG officials." Baker cites these requests as beginning in 1951, but becoming especially heavy towards the fall of the Arbenz government in 1954. There were apparently about two dozen such cases altogether in the records he inspected. This material indicates that the revolutionary activities, specifically those of the CNGG, saw this arm of the military as a potentially dangerous threat to efforts to alter the social structure of the country.[21]

The innovation in the commissioner system was to convert what had been a device for local control into a widespread active spy network. It was the duty of the commissioner to report on the activities of the local people. Incidents that seemed to have any interest for the military, and this included activities of a political nature, were reported. This became especially active under the intermittent periods of martial law. The procedure was changed under the Peralta regime so that the information came directly to the chief of state's general staff. While the change in activity of the commissioner succeeded in establishing a network of information and control over much of the nation, it operated differently in different regions. In the manner here described, it was particularly important to the south coast and the *oriente*. The research team found little evidence of this kind of activity in the western departments. In the northeast, where guerrilla activity was overt, the term "military commissioner" applied to a rather different type of individual. There he was a one-man army who moved from one settlement to another, on the lookout for evidence of guerilla activity. In this case, the commissioner was occupied full time in his task and was paid for it.

Response to the commissioner-turned-spy was, as might be expected, suspicion. *"Orejas"* (ears), as they are known in Guatemala, are quite familiar and every government within living memory has had some. With the increasing antagonism that accompanied the expanded role of the commissioners, peasants were encouraged by their more revolutionary or radical friends to do away with particularly obnoxious commissioners. The guerrilla bands began to report that they had killed specific commissioners as

TABLE 1

MILITARY SCHOOL (*POLITÉCNICA*) ENTERING CLASSES AND GRADUATES WHO HAVE REACHED COLONEL'S RANK AND WHO HAVE TAKEN ADDITIONAL ACADEMIC DEGREES.

Year (Promotion)	Entering Students			Graduates				Colonel in 1964				Taken Additional Degrees	
	TOTAL	New	Line	TOTAL	New	Line	TOTAL	New No.	New %	Line No.	Line %	No.	%
1920 (1 & 2)	31	31	0	22	22	0	16	16	72.7	0	0	2	9.0
1921 (3 & 4)	32	32	0	21	21	0	14	14	66.6	0	0	2	9.5
1922 (5 & 6)	43	43	0	31	31	0	22	22	70.9	0	0	1	3.2
1923 (7 & 8)	19	19	0	10	10	0	6	6	60.0	0	0	0	—
1924 (9 & 10)	36	36	0	18	18	0	15	15	83.3	0	0	0	—
1925 (11 & 12)	23	23	0	14	14	0	8	8	57.1	0	0	2	14.2
1926 (13 & 14)	22	22	0	6	6	0	3	3	50.0	0	0	2	33.3
1927 (15 & 16)	62	62	0	21	21	0	16	16	76.1	0	0	1	4.7
1928 (17 & 18)	27	27	0	18	18	0	10	10	55.5	0	0	1	5.5

TABLE 1 (continued)

MILITARY SCHOOL (*POLITÉCNICA*) ENTERING CLASSES AND GRADUATES WHO HAVE REACHED COLONEL'S RANK AND WHO HAVE TAKEN ADDITIONAL ACADEMIC DEGREES.

Year (Promotion)	Entering Students			Graduates			Colonel in 1964					Taken Additional Degrees	
	TOTAL	New	Line	TOTAL	New	Line	TOTAL	New No.	New %	Line No.	Line %	No.	%
1929 (19 & 20)	36	36	0	13	13	0	7	7	53.8	0	0	1	7.6
1930 (21)	33	33	0	17	17	0	16	16	94.1	0	0	1	5.8
1930 (22)	32	32	0	18	18	0	15	15	83.3	0	0	1	5.5
1931 (23 & 24)	81	81	0	48	48	0	38	38	79.1	0	0	4	8.3
1932 (25 & 26)	34	34	0	28	28	0	21	21	75.0	0	0	4	14.2
1933 (27 & 28)	38	38	0	23	23	0	20	20	86.9	0	0	0	–
1934 (29)	33	33	0	19	19	0	11	11	57.8	0	0	1	5.2
1935 (30 & 31)	40	40	0	24	24	0	15	15	62.5	0	0	4	16.6
1936 (32 & 33)	39	39	0	21	21	0	17	17	80.9	0	0	1	4.7

TABLE 1 (continued)

MILITARY SCHOOL (POLITÉCNICA) ENTERING CLASSES AND GRADUATES WHO HAVE REACHED COLONEL'S RANK AND WHO HAVE TAKEN ADDITIONAL ACADEMIC DEGREES.

Year (Promotion)	Entering Students			Graduates			Colonel in 1964					Taken Additional Degrees	
	TOTAL	New	Line	TOTAL	New	Line	TOTAL	New No.	%	Line No.	%	No.	%
1937 (34 & 35)	24	24	0	17	17	0	7	7	41.1	0	0	2	11.7
1938 (36 & 37)	26	26	0	20	20	0	15	15	75.0	0	0	1	5.0
1939 (38 & 39)	53	53	0	43	43	0	27	27	62.2	0	0	9	20.9
1940 (40 & 41)	28	28	0	21	21	0	10	10	47.6	0	0	1	4.7
1941 (42)	8	8	0	8	8	0	6	6	75.0	0	0	1	12.5
1942 (43)	41	41	0	28	28	0	5	5	17.8	0	0	8	32.1
1943 (44)	29	29	0	25	25	0	10	10	40.0	0	0	7	28.0
1944 (45)	36	36	0	24	24	0	11	11	45.8	0	0	3	12.5
1945 (46)	35	21	14	27	13	14	18	6	40.0	12	85.7	1	3.7

TABLE 1 (continued)

MILITARY SCHOOL (*POLITÉCNICA*) ENTERING CLASSES AND GRADUATES WHO HAVE REACHED COLONEL'S RANK AND WHO HAVE TAKEN ADDITIONAL ACADEMIC DEGREES.

Year (Promotion)	Entering Students			Graduates			Colonel in 1964					Taken Additional Degrees	
	TOTAL	New	Line	TOTAL	New	Line	TOTAL	New No.	New %	Line No.	Line %	No.	%
1946 (47)	63	50	13	43	31	12	31	19	61.3	12	100	2	4.6
1947 (48)	76	48	28	49	26	23	17	0	0	17	74.0	2	4.0
1948 (49)	59	35	24	32	10	21	16	0	0	16	75.2	0	0
1949 (50)	50	31	19	24	7	17	16	0	0	16	94.0	0	0
1950 (51)	42	32	10	16	8	8	6	0	0	6	75.0	0	0
1951 (52)	56	36	20	31	12	19	18	0	0	18	99.7	0	0
1952 (53)	54	38	16	29	17	12	10	0	0	10	83.2	0	0
1953 (54)	65	57	8	14	8	6	6	0	0	6	100	0	0
1954 (55)	44	40	4	12	9	3	3	0	0	3	100	0	0

TABLE 1 (continued)

MILITARY SCHOOL (POLITÉCNICA) ENTERING CLASSES AND GRADUATES WHO HAVE REACHED COLONEL'S RANK AND WHO HAVE TAKEN ADDITIONAL ACADEMIC DEGREES.

Year (Promotion)	Entering Students			Graduates			Colonel in 1964					Taken Additional Degrees	
	TOTAL	New	Line	TOTAL	New	Line	TOTAL	New No.	%	Line No.	%	No.	%
1955 (56)	47	47	0	22	22	0	0	0	0	0	0	0	0
1956 (57)	60	35	25	41	23	18	15	0	0	15	83.3	0	0
1956 (58)	11	11	0	5	5	0	0	0	0	0	0	0	0
1957 (59)	45	45	0	19	19	0	0	0	0	0	0	0	0
1958 (60)	87	87	0	45	45	0	0	0	0	0	0	0	0
1959 (61 & 62)	68	68	0	32	32	0	0	0	0	0	0	0	0
1960 (63 & 64)	33	33	0	9	9	0	0	0	0	0	0	0	0
1961 (65)	14	14	0	8	8	0	0	0	0	0	0	0	0
1961 (66)	14	14	0	—	—	—	0	0	0	0	0	0	0

TABLE 1 (continued)

MILITARY SCHOOL (POLITÉCNICA) ENTERING CLASSES AND GRADUATES WHO HAVE REACHED COLONEL'S RANK AND WHO HAVE TAKEN ADDITIONAL ACADEMIC DEGREES.

Year (Promotion)	Entering Students			Graduates			Colonel in 1964					Taken Additional Degrees	
	TOTAL	New	Line	TOTAL	New	Line	TOTAL	New No.	New %	Line No.	Line %	No.	%
1962 (67)	33	33	0	—	—	—	0	0	0	0	0	0	0
1962 (68)	22	22	0	—	—	—	0	0	0	0	0	0	0
1963 (69 & 70)	69	69	0	—	—	—	0	0	0	0	0	0	0

SOURCE: Francisco A. Samayea, *La Escuela Politécnica a Través de su Historia* vol 2. Guatemala, 1964. This table was prepared by Jerrold Buttrey.

TABLE 2

Issue		Students	Graduates
Labor Unions	In favor	7	6
	Against	17	19
	Indifferent	6	4
Political Parties	In favor	14	8
	Against	12	20
	Indifferent	4	2
Treat Indians as Equals[a]	Yes	11	6
	No	16	20
Strong Friendship with the United States	In favor	1	9
	Against	16	14
	Indifferent	3	7

[a] Apparently the question refers to how the subject thinks the Indians *ought* to be treated, but this was not clear in Toledo's text.

a service to the peasants. In some instances, however, commissioners were themselves sympathetic to the political concerns of the peasants and presumably provided the military with little useful information.

The other major step taken by the army, the civic action program, was designed to simultaneously gather intelligence about provincial areas where there was little current control and, in so doing, provide a better image for the military in the eyes of the civilian population. The civic action programs and counter-insurgency were closely coupled activities, the former being one rather specialized phase of the latter. While used much earlier in the Philippines to control the Huks, Guatemala was the first country in Latin America to actively undertake such a program.[22] The Guatemalan army had for years participated in limited civic functions. The most important were road building and the extension of telegraph service. During the 1930s, such emphasis was placed on this that for a time a special alternative degree was offered in road engineering at the *Escuela Politécnica.* one of the outstanding features of Ubico's administration was the extension of the road system to many formerly inaccessible corners of the country. This was done in large part under the direction of army officers.

The expansion of civilian ministries under the post-1944 governments led to a reduction of army participation in much of this kind of work. In 1960, however, the Inter-American Defense Board approved a resolution to use military personnel and equipment for purposes of economic development, education, and highway settlement work, insofar as such work did not interfere with the civilian agencies and regular military tasks.[23] While this resolution was approved on December 1, 1960, in the previous month of the same year the United States had already sent a civic-action team to Guatemala at the request of Ydígoras. Ydígoras openly supported its development. In 1964, a committee in each locality was set up to be responsible for determining what projects would be carried out. For the most part, the some 240 committees that were set up were inoperative by 1966.

Reportedly the most active and probably successful of the various attempts were in inoculation, school lunches and literacy.[24] The inoculation program is supposed to have reached some 30,000 people in the department of Izabal in 1964. Mobile medical teams reached various places irregularly. The medical program, started much earlier, had proved so successful that it had run into objections from the Ministry of Public Health and had to slow down. From 1963 until 1966, the school-lunch project expanded from "740 schools and 78,000 children to 3,320 schools and 338,775 children." The account of the *Dirección de Desarrollo* Socio-Educative Rural for 1965 states that approximately 75 percent of the rural-school population received hot lunches. But note that only 26 percent of all rural children 7 through 14 were enrolled in school.

Perhaps the strongest arm of the civic-action program has been literacy. The army printing plant (with strong support from AID) turned out 2 million sets of first-reader series, together with workbooks, teaching aids, charts and so forth during the 1963-65 period. In an analysis of the total national literacy effort for the month of January 1965, it develops that of the 64,589 students recorded, 13,631 were receiving instruction from military personnel in the civic-action program. The greatest number of these were in Sololá, Huehuetenango and Alta Verapaz, only the last of which is an area of particular concern in the efforts of the insurgents. The total effort, however, was reaching only 2 percent of the illiterate population and of those enrolled, between 30 and 40 percent passed the program successfully.

Evaluation of the civic-action programs is as difficult as is the evaluation of any military action. Most of the information is hard to come by and, even though civic-action officers of both the Guatemalan and U.S. military were cooperative to the research team, some crucial information is unavailable. There is little question, however, but that such activity has been carried on and that it could not help but have had some effect of the kind for which it was designed. Whether it profoundly changes the traditional suspicion of the peasant towards the military is an open question.

Given the growth in strength of the military, their increased incorporation and professionalization, and the threats that they perceived due to the cumulation of arms in provincial areas and the advent of the guerrillas, one further factor has contributed to the tendency toward regnancy. This was the first year of practice rule that they had from 1962 to 1963, and then the three years of overt rule, from 1963 to 1966.[25] Following the public disturbances in March 1962, the Ydígoras government was all but taken over by military officers. Cabinet and other central posts were occupied by officers and essentially the president was allowed to play only a superficial and vocal role. Finding that they were able to handle matters at least as well as, if not considerably better than Ydígoras had, they then took over completely in 1963. In a real sense, the takeover was not merely military, since it had the strong support, if not the overt cooperation, of many sectors of the population. But that it was militarily led and that the government continued to be militarily staffed meant that it was a reasonable approximation of what a military government would look like. The three years of open rule confirmed what the military had learned in the previous year of covert control. They could handle it just as well as their civilian predecessors. The fact that not too many steps in development were taken was explained as an attempt to avoid the impression that the military government wished to remain in power. The chief of state, Enrique Peralta, refused for this reason to take the title of president, and being assured of the elimination of the really undesirable candidates (from the military point of view these included Juan José Arévalo, Francisco Villagrán Kramer and possibly Mario Méndez Montenegro), the election of a civilian government was overseen in a traditionally democratic manner.

If there is a tendency toward regnancy, as is proposed here, why did the military permit a civilian government to reassume power? The answer lies in at least five areas. First, the military did not give up some crucial powers, such as the freedom to continue to handle the guerrillas as they pleased and to name the minister of defense. Second, it was public knowledge that a sizeable portion of the conservative officers were deeply suspicious of a "leftist" civilian administration and were constantly threatening, along with conservative civilians, to topple it. Third, since the time the Guatemalan military committed itself to act sheerly as an interim government, two other major Latin American countries were taken over in such a way as to leave no doubt that a military regime would continue to exist indefinitely. In Argentina and Brazil, military governments had made it clear that they did not regard the immediate return of a civilian democratic government to be at all desirable for the welfare of the country as a whole. Fourth, the personality of Enrique Peralta Azurdia must be considered a factor. This officer had, on previous occasions, ample opportunity to become chief of state but actually avoided them. His first opportunity followed the 1944 revolution, at which time he was favored for the new presidency. He rejected the offer, however, and consistently showed himself to be unwilling to assume such a permanent position thereafter. Placed in the temporary seat of power, it seems reasonable to see his subsequent actions as being consistent with his earlier predisposition.

Finally, the position of the United States, especially influential in Caribbean politics and relatively less so in Brazil and Argentina, was that it did not wish to support a military dictatorial government. In addition to wishing to appear as if it were not influencing the Guatemalan political situation, it did not want to be accused of supporting military dictatorships. Presumably in good faith, it took the policy position that a civilian, democratically elected government would be better in the long run, especially if the military kept to its task of running down the guerrillas. Following the resumption of civil government in 1966, the United States made every effort to discourage another military coup.

If it is not possible to fully evaluate these five factors, we can, however, ask what would happen were they different. In the first place, given its current power, the military is not likely to give up its power and control its own position. Second, it is quite possible for the conservative element of the military to take over the direction of the whole, particularly if the civilian government proves effective. Third, Brazil and Argentina now stand as models of what a military government may attempt should it so wish. Fourth, there is absolutely no reason to think that the next military leader will be reluctant, as was Peralta Azurdia, to assume dictatorial powers. And finally, the United States, if it is sufficiently afraid of the "Communist" guerrillas and if it is true to form, will automatically opt for an incumbent government that promises to "achieve stability and democracy."

In terms of the total power structure of Guatemala, it is erroneous to think of the military acts merely in some predestined, cyclical manner. The role of the military in Guatemalan public affairs has changed steadily and the change has been in one direction. While it has broadened its position in the society at large, it has consistently consolidated its mechanisms and bases of control. It is in a position to take over the government whenever conditions indicate that it should and it is capable of ruling for an indefinite period. It is capable of thus providing the population's interest, motivation and bases and mechanisms for political action do not grow. In this era of world history, these "ifs" warrant serious attention.

TABLE 3

Issue		Students	Graduates
Religion	Practising Catholic	4	4
	Non-practising Catholic	20	13
	Protestant	2	1
	No religion	4	12
Political Preference	With Liberals	9	8
	With Conservatives	3	1
	With October 1944 Revolutionary Movement	12	9
	None	6	12
The best government for the country would be:	Civil	13	14
	Military	17	12
	Mixed	—[a]	4
Socio-economic preference preference	Free Economy	19	16
	Directed Economy	5	9
	Indifferent	6	6

[a]"Mixed" category not included in student questionaire.

NOTES

1. The materials upon which this analysis is based were collected to a great extent by Jerrold Buttrey as a part of a broader research project on the contemporary social structure of Guatemala under the direction of the present writer. Buttrey did most of his work during the summer of 1965 but has made frequent visits to Guatemala both before and since that time. While indebted to him for much of the data and ideas utilized herein, we must assume responsibility for the form of analysis and conclusions reached. Buttrey's work in 1965, as well as much of the general project of which this study is a part, was made possible through a grant from the Ford Foundation to the Institute of Latin American Studies of the University of Texas. The cooperation of the Seminario de Integración on Social Guatemalteco and the Consejo Nacional de Planificación Económica of the Guatemalan Government was central to the research and is hereby gratefully acknowledged. In keeping with anthropological field research practice, informants remain anonymous, but their active participation in the research was, quite obviously, central to its success.

2. P. Zamora Castellanos, *El grito de independencia* (Guatemala: Tipografia Nacional, 1935).

3. There are reports of using military positions to enhance one's private income. Most favored jobs within the armed forces include those related to the handling of supplies and running commissaries. There is no reason to imagine that Guatemalan officers are any less subject to temptation than those in other armed forces in this regard. The present subject does not concern itself with this subject, however, and therefore we can only assume that the level of dishonesty within the military is no different from that in the population at large.

4. The newspaper *El Imparcial* on November 24, 1960, carried the report that President Ydigoras had announced that two national estates would be divided among deserving members of the military. It seems likely that "deserving" in this context refers to the role the officers played in the November 13 attempted military coup against the Ydigoras government.

5. The writer recalls a discussion he had with a member of Panama's oligarchy in the Union Club in Panama City in 1953. His host offered a fairly involved but well thought out exposition of how the various "forces" or "interests" in Panama could and,

according to the speaker, would undertake a guerrilla war to eliminate the oligarchy and eventually United States control in the country. Vietnam's struggle against the French was the explicit case in point at that time.

6. It may be mentioned at this point that, while cooperation was offered to the study by a number of elements in the officer corps, a more common reaction to inquiries or requests for permission to obtain information was one of distrust. It was not possible in the time available to obtain contemporary data on the enlisted forces or on details of the sociological background of the members of the officers' corps. It is perhaps an indication of the very corporate quality here under discussion that a perceived threat to any part of the military establishment is seen as a threat to the entire organization.

7. El Servicio de Analfabetización del Ejército, "La alfabetización en el Ejército: estudio sobre la contribución del Ejército en la lucha contra en analfabetismo en Guatemala," mimeographed (Guatemala: September 15, 1961).

8. With the downfall of Ubico and the institution of the revolutionary regime, all ranks above that of colonel in the Guatemalan army were abolished. Those reaching colonelship have, then, achieved the highest rank the army has to offer.

9. Mario Monteforte Toledo, *Guatemala: Monografía Sociológica* (Mexico, 1959).

10. Ibid.

11. The question as to this alliance was brought to my attention by Jerrold Buttrey. See Ronald M. Schneider, *Communism in Guatemala, 1944-54* (New York: Praeger, 1959).

12. R. K. Baker, *A Study of Military Status and Status Deprivation in Three Latin American Armies* (Washington, D.C.: The American University, Center for Research in Social Systems, 1966).

13. Anonymous, *Relatos del Normalista y Soldado, Verdaderas Causas de la Caída del Poder Público del Sr. Lic. Manuel Estrada Cabrera* (Quetzaltenango: Tipografía Occidental, 1928).

14. Jerrold Buttrey, "The Guatemalan Military, 1944-1963: An Interpretive Essay," unpublished manuscript.

15. J. M. Orellana, 1922-27; Lázaro Chacón, 1927-31; Jorge Ubico, 1931-44; Federico Ponce, 1944; Jacobo Arbenz, 1950-54; Carlos Castillo Armas, 1954-56; Miguel Ydígoras Fuentes, 1958-63; Peralta Azurdia, 1963-66.

16. John J. Johnson, *The Military and Society in Latin America*

(Stanford, Calif.: Stanford University Press, 1964) and Irving L. Horowitz, "The Military Elite," *Elites in Latin America* Seymour M. Lipset and Aldo Solari, eds. (New York: Oxford University Press, 1967), pp. 146-89.

17. Department of Defense, *Military Assistance Facts* (February 15, 1965).

18. Willard F. Barber and C. Neale Ronning report that in 1959 the United States Congress amended the Mutual Security Act to provide that "internal security requirements shall not, unless the President determines otherwise, be the basis for military assistance programs to American republics." In a State Department bulletin of March 11, 1963, assistant secretary of state Martin stated that the improvement of Latin American national security was one of the steps that the United States was taking to combat the spread of Communist subversion in the hemisphere. A year later, this was expressed as a matter-of-fact doctrine in a State Department memorandum entitled *Points in Explanation of U.S. Military Assistance Program for Latin America*: "this administration is seeking to orient the military assistance program in Latin America away from the outmoded concept of hemispheric defense towards greater emphasis on meeting the internal subversive threat." Two years before, in its joint resolution of October 3, 1962, Congress had already called for immediate steps, "by whatever means may be necessary, including the use of arms," to prevent Cuba from extending communism in the hemisphere.

19. See, among others, A. Rivera, "Llamamos a la toma del poder, dicen las guerrillas," *Economía* 2 (March-April 1965): 29-33; Daniel James, "Subversive Document Revealed," *The Latin American Times* 1 (1965): 18; A. Howard, "With the Guerrillas in Guatemala," *New York Times Magazine*, June 26, 1966; and A. Gilly, "The Guerrilla Movement in Guatemala," *Monthly Review* 17 (1965): 7-41.

20. G. A. Moore writes that "the military commissioner . . . has been present in the village for the last generation, and he acts to intervene as a direct arm of the army whenever that institution seeks to influence action on a local level. Thus on the one hand, he and his four assistants act as a police force during an official state of siege, and also act as an information agency. When for example, the military regime sought to change the municipal corporation in 1963, this was the Army's means of penetrating this particular village. The commissioner's role itself is given no particular ideologic content

save that which accompanies any military training. The commissioner retains his army rating and owes obedience and loyalty like any good soldier. Complaints directed against him by the villagers stress his overemphsis on military duties at the expense of local etiquette." G. A. Moore, *Social and Ritual Change in a Guatemalan Town*, Ph.D. disser. Columbia University (Ann Arbor, Mich.: University Microfilm, 1966), p. 359.

21. Baker, *A Study of Military Status*, pp. 43-44, 101, 117.

22. H. F. Walterhouse, "A Time to Build: Military Civic Action—Medium for Economic Development and Social Reform," *Studies in International Affairs* Institute of International Studies, University of South Carolina 4 (1964).

23. Willard F. Barber and C. Neale Ronning, *Internal Security and Military Power: Counter-Insurgency and Civic Action in Latin America* (Columbus, Ohio: Ohio State University Press, 1966).

24. Jere Weaver, *Political Style of the Guatemalan Military Elite* Ph.D. Diss., University of Pittsburgh, 1969.

25. Buttrey, "The Guatemalan Military."

6
Military Organization and Conspiracy in Turkey

Kenneth Fidel

Since the end of World War II, military seizure of political power has become a recurrent phenomenon in the developing world. Over the past 25 years, the list of nations that have experienced military power seizures has grown increasingly longer. Social scientists have not overlooked the military revolt as a concomitant of development; 'in both national studies and cross-national comparisons they have noted the importance of the military in the development process and the correlation between nation-building and military politics.[1] For the most part, social-scientific interest in military revolt has been primarily with the political preconditions for military insurrection and the effects of successful power seizure. In most instances, the relationship has been posited in terms of the military as the independent variable and development as the dependent variable. In this chapter, development is viewed as the independent variable and the form and substance of military politics as the dependent variable. In effect, military revolt is viewed as a function of development and development processes.

Much of the social-scientific literature has also overlooked variations in military organization and insurrection.[2] This chapter is primarily concerned with one type of military revolt—that carried out by conspiratorial military groups in large, bureaucratically structured military organizations. As such it is intended as a segment of a larger theory of military politics. We are concerned with three topics: (1) the social-structural conditions producing conspiratorial military groups, (2) their recruitment base and (3) the dynamics of conspiratorial organizations.

Materials used are drawn from a case study of the 1960 Turkish military revolt and the conspiratorial group that planned the coup. The main body is divided into three sections that deal with the following topics respectively: First, there is a discussion of Turkish development showing how the impetus to military discontent stemmed from changes in Turkish social structure and the declining position of the officer corps as a social class. Second, there is a discussion of the officer corps as a segmentalized group in which different categories have varying interests, political outlook and political opportunity. Changes in the social structure and its concomitants are shown to have differential effect on different segments of the officer corps. Third, there is a discussion of the sociology of conspiratorial military groups showing how their existence is patterned by secrecy, illegitimacy and lack of access to normal channels of political communication and influence. There are also discussions of the dilemmas of conspiratorial group existence, recruitment, organization, leadership, ideology and strategy and tactics.

TURKISH DEVELOPMENT AND SOCIAL STRUCTURE

After nearly 40 years of existence, the first Turkish republic was brought to an abrupt end by a military coup and the supplantation of the civilian regime by a military junta, the National Unity Committee. Although the republic had been founded by military men and the armed forces had been continuously involved in both formulating and enacting public policy, it had never before experienced overt military intervention. As late as 1955, civil-military relations appeared to have stabilized with the principle of civilian domination of politics permanently established. During the following five years, established patterns of civil-military relations deteriorated and the principle of civilian domination of politics was destroyed. The 1960 revolution was more than an expression of military discontent with a civilian regime; it was the culmination of a historical era in which changes in the Turkish social structure had radically altered every major facet of the political culture. The thrust of the revolt, however, was not the establishment of a new order reflecting a newly emerged social structure, but an attempt to reconstitute an obsolete coalition and restore the old order.

In this instance the old order was the socio-political culture that prevailed as an outcome of the Kemalist development program. In most general terms, the goals of that program were to replace moribund Ottoman institutions with borrowings from Western society and have Turkey develop economically through the mobilization of internal resources. To carry out the program, a number of basic orientations towards the population were adopted; specifically these were etatism, secularism, modernization, authoritarianism and centralization. Moreover, the Kemalist program was not universally applied. On the basis of a socio-political analysis that identified the major centrifugal forces potentially fragmenting the nation as the independence and isolation of urban regions, Kemal Ataturk chose to weld the nation into a single entity by concentrating development effort in urban regions and linking the cities physically, culturally and politically to the capital.[3]

The rail network was extended to every city and designed to provide direct transportation from every region of the country to the new capital at Ankara. In the cities, development funds were used to construct schools, baths, public buildings, streets and sewers, thus providing urban populations with common amenities of urban life. Cultural programs stressing Turkish nationalism were organized in the capital and sent to perform in public cultural centers built in urban centers. The educational program was standardized providing a common base of knowledge for all students. In sum, the urban-development program served to physically and culturally unify a previously diverse population.

Political unification was accomplished through centralization of all government activities and strengthening of the civil service. Every facet of local administration was placed under the control of national ministries in the capital. Local budgets were subject to ministry approval and budgetary funds were allocated by national officials. Local administrators were members of a national civil service and owed primary allegiance to ministry heads.[4] The development of loyalties to traditional local leaders was precluded through a system of periodic transfer to other parts of the nation. Within the cities and towns, the civil servants represented the national government rather than the local constituency. This role was not limited to political acts only; civil servants also acted as bearers of the new Western culture of which they were expected to be living examples.

The important political and cultural roles assigned civil servants enhanced an already high status rooted in Ottoman tradition. Moreover, as a group, civil servants benefited from urban development and special considerations granted them by the government. As a result, government workers emerged as a privileged and honored segment of the Turkish population. The military shared the status of government workers.

The military role in the Kemalist program was as important as that of government workers: on the cultural level the officer corps provided personal examples of Westernized life styles; retired officers provided a major recruitment base for political and government positions; most important, however, the military enforced government power throughout the nation and guaranteed local compliance with government edicts.[5] The military role was by no means limited to the operational level of Kemalism. Although the military was barred from active political participation, Ataturk maintained a consultation relationship with important military leaders who kept him informed of impending legislation, and these men exercised an informal veto power over major government acts.[6] It was during this period that the military began to view itself not only as the chief protagonist of development but as the vanguard of the reform movement as well, a self-image that continues to this day.

Strong personal and ideological ties between the military and Ataturk's Republican Peoples party continued throughout the forties. However, after Ataturk's death, the party lost much of its charismatic appeal, particularly for younger officers. Thereafter military support for the Republican Peoples party stemmed more from tradition and economic interest than charismatic identification, and the strength of ties was considerably reduced. By the late forties, many younger officers viewed the party as a deterrent to development and the emergence of a truly democratic political system. Party suppression of potential political opposition met with resistance from junior officers and, by 1950, segments of the officer corps were on the verge of revolt against single-party rule. In part the ability of the Democratic party to take office after the 1950 elections was a function of informal military intervention.[7]

The effects of the Kemalist program were not limited to the development of an entrenched class of government officials. In urban regions the extension of the rail network and construction of public facilities created a resurgence of commerce that had all but disappeared during World War I and the postwar revolutionary period. Government-sponsored industries provided new goods that were marketed primarily in urban areas and the availability of funds from newly formed government banks lent impetus to commercial processes. Within Ankara the influx of civil servants created a new urban real estate market and stimulated both land speculation and a construction boom. All of the above helped to create a new Turkish urban elite of wealth that has since supplanted older minority-group commercial elites.[8]

Important social change also occurred in the rural regions of the nation. However, as rural regions were largely unaffected by the development program and isolated from urban centers, social change there took place within a traditional, antisecular milieu. Reflecting this milieu, social change in rural regions occurred along traditional lines of Near Eastern peasant values and consisted of the redistribution of lands formerly attached to the sultanate, definition of village boundary lines and the emergence of a class of landed elites.[9]

The elite status of the landed was rooted in both ownership of property and a necessary political alliance with the Republican Peoples party. As a result of the latter, they played a dual role: they participated, often at high levels, in the national government and the modernization movement while also representing their own and their constitutents' rural, traditional interests. As such, they played the role of political brokers in the rural regions; and, without their assistance, relations between the peasantry and the central government, in the past always tenuous, would have degenerated into open rebellion and consequent military repression. The brokers' role led to political entrenchment in national politics and extended-term political domination of the rural regions.[10]

From its founding shortly after the revolution to the 1946 elections, the Republican Peoples party was an amalgam of representatives of the military, government workers, the urban commercial elite and the rural rich. Each group was represented in both the party and the government.[11] Despite the existence of this coalition, party and government programs were primarily aimed at induced transformation of urban regions. In the area of individual and collective freedoms, the party favored strict social control. Republican governments passed laws limiting freedom of association, the creation and existence of new political parties and the rights of individuals within already existent associations. The best-known examples are the laws forbidding formation of new political associations, limitation of the rights of workers to organize or strike and the destruction of the religious orders. Under Ataturk, the government imposed new cultural norms upon the population, with severe punishment as the cost of nonconformity.[12]

In the field of economics, the Republican governments pressed an etatist approach to development. Large sums of money were appropriated for the development of state enterprises and selected areas of the economy were closed to private investment. The urban regions were favored with public works, while rural regions were left isolated and underdeveloped.

While the thrust of the Republican Peoples party program favored urban populations and government workers in particular, representatives of the rural elites retained their ties to the party. The continued coalition between disparate urban and rural interests was rooted in the perquisites that accrued to rural elites as a result of political participation and a veto power over proposals for rural reform. It was precisely at the point that urban segments of the party leadership pressed for significant land reform that rural elites withdrew from the party and formed the Democratic party under the leadership of Adnan Menderes.

Although the first defectors from the Republican Peoples party were the landed rich, they were soon joined by representatives of urban commercial elites, free professionals, intellectuals and the military. With these new elements, the Democratic party program was expanded to include not only rural issues but issues of personal and corporate freedom and free-enterprise development. The party supported policies favorable to groups involved in the open market and inimical to fixed-income groups such as government employees and the military.

By 1950, the Democratic party had sufficient popular support to sweep the national elections and assume power with a legislative majority. Once in power it instituted a program that was in many respects the opposite of the Kemalist program. Etatist policies were replaced with emphasis on private investment and the opening of previously restricted investment opportunity. Import and credit restrictions were loosened and large amounts of United States money flowed into the country by way of government loans and gifts. Restrictions on freedom of association were eased. Previously outlawed religious practices were once again allowed and religious instruction in public schools was instituted.

Despite the presence of urban groups in the Democratic party, the bulk of party support came from rural regions, and the rural-development program comprised the major facet of party policies during its tenure in office. The rural infrastructure underwent major expansion including electrification, irrigation and drainage projects and road-building. Road-building in particular had a significant effect in that it allowed previously isolated villages access to urban centers and created new cultural and commercial ties. Concomitant with the road-building program large numbers of automobiles, tractors, trucks and buses were imported. Buses provided mass transportation throughout the rural regions, while trucks allowed villagers to market perishable foodstuffs in newly available urban markets. As a result, truck farming became a viable commercial venture in areas not contiguous to major urban centers. Large amounts of money began to flow into rural regions where it was used for consumer and investment purposes. This new wealth was largely undiluted as the Democratic party passed legislation exempting agricultural income from taxes. All of these developments led to a period of relative prosperity in the rural regions, accompanied by an increased demand for consumer goods, increased imports and inflation.

THE MENDERES REGIME: A CASE OF POLARIZATION

From the Kemalist revolution of the 1920s to the mid-1950s, Turkey was rapidly becoming a pluralistic society. During the intervening years Turkey experienced the development of a multiparty political system, the growth of an industrial and distribution economy, the expansion of educational opportunity (especially in urban areas), the appearance of modern mass-communication systems, the increasing urbanization of the population both demographically and culturally, the emergence of new intermediary social classes and the formation of new interest groups. Turkey appeared to be developing into a modernized pluralistic state along the model of European democratic states.

In 1950, the Democratic party, headed by Adnan Menderes, was swept into power by a combination of rural and urban support. Support for the Democratic party among the rural peasantry stemmed from a number of factors: its opposition to the long-incumbent Republican Peoples party, which had tended to ignore, if not suppress, peasant interests; the emphasis on tradition and religion; and the vague hope of an improved lot under a new administration. Another source of support was the landed rich. Their backing was based on the Democratic party's promise of higher agricultural prices and the knowledge that a party emphasizing the Islamic tradition could bring few changes in either the land-tenure system or the rural power structure. Within the cities, the Democratic party received the backing of both the large and small business interests and the growing professional groups. De-emphasis on public investment in industry and easy credit for private investment secured the support of business, while a policy allowing free importation of consumer goods and greater personal freedom assured middle-class backing.

The Republican Peoples party, founded by Ataturk, provided the major opposition. After having dominated politics for 27 years, the Republican Peoples party had finally been replaced. In rural areas Republican Peoples party support tended to be based on the individual's charismatic identification with Ataturk and the Kemalist revolution.[13] Urban support had a more solid base. It was an amalgam of relatively small but highly important groups that included the military, the intelligentsia, the government bureaucracy, fixed-salaried, white-collar workers and the incipient working class. Throughout the first five years of Democratic party rule, Turkey maintained its pluralistic nature.

In the latter stages of the Menderes regime (1956-60), the pluralized Turkish society began to show the deleterious effects of Menderes' economic policies—spiraling inflation, lack of planning and increasing national debt. The urban groups which had opposed the Democratic-party government from its inception increased their attacks upon the regime while slowly, as a consequence of economic hardship, urban supporters began to desert to the opposition. As opposition to the government grew more powerful and more vocal, the regime was forced to resort to repressive measures. In order to maintain a clear majority, the Democratic party was reputed to have falsified the 1957 election results. Next there followed a series of laws suppressing the opposition press and open criticism of the government. The assets of the Republican Peoples party—the major opposition and the government's most vocal critic—were confiscated. Political meetings were banned. Finally, a special committee of the assembly (having extraordinary investigative and penalizing powers) was formed to suppress all opposition to the government. Those urban supporters who might have remained loyal to Menderes for economic reasons deserted as a result of the political repression.

By 1960, the Menderes regime had caused Turkish society to polarize along the lines of support for or opposition to the regime. Peasants, landowners and the religious elements supported the Menderes government and its policies while the urban population, the press, the intelligentsia and the armed forces opposed the regime. The two camps were composed of three traditionally rival groups: (1) the urban population as opposed to the rural population, (2) the military as opposed to the religious sector and (3) the Westernized intelligentsia as opposed to the tradition-oriented. The military allied itself with modernizing urban interests in opposition to the government, which catered to rural traditional interests.

The conditions of Turkish society during the latter half of the Menderes regime were such as to frustrate the political and ideological desires of the armed forces, making them hostile to the government and prone to revolt. During this time, some military leaders openly expressed their opposition to the government. The scene was set for a military coup as early as 1958; however, the provocation was not supplied until 1960.

The spark that ignited the coup was provided by the economic crisis of 1959-60. The United States had cut back on its foreign aid, and a stabilization loan by the Organization for Economic Cooperation and Development had failed to ease the country's monetary crisis. Government attempts to ease the crisis were largely inadequate. In the same period, student riots broke out in connection with the suppression of free press, university freedoms and rival political parties. In neither case did the Menderes regime deal adequately with the situation; the economic crisis worsened and the rioting increased. The Menderes government used the military to suppress the rioting, but it became evident that many in the military were supporting the rioters.

When the coup occurred it was neither spontaneous nor hastily organized. In preparation, the revolutionary ogranization infiltrated the personnel section of the army and then proceeded to assign fellow conspirators to key positions in major cities. Relations were established with other conspiratorial groups in different sections of the country and in other branches of service. Possible military opposition to the coup was effectively neutralized by coopting the elite of armed divisions through to be loyal to the Menderes regime. No organized resistance confronted the conspirators. Before dawn on May 27, 1960, the commander of the presidential guard arrested the president. Revolutionary units in Ankara, Istanbul and Izmir arrested the cabinet, key government officials and Democratic party representatives in the assembly, while others occupied the government radio stations. By noon, the actual military phase of the operation had been concluded with little disruption to the life of the nation.

Polarization and Pluralization in Turkey

Pluralization in Turkey has been urban rather than national in character. From the point of view of the urban sectors, pluralistic politics can only occur when the rural sector plays a subordinate role in national politics. When the rural sector won control of the government, the nation moved rapidly toward an urban-rural polarization. Policies sponsored by the rural sector, such as cheap money, investment in agriculture, construction of a rural infrastructure and the exemption of agricultural income from taxation, were in direct conflict with urban interests. In reaction to the excesses of rural dominance, the urban-interest groups solidified and proceeded to attack the government with every means at their disposal: the urban-controlled press became hypercritical of government policies, business groups sent money abroad; after years of acrimonious debate, the urban-based Republican Peoples party left the assembly. The economy, gripped by uncontrollable inflation, stagnated, and politics became antipolitics.

When polarization occurred, the military elite, who were traditionally allied with the urban sectors, participated in the solidification of urban interest groups in opposition to the rural-oriented government.

The 1960 revolution occurred at the point of national polarization along the rural-urban axis and its underlying causes were rooted in the systematic frustration of military interests concomitant with the breakdown of interest-group politics during the latter years of the Menderes regime. Moreover, there was little hope of the situation changing; for despite the continued holding of national elections, legitimate means of replacing the government were denied by the preponderance of the rural electorate.

The discussion of gross societal factors predisposing segments of the Turkish military to overt intervention provides a description of the preconditions for revolution. Why the insurrection took one form rather than another and why certain military personnel and not others participated are questions that have not yet been dealt with. A complete investigation of the causes of the 1960 revolution must also examine the social structure of the military institution and the dynamics of the conspiratorial organization that executed the seizure of political power. This entails developing linkages between the structure of military organization, life conditions of career officers, the political culture and the dynamics of politicized military groups—in effect, the exposition of a theory of political involvement by members of large military organizations.

MILITARY PROFESSIONALISM AND
POLITICAL INVOLVEMENT

The Dual Role of Career Officers

Students of military sociology have shown that the occupation career officer has dual-role components: professional officer and public servant.[14] The professional component of the military role focuses on the management of violence—both external and internal—and in most nations the military dominates the means and skills of violence.[15] Where other means of internal political conflict-resolution exist, there may be little need or call for violence in the political culture. However, when systems of reconciliation break down, violence may become the dominant mode of conflict resolution and the military may become the final arbiter of political confrontation. Thus, although the professional military role does not overtly engage the soldier in politics, access to the means of violence implies ultimate inclusion in the political arena.

The public servant role of the professional soldier more openly involves him in political activity. As servants of the state, soldiers are professionally dedicated to the protection of national interests and reside in a nationalistic environment. While the task of defining national interests normally falls to others, when the military as a whole or some important segment of the military finds itself irrevocably opposed to the government, that function may be usurped. The public servant role of the military also allows for legitimate participation in defining the national interest and as such makes career officers political beings and the military organization a political institution.

In other words, both role components of the career officer converge to make the professional soldier an active participant in the political culture. Moreover, domination of the means of violence provides the potential for making the military the final arbiter of politics, not merely in the sense of resolving issues that are otherwise irresolvable within the ongoing political system but also in the sense of the military being capable of providing its own definition of national interests and imposing this definition on the nation.[16] The latter represents the militarization of politics.

Under what conditions the military chooses to use violence as a technique for imposing a definition of national interests on the political culture is an empirical question. In their cross-national study of political instability, the Feierabends found that political aggression was closely related to systemic frustration. Systemic frustration was defined as including those situations in which large strata of the population experience expectations, needs or aspirations which remain unmatched by equivalent levels of satisfaction. This type of gap between need or demand and achievement may most easily be identified among the ecological variables of political systems, especially socio-economic variables.[17]

The same conditions that led to the polarization of Turkish society during the latter part of the Menderes regime also led to systemic frustration among an important segment of the Turkish military and the reactions of this group were aggressive. Furthermore, the mode of aggression was a function of access to channels of political involvement differentially available to segments of the military.

Cleavages in Military Organization

Cleavages within the military can be observed along at least two dimensions: those that result from the structure of society and those that inhere in organizational structure. A third dimension along which cleavages occur is the interaction between societal and organizational features of the military leading to internal segmentation along the attitudinal dimension. The multiplicity of groups formed by cleavages along these three dimensions precludes large, well-developed military institutions from being characterized by complete internal solidarity, monolithic command structure and internal cohesion or consensus. Furthermore, complete communality of collective interests and definitions of national interests does not prevail. Studies of other large organizations have borne out this point.

The problem is to delineate important lines of cleavage within the Turkish military and show how the political culture during the latter half of the Menderes regime provided systemic frustration for important groups created by internal cleavages. There is also interest in the manner in which frustrations are translated into politically aggressive behavior and the way in which differential access to modes of political involvement fashions the nature of political acts—in other words, to trace the alienation of the 1960 revolutionary group to the Menderes policies and the mode of intervention to organizational features constraining modes of political involvement.

As in any bureaucratic organization, hierarchical ordering of strata provides the basic dimension along which structural differentiation obtains in military organization. Rank differences specify differential roles with varying rights, privileges, duties and obligations. While rank provides an array of strata, the most important line of cleavage is that between officer and enlisted man and it will suffice to deal only with the officer corps.

Within the officer corps there are distinctions based on rank that create different strata and lines between them are almost as rigid as those created by the distinction between officers and enlisted men. The officer corps can be divided into three distinct groups: low-ranking or junior officers—second lieutenant through captain; middle-ranking officers—major through colonel; and high-ranking or senior officers—generals. Each of these three strata differs in terms of age, salary, career and mobility potential and command or duty responsibility.

Junior officers are most often younger men; promotion policies in the Turkish military provide almost automatic advancement to the rank of captain and it is only at the higher grades that questions of age and time in grade become important indicators of career lines. Lacking rank and seniority, junior officers are severely limited in the nature and type of assignment available. Most often, junior officers are assigned to large units and lack authority and command. Junior officer salaries are low, providing a standard of living closer to that of lower-level white-collar workers than other professionals of comparable education. Consequently, status deprivation stemming from decreasing purchasing power and living standards is most keenly felt in this group.

Middle-ranking officers can be divided into two types: those whose mobility is limited and present rank obtained only after many years in junior grades and those of high mobility who are promoted to the middle ranks as a prelude to further promotion to senior positions. While the former are likely to retire as middle-ranking officers, the position of the latter is temporary and a stepping-stone to further advancement. Differential career patterns can be readily distinguished by the types of duty assignments men draw and the amount of special education they are afforded. Nonmobile middle-ranking officers are most often placed in line positions and assigned to field units throughout the country. Specialized education is limited to those areas directly related to line duties, that is, infantry school, artillery school and tank school. The upwardly mobile are assigned to staff duties, spend much of their time at posts in and around major urban centers and attend staff-officer schools in either Istanbul or Ankara. A staff officer's education is preparation for important later assignments, and selection for admittance to these schools is an indication of positive evaluation by superiors, implying future upward mobility.

Differential duty assignment provides different life styles and reactions to social conditions. Nonmobile middle-ranking officers are usually posted to command positions in rural areas. Within small military encampments they represent an elite group. Moreover, in rural areas, military salaries are more than adequate to provide a relatively high standard of living. Consequently, these men may not perceive status deprivation or react violently to changes in relative status and living standards occurring in urban regions. The situation is only slightly different in large military encampments. Although middle-ranking officers do not comprise an elite in these places, they are surrounded by fellow officers sharing essentially similar living standards and thus may also be oblivious to the changing urban situation.

The conditions under which upwardly mobile middle-ranking officers live are considerably different. Assigned to staff and headquarters positions, they represent the lowest rung of power and status within their units. Moreover, they often live in urban areas and are affected by price fluctuations, housing shortages and inability to obtain newly available consumer goods. The contrast between their standard of living and that of newly affluent urban groups, such as professionals and commercial elites, is starkly apparent. As a result, perception of status deprivation is more likely among men in this category.

The general-officer level, rather than being a segment of the rank continuum, is distinctly different from subordinate groups. Promotion to general represents a radical departure from usual appointment practices and only a very few men, carefully selected and trained, ever achieve this rank. Those who attain this rank represent an elite group having special perquisites that are not available to other officers: their pay is high, special services such as personal transportation and household help are regularly available and they have high status within the local community whether it be urban or rural.

Unlike their subordinates, generals participate in the urban civilian community without suffering status deprivation. Their salaries and special benefits allow them to maintain reasonable living standards while their power within the military, and by implication the government, provides social status. In personal relations with civilians and most government officials, official etiquette demands that generals receive deference.

The duties and past associations of generals often place them in close contact with government and political officials. Both formal and informal contacts stem from participation or interaction with political bodies such as the National Security Council, the Defense Ministry and various legislative committees concerned with military affairs. Other contacts with civilian officials stem from diplomatic missions and functions and the social life of higher government officials in urban regions. Such contact often makes political involvement through formal and informal channels available to generals.

Contact with civilian sectors of the population makes generals more aware of civilian viewpoints and more sensitive to political issues than other officers. Furthermore, participation of the Turkish military in international military organizations such as the North Atlantic Treaty Organization and the Central Treaty Organization has made general officers aware of and concerned with international issues and Turkish international status. This redounds upon their views on internal political issues and conflict resolution: general officers are prone to consider political activity not merely in terms of internal effect but also in terms of effect upon international stature and position within the international political arena.

The discussion of group differences rooted in rank has also implied a number of differences that inhere in other aspects of military participation. Some implications of urban versus rural assignment and staff versus line assignment have already been discussed. Other differences inhere in the nature of the duty assignment and service branch. For example, while army officers may be assigned anywhere within the nation, most air bases are near major cities, making most air force officers urban residents. The contrast is even greater when one considers post assignments within the navy. The naval academy is located within the Istanbul area and the major naval bases are at Istanbul and Izmir—two of the nation's three largest cities.

The military organization may be a microcosm of the larger society. While the professional officer corps probably does not fully reflect the total array of subsegments of the population, it is representative of much of the nation, including within its ranks men of urban and rural backgrounds and middle-class, working-class and peasant origins. The extent to which social structure cleavages are significant is presently a moot question. While childhood socialization patterns may have an important bearing on later life, similarities of professional socialization may minimize differences rooted in premilitary residential and social-class life styles.

Attitudinal cleavages result from the interaction of structural and organizational cleavages dividing the officer corps. The focus of interest is two attitudinal parameters: alienation from politics versus nonalienation from politics and politicized versus nonpoliticized.

Alienation from politics implies a lack of commitment to the government and the existent political system. Lack of commitment is not used here in the neutral or apathetic sense; instead it denotes feelings of antipathy and antagonism. Those officers who are alienated from politics represent real or potential enemies of the government and the existent political system, either in their unwillingness to defend it or willingness to attack and destroy it. The ability to carry out the latter is in part a function of degree of politicization.

Politicized individuals are those whose concern with political matters is potentially translatable into political activity. While a natural dichotomy exists between the politicized and the nonpoliticized, a continuum of politicization exists, ranging from those who are merely concerned with politics to those who are actively engaged to the point where it is their primary activity.

Such factors as urban residence, staff officer duty assignment and junior or middle rank are most likely to produce feelings of status deprivation. Status deprivation, in turn, can be expected to produce alienation from politics, which may also lead to politciization. As these groups may also lack access to legitimate channels of political involvement, individuals may be expected to seek other channels, and these are most likely to be illegitimate or *conspiratorial.*

While not all general officers have access to legitimate channels of political involvement or, barring that, informal channels, these are usually denied middle- and junior-ranking officers. Thus, during the Menderes regime, after nearly ten years in office, the process of rewarding friends and punishing enemies had led to a situation in which the majority of influential public officials were staunch government supporters. There was little opportunity for contact between political officials and military men who opposed the government. Lacking access to even informal involvement in politics, alienated and politicized officers had no recourse but to turn to conspiratorial activity.[18] This was most true at the middle- and junior-rank levels.

The Menderes policies, leading to polarization along the urban-rural axis, created the general conditions for urban discontent and status deprivation among junior- and middle-ranking officers stationed in urban regions. During the Menderes years, many of the developmental functions of the military were curtailed while aspects of the Kemalist reforms, such as subordination of religious interests and outlook, were abandoned. Economic expansion was only selectively beneficial, as new goods introduced into the market were unavailable to fixed-income groups. Yet another effect of the Menderes policies was the creation of new elites of wealth, accompanied by a burst of consumer spending and indulgence in leisure activities that offended the puritanical ethos of the military. In large cities, night life similar to American café society emerged in luxury hotels and newly developed resort areas. Expensive European and American cars appeared, for the first time, on Turkish streets and roads. Luxury homes were built on prime city real estate and furnished with expensive appliances and furniture. Menderes boasted that every quarter of the city now contained millionaires. As a fixed-income group, the military was largely excluded from participation in the new consumer culture. Puritanical morality was further offended by corrupt practices. Official corruption had not been previously unknown; rather, new wealth increased both the scale and visibility of public corruption.

Economically unable to participate in the new middle-class culture of consumption, urban-based segments of the military perceived relative status deprivation and became alienated from the Menderes regime.[19] Politicized individuals desiring to alter the situation, yet unable to act within the boundaries of legitimate political activity, turned to conspiratorial involvement. The impetus to revolt stemmed from societal conditions and the lack of access to ongoing political activities. The organizational format that the revolt assumed and the personnel involved were functions of military organization and the career patterns of professional officers.

CONSPIRATORIAL GROUPS

Three polar concepts provide the parameters that distinguish conspiratorial groups from other politicized military groups. These are: (1) access versus lack of access to channels of political communication; (2) legitimacy versus illegitimacy; and (3) public versus secret. Conspiratorial organizations can be defined in terms of the extremes of each of these conceptual dichotomies.

First, although conspiratorial groups attempt to influence or change the political culture, their members lack access to legitimate channels through which political influence is exerted. There is little or no contact with individuals or groups capable of exerting formal or informal political influence, and efforts to establish such contacts are minimal. As a result, unless exposed, conspiratorial groups are invisible to both political and military leadership. Lack of contact with legitimate or informal political personages also limits the strategies available to conspiratorial military groups. Unable to influence the political culture through existent channels of political communication, conspiratorial groups are limited to strategies of displacement or supplantation. Second, conspiratorial groups are illegitimate in two senses of the term: the men participating are legally barred from active political participation; and the modes of organization and political involvement are illegal, and participation would be serverely sanctioned if discovered. Third, conspiratorial groups are secret societies. The members share knowledge that is barred to the general population. However, conspiratorial military groups differ from the associational form that Simmel describes, in that membership is limited to individuals who share a single occupation and institutional identity. Consequently, patterns of association also differ from those Simmel describes as characteristic of secret societies.[20]

The characteristics that differentiate conspiratorial groups from other politicized military groups also create internal tensions, dilemmas and problems of organizational cohesion and maintenance that must be dealt with if the group is to survive and achieve its objectives. The manner in which these are handled vitally affects the life history and character of conspiratorial groups and, in the case of a successful *coup d'état*, partially determines the course of post-revolutionary events.

The School System and Politicization

While the effects of the Menderes policies were felt throughout the military, conspiratorial activities were not common to all segments of the military, nor even necessarily to those most affected by the newly emergent culture of wealth—middle- and junior-ranking officers stationed in urban regions. Conspiratorial involvement throughout the post-World War II era was most often located or initiated within the military-school system. In particular, those schools providing advanced training for upwardly mobile officers were seedbeds of conspiratorial group organizations. A 1946 conspiratorial group was formed at the War School located at the Yildiz compound in Istanbul. This group later merged with yet another organization composed of faculty at the General Staff College, which is also located at Yildiz. The group that overthrew the Menderes regime had its origins in schools at Yildiz, the Tuzla Air Force School and the Military Academy at Ankara. Post-1960 coup attempts, the abortive revolts of 1962 and 1963, were also products of the military school system—most participants were students at the Ankara Military Academy, and Talat Aydemir, organizer of both revolts, was commandant of the school prior to forced retirement in 1962.[21]

Military schools are not the only breeding ground for conspiratorial groups; any military post can serve the same function, as the number of conspiratorial groups that formed at the Elazig artillery battalion (in east-central Turkey) illustrates. The conditions of post life, in which officers are thrown into close and intimate contact, are conducive to group formation and the nurturing of discontent. However, the status position and career lines of officers regularly stationed in urban regions or attending advanced military schools exacerbate alienating conditions, making conspiratorial-group formation more likely to occur among these men and in the school or postschool environment.

If the military live in a nationalist environment, the nationalism is heightened within the school atmosphere. The curriculum at military schools invariably includes history courses that trace national political development and emphasize the role of the military in bringing about democratic reforms. Particular attention is paid the Kemalist reforms and their role in transforming the nation from the bastion of traditionalism to the first newly developing nation. There is a consideration of present social issues and conflicts that causes students to reflect on present developments and their personal role in shaping contemporary and future events. In effect, the public-servant role of the military is made salient and nationalist values are stressed.

Heightened personal concern with national issues is less a manifest function of the curriculum than a latent function stemming from informal discussions among students and faculty and personal introspection. While the formal curriculum is not, in and of itself, an impetus to conspiratorial activity, the atmosphere created by juxtaposition of nationalist concern and the outward manifestation of urban affluence, immediately outside of the military compound, makes for simple recognition of national problems, and vast differences in living standards between different sectors of the population—a recognition that might not occur in a less nationalist-charged atmosphere or a location physically isolated from the extremes of urban affluence and poverty. For these reasons, conspiratorial activity is more likely to occur in urban schools than those located in outlying areas of the nation.

The military school also provides a suitable physical setting for conspiratorial-group formation. The grounds are sealed off from civilian intrusion and provide ideal conditions for secret meetings. Moreover, school-cohort groups are in continual interaction. The daily round of activities provides ample opportunity for students to speak privately with one another and ascertain individual feelings and beliefs. Thus it is possible to locate those within the cohort who share similar beliefs and aspirations, diagnoses of national ills and suggested therapies for those ills. Finally, the shared school experience provides a basis of friendship and common trust that permits free discussion and interpersonal reliance in dangerous or delicate situations.[22]

Differential location is not the only explanation of why conspiratorial activity occurs in some schools but not in others. There are numerous urban-located military schools that have never experienced the development of conspiratorial groups. School faculty may be an important factor. Instructors may act as catalysts to conspiratorial activity through presentation of course materials and informal discussions outside of the classroom. Whether or not instructors intentionally instigate conspiratorial activity is unknowable. The illegitimacy of such acts and potential sanctions makes open admission of such intentions unlikely. There are a number of examples indicating close connections between school faculty and conspiratorial activity. Talat Aydemir, while commander of the Military Academy in Ankara, structured school curriculum and extracurricular lecture series so that students were bombarded with materials suggesting conspiratorial involvement and revolutionary activity.[23] Furthermore, throughout the post-World War II era school faculty participated in conspiratorial groups and there is no reason to believe that teaching and administrative duties were unaffected by political views.

The variety of schools at which conspiratorial activity emerged suggests that the phenomenon is not the product of any particular class or cohort group but inheres in the student status.[24] Besides heightening nationalist feelings and bringing national and personal issues into clear focus, school attendance has other meanings as well. For those attending the military academy, it is a period of military socialization likely to have a profound, if temporary, effect on self perception as an agent of social change. Attendance at other schools, such as the Staff College or the War School, is indicative of upward mobility and a future role in military decision-making. This may lead to a sense of personal and national destiny through radically altering the course of national history, making for personal ambitions that cannot be fulfilled through legitimate participation in political affairs.

Political absolutism stemming from alienation is transformed into conspiratorial activity by the very factors that make for unrealistic appraisals of political conditions—isolation from ongoing political processes and the absence of channels for direct political involvement. Those most susceptible to political alienation and absolutism are upwardly mobile middle- and junior-ranking officers presently or recently in the highly charged nationalist atmosphere of military schools and living in urban areas. These men are also most aware of political events and most frustrated by inability to influence them.[25] Given these conditions, conspiratorial involvement employing strategies aimed at displacing or supplanting the government becomes the only viable form of political activity.

Conditions that prevail at military school may also provide the student with an unrealistic view of national politics: national goals may be escalated out of proportion to what is realistically possible for the nation to achieve; social problems and the culpability of government, political and military leaders may be exaggerated; and standards of personal and political morality that are unreasonable within the current political culture may be used to evaluate people and parties. Political unrealism easily leads to political alienation and an absolutist view of politics.[26]

The Dilemmas of Secrecy

Illegitimacy of conspiratorial organization and activity imposes the need for secrecy which, in turn, imposes limitations on every facet of organizational existence including recruitment, organizational structure and planning. Secrecy also hinders the formation of conspiratorial groups and, once formed, makes continued organizational maintenance imperative lest dissolution or factionalization expose all members, past as well as present, to official sanctioning. Political compromise, while often unavailable in conspiratorial group interaction with the regime, is a primary technique for obtaining internal cohesion and solidarity, requisites for continued organizational maintenance and preventing exposure or betrayal. However, conspiratorial-group solidarity may be transitory, lasting only as long as cohesion is dicated by fear of exposure and potential sanctions. For example, after the 1960 revolution, despite attempts to maintain a facade of group solidarity, the ruling junta was factionalized by issues left unresolved during the period of conspiratorial-group activity.

Secrecy also provides a dilemma for recruitment. To be politically effective, conspiratorial groups must recruit as widely as possible. Open recruitment, however, increases the possibility of exposure. Moreover, it is precisely those who may be most useful to conspiratorial activity and most likely to betray group existence. Those most prone to joining secret, illegitimate groups may also be the officers with the least potential for effective political activity.

Another dilemma of secrecy is its effect on conspiratorial organization. To implement important political change, a viable political organization must be developed. Such an organization requires large numbers acting in a coordinated manner. Furthermore, there must be interaction between members and communication between affiliated groups. Without freedom of communication, neither coordinated action nor effective implementation of strategies of involvement is possible. Yet the requisite of maintaining secrecy makes free communication between groups and members impossible. Lines of communication must be guarded and protected lest nonmembers become aware of the organization's existence and betray it.[27] As a result, conspiratorial-group effectiveness is limited by inability to sustain an uninterrupted flow of information within the organization.

The 1960 conspiratorial group was continually hindered by problems of communication. The need to maintain secrecy precluded use of the telephone or mails and limited communication to interpersonal interaction. Coordinating the activities of the Istanbul and Ankara groups required a constant flow of couriers between the two cities, and this tended to arouse the suspicions of commanding officers and acquaintances. In a few instances public means of communications were used to relay coded messages. However, this technique ' was problematic, as messages were sometimes misinterpreted.[28] Group meetings presented a similar problem; a large number of officers gathering at a house or public garden invariably aroused suspicion. Consequently, the size of gatherings was limited and meetings were held outside of the city or in secluded areas, in which case large numbers of officers seen traveling to an out-of-the-way place were also cause for suspicion. There was not one large meeting that did not come to the attention of the regime. Colonel Koksal, in a newspaper interview in *Cumhuriyet* on July 18, 1960, revealed that President Celal Bayar would question him about the proceedings of the very meetings at which the sonspiratorial group planned the revolution. In effect, not only did the regime know of the meetings, it also knew who had attended them.

The need to maintain invisibility also affects implementation of plans and strategies. Overt political activity cannot be identifiable as an act of the conspiratorial group, lest such a connection lead to an investigation and exposure. Only at the point at which definitive political action is taken, such as the point of revolution, can the veil of secrecy be lifted and conspiratorial activities linked to the organization.

Yet another dilemma associated with illegitimacy and the need to maintain secrecy is the problem of internal social control and sanctioning processes. While close internal control is requisite within illegitimate organizations, the ability of any member to expose the group makes such control superfluous and ineffectual. Sanctioning a member risks alienating him and provoking betrayal. Consequently, although internal social control is necessary, it is also impossible to maintain. This does not mean that sanctions are unavailable. The most brutal sanctions, political murder and the threat of assassination, are viable techniques of internal control However, the use of brutal sanctioning techniques is also likely to cause disgruntled members to attempt avoiding punishment by exposing the group prior to imposition of sanctions.

Ostracism is also available as a sanction; however, its use is limited to those instances in which the individual is dedicated to revolutionary goals and the depth of personal involvement in conspiratorial activities precludes betrayal. The case in point is that of Colonel Alparslan Turkes.[29] Upon being retired by the Menderes regime, General Cemal Gursel, titular head of the 1960 conspiratorial group, left for his home in Izmir. Fearing the general was being watched, conspiratorial group leadership forbade any contact with Gursel. A few days later, a rumor to the effect that Turkes had visited the general circulated throughout the group. As a matter of precaution and a form of sanction, a decision was taken to ostracize Turkes from conspiratorial activities. Imposition of the sanction lasted until a few days before the coup, when Turkes was called on to participate in final planning and preparations.

Restrictions that secrecy imposes on conspiratorial groups both maintain existence and hinder achievement of goals. Organizational maintenance resulting from protective measures obtains at the cost of impaired organizational functioning. The resultant extension of organizational life is problematic in that extended longevity increases the likelihood of betrayal and exposure. Secrecy in conjunction with extended organizational longevity also creates organizational problems that in other circumstances might be inconsequential but here under the conditions of conspiratorial-group life, they are critical. Over time, anticohesive factors may emerge. Interpersonal enmity, distrust and competition that did not exist at the time of group formation may emerge as a result of extended organizational longevity and inability to attain group goals. In time, issues and problems that were previously unperceived may threaten internal cohesion and solidarity. Thus, the very techniques that maintain conspiratorial organizations may also cause their demise.

Equality

Sharing conspiratorial secrets makes conspiratorial group members equal—equal in the sense that illegitimate activity, if exposed, would lead to a common fate. Equality is also rooted in shared knowledge that is denied to other members of the community. Given equality of knowledge and fate, equality of status follows.

As Simmel perceptively pointed out, egalitarianism in secret societies is a function of separation from the larger society and can continue only as long as members are able to mask their public identities or seclude themselves. While this is possible in a heterogeneous group, it is impossible in homogeneous military conspiratorial groups. Although certain aspects of identity lose salience in conspiratorial groups, institutional identity cannot be hidden. Every participant is known to other members as both an individual and an officer of a given rank and status. The source of knowledge is threefold: first, every officer wears his rank on his uniform; second, within the military community, personal status and reputation quickly disseminate throughout the professional officer corps; and third, the need to maintain secrecy limits membership and recruitment to those who are known and trusted.[30]

With the knowledge of institutional status and position, it is impossible to avoid impingement of rank upon egalitarian attitudes. Both level of participation and military rank establish status within conspiratorial groups, destroying even the potential for egalitarianism. Once admitted to the inner circles of conspiratorial groups, high-ranking officers invariably assumed important roles in group decision-making. In 1950, General Belen was able to overrule previously agreed-upon plans for a coup. Even though General Madanoglu was only admitted to the inner core of the 1960 group immediately prior to the revolt, he played an important role in planning and executing the coup. For this reason, Talat Aydemir (in planning two revolts) was wary of admitting high-ranking officers to the conspiratorial coterie.

In a similar fashion, bureaucratic position also impinges upon egalitarianism. Conspirators occupying key positions within the military ogranization are, by dint of their institutional function, more important and powerful within conspiratorial organizations than others occupying less important posts. For example, Sitki Ulay, commandant of the Ankara Military Academy, was incorporated into the leadership cadre at the time he joined the conspiratorial group. General Ozdelik, martial law commander of Istanbul, was brought into the conspiratorial group on the night of the 1960 revolution. At that time, he was asked to take command of revolutionary forces in Istanbul.

While conspiratorial activities provide an alternative source of status and power within the group, they do not confer institutional rank and position on the individual. Consequently, tension exists between claims to status and authority rooted in conspiratorial participation and claims rooted in military status and position.

Men whose leadership status stemmed solely from participation were constrained to maintain their position within the organization through often nonessential activities such as meeting attendance, intragroup communication and recruitment. Performing nonessential functions and lacking institutional power, these men often found their leadership roles tenuous. Unable to serve a critical operational function within the group, participatory leaders tended to be primarily concerned with ideological issues and questions of postrevolutionary government. At meetings they often advocated revolution rather than reconciliation and prolonged military rule rather than immediate elections. Exposition of these political positions continually led to clashes with senior officers and men whose ideological positions were less absolutist. It was precisely these issues which served as the major anticohesive force within the group and at times even threatened the continued existence of the revolutionary movement.

Within conspiratorial military groups, competitive claims to status and authority stem from a poorly defined relationship between the organization and the military institution. If the group views itself as an adjunct of the military institution, and such factors as exclusive menbership and an ideology rooted in military definitions of political issues favor this view, then status rooted in institutional rank and position is consonant with the membership's world view. However, when the group defines itself as distinct from the military institution, a view buttressed by alienation from the political stance of institutional leaders, then conspiratorial-group status and authority stemming only from participation are legitimate. Resolution of tensions stemming from competing claims to conspiratorial leadership is dependent upon clarification of the relationship between conspiratorial involvement and military affiliation, and this is a function of military reaction to the conspirators and the strength of professional identification.

In the case of the 1960 conspiratorial group, the dilemma of institutional affiliations was resolved, in part, by the course of events. The Menderes policies served to promote military sympathy for the revolutionary movement. As a consequence, large numbers of officers were politically available and willing to join a revolutionary group. Career officers whose professional identification was strong were recruited, including a number of high-ranking officers occupying important institutional positions. Moreover, during the latter months of conspiratorial planning, the military high command gave the group tacit support.[31] As a result, the question of the conspiratorial group's relationship to the military organization was never fully resolved. Ties to the military institution were maintained while the independent political facet of the group continued to exist. The group was neither an independent political force nor a tool of the military high command.

Legitimacy represents another aspect of the dilemma imposed by the absence of a clearly defined relationship to the military institution. One the one hand, severing ties with the military denies the very social status that military conspirators view as their legitimate entree to politics—that of apolitical, nationalist-oriented, public servants whose foray into politics is inspired solely by objective and impersonal criteria. On the other hand, submission to military authority ultimately places conspirators under the authority of the chief of staff, thus acknowledging that conspiratorial political activity is essentially illegitimate and unwarranted. Neither position is fully tenable and tensions resulting from competing claims to authority remain irreconcilable and a fact of conspiratorial-group existence.

Egalitarianism is also destroyed by the development of organization. Increasing group membership requires the establishment of a formal organization to coordinate group activities. The very characteristics of organization are inimical to egalitarianism: hierarchical structure places some men in decision-making positions while excluding the bulk of membership; transmission of decisions to the membership establishes command functions; and the need to protect the organization from exposure limits information and activities to a select few men. Furthermore, there is no reason to believe that the "Iron Law of Oligarchy" does not hold as a result of leadership participation in spheres of political interaction that are closed to most members.[32] Organization leaders may develop personal interests that differ from those of the membership. Although the total membership shares the risks of conspiratorial participation, the emergence of conspiratorial organization may result in unequal distribution of benefits.

The development of differential interests, resulting from establishing of organization and unequal distribution of power and authority, may also lead to internal differences rooted in divergent personal goals and approaches to goal attainment. While this may lead to organizational factionalization, there are also pressures for organizational maintenance that preserve the group despite lack of internal cohesion. The illegitimate nature of the group and need to guard against exposure have already been mentioned. Another is belief that at the crucial moment a leader or coterie sharing a particular viewpoint will be capable of subordinating opposing individuals and approaches, coopting the total organization rather than some fraction of it.[33] Consequently, the critical point in conspiratorial group life is not its inception but its climax—the point at which a definitive move is attempted and opposing factions, previously bound together, engage in a decisive confrontation determining the dominant political position. The outcome of this confrontation is, in part a reflection of previous patterns of internal inequality, but more importantly it is also the resolution of the question of inequality of fate that inheres in conspiratorial organization.

Conspiratorial Group Recruitment

The illegitimate nature of conspiratorial-group activity limits recruitment and the ultimate size of conspiratorial groups within the military. The need for secrecy imposes a filtering process upon recruitment activity that allows only a select group to become aware of the existence of the conspiratorial organization.

The first filtering process is friendship, as it provides the only basis of trust that allows a conspirator to approach another person with a solicitation to join an illegal organization and participate in illegitimate and negatively sanctioned activities. Trust is a second filtering process. The officer solicited for group membership must be perceived as a person who will neither willingly nor unwillingly betray the group. Correlative with trust, the potential recruit must also be esteemed for his good judgment, as every member is also a potential recruiter. As indicated earler, shared school experiences are likely to provide the types of interpersonal relationships requisite for conspiratorial-group recruitment.

The common denominator of potential recruits is shared beliefs and a common outlook, not in the positive sense of sharing a common vision of the "new society," but in the negative sense of being dissatisifed with the present one.

Complete congruence of belief was not requisite; none of the known conspiratorial groups displayed a complete consensus of opinion. However, a minimal requirement was recognition of the importance of those issues which coalesced the conspiratorial group and willingness to provide a therapy for perceived ills.

Finally, propinquity serves as a filter through which selected individuals are recruited for group membership. Only those who are close at hand can be approached and examined as potential members. The necessity for secrecy and accurate judgment limits recruitment to men stationed in the same vicinity as the conspirators. The large number of men stationed at major military encampments in urban centers makes recruitment there easier, as a large number of potential members are available. Remote posts, where officers are isolated from the civilian population and the urban culture, make for intense friendships potentially leading to the development of conspiratorial coteries. However, organizational size is limited, and distance from the political center reduces the potential for effective political action.

Two distinct recruitment patterns characterized conspiratorial groups in the Turkish military. One allowed members to freely approach and recruit among friends and acquaintances. The second consisted of group members nominating potential recruits, followed by a collective decision on suitability for membership. The latter represents selective recruitment. Recruitment selectivity is directly related to perceived illegitimacy, as available materials indicate that most stringent recruitment techniques prevailed when the climate of military opinion was unfavorable to revolution. When a favorable

climate of opinion predominated, open recruitment swelled the
ranks of conspiratorial organizations and restrictions on recruitment
were eased.

Selective recruitment is also closely tied to the emergence of
political strategies and tactics. Once the form of a general plan is
agreed upon, it may become necessary to recruit individuals
occupying key institutional positions, the duties of which are
requisite to goal attainment. The only alternative to recruitment of
institutionally important individuals is gaining control of these
positions through placement of group members. Both of the above
strategies were practiced by the 1960 conspiratorial group.

Irrespective of the prevailing climate of military opinion,
leadership consensus is requisite for recruiting general officers. Their
status precludes complete sharing of conspiratorial secrets, and
access to government officials and agencies makes them potentially
dangerous. For involved officers, the risks are too great to entrust
career and civil status to an outsider whose interests may be radically
different from theirs.

Of the generals involved in conspiratorial organizations, none
were every fully privy to the secrets of the groups that coopted
them. Instead, their contact with these groups was limited and core
leaders viewed the generals as titular or figurehead leaders.
Limitations on contact between general officers and conspiratorial
groups serve other functions as well. As in every instance about
which sufficient materials are available, conspiratorial groups were
formed by men below the general officer rank, and exclusion from
the group's inner circle precluded pre-emption of all leadership roles
by generals.[34] In effect, it was a technique used by middle-ranking
leaders to preserve control over conspiratorial organizations.

Differential perception and interest provide yet another reason
for excluding generals from conspiratorial organizations. Having
access to high military and government officials, many of whom may
also be personal friends, generals may be more interested in
compromise than junior officers. In the event of a revolution, they
may insist upon saving or retaining old colleagues and friends that
junior officers want removed. Generals may also want to occupy
government positions that junior officers have already assigned to
themselves or others. Finally, in the event of internal dissent, they

may betray the conspiratorial organization to existent authorities.

The group that organized the 1960 coup had a fairly open recruitment policy. While there is no available estimate of membership at the time of the coup, it is apparent that the conspiratorial network consisted of several hundred men. Tactically, the group may have been too large, as many members could in no way assist in execution of the revolt, and excess membership only increased the possibility of exposure. There were a number of reasons for a policy of overrecruitment. In a climate of discontent and revolution, by accepting new members the conspiratorial organization was able to maintain itself as the revolutionary vanguard and prevent other groups from forming or revolution-oriented officers from joining other organizations. Expanded membership also increased revolutionary sentiment within the military, as new recruits became propagandists for the organization. Finally, by continuing to accept new recruits, the revolutionary organization was able to stave off the possibility of disgruntled applicants exposing the group. In effect, the dysfunctional policy of overrecruitment helped maintain the revolutionary movement intact.

Conspiratorial Group Organization

Available information indicates that throughout the decade and a half of conspiratorial-group activity under consideration, typical organizational patterns emerged. While the group was new and small it met as a unit and decisions were reached through group discussion and consensus. However, with increasing size, group meetings became dangerous and organization became requisite for maintaining secrecy.

While the original organizational format was democratic—with elected officials filling specific posts and total membership apprised of major decisions and events—in time a gap between members and leaders developed and conspiratorial involvement became limited to group leaders, whose identity was often unknown to the general membership.

Considerations of security led the 1960 group to adopt a

cell-system organization. Every cell, isolated from other cells and the larger organization, existed as a separate entity, thus protecting the total group from exposure of a single cell and individual members from exposure of the conspiratorial group or some segment of it. Group structure limited the dangers of illegitimate activity, thereby limiting not only the threat to individual members but the threat to the revolutionary movement as well.[35]

The effectiveness of cellular organization is clearly indicated by the one case of a disgruntled potential member exposing the organization. A Major Kuscu, rebuffed and refused admission to the cell he had made overtures to, informed the defense ministers and Menderes' personal aide of the conspiratorial organization and the identity of cell members. The cell was arrested and its eight members imprisoned for eight months while an investigation was carried out. Of the arrested, only one man, Faruk Guventurk, knew the names of other conspirators, and he refused to disclose any information. All were released for lack of information, and the conspiratorial organization survived despite exposure of a cell.

The cell system had other functions as well. As recruitment was most often based on personal friendship, individual cells tended to be composed of men who knew and trusted one another and this lessened the potential for internal disintegration resulting from personal animosity. Another function was to maintain the leadership position of early conspirators. New members were absorbed by the cell that recruited them and excluded from even attempting to assume decision-making positions within the larger organization. As a result, personal competition for leadership was limited to the cell, where previously established patterns of interpersonal relations determining leader-follower relations prevailed. Significantly, divisive questions of leadership did not emerge until after the revolution.

Cell-system organization also allowed a greater degree of central-committee control over group activities and individual participation. Cell leaders, in touch with organization leaders, received orders that were then carried to the general membership. There was little opportunity for the membership to react to or oppose organizational policy, and dissent or disobedience was limited to small groups.

Leadership

Outside of public politics, conspiratorial groups are insusceptible to events occurring in the political milieu and irresponsible to any broader public. In these circumstances, the quality of leadership is critical to maintenance of group existence and development of strategies and tactics. Given the centralized organization of Turkish conspiratorial military groups, leadership functions were the determinant factor in devising and carrying out revolutionary plans. There are four bases of conspiratorial-group leadership: participation, institutional position, rank and popular support. Participation in conspiratorial-group activity allows the individual to circulate among other conspirators, be present at group meetings and help shape conspiratorial-group decisions. In this instance, leadership is a function of having a voice in organizational affairs. As participation increases, so too do the circle of acquaintanceships within the group, knowledge of group secrets and influence in decision-making processes. Those who were original members often assumed leadership positions in the expanded organization. Having been present at the formative stage, these men were able to place themselves in key positions and participate in original group decisions. As a result, there was continuity of important conspiratorial personnel between 1946 and 1960.

Institutional position may also affect both participation and leadership. Those who occupy important institutional positions automatically become important to the conspiratorial group. Access to important men, control of bureaucratic functions and access to information increase their value to the conspiratorial group, and these men are immediately coopted into the leadership cadre. Upon joining the conspirators, Ulay—commandant of the Ankara Military Academy—was immediately made a member of the decision-making committee. Command of the students, who later played a key role in the 1960 revolution, was the basis of his leadership role in the conspiratorial group. Similarly, Suphi Karaman's appointment to the general staff personnel section assured his position as a conspiratorial group leader. Control over personnel-assignment policy made Karaman's participation necessary for the successful execution of conspiratorial group plans.

Closely associated with institutional position are rank and associated command. High-ranking officers may command large armed units which may be enlisted, in toto, for revolutionary purposes.[36] Troop command, in conjunction with the respect and obedience due a ranking officer, automatically makes one a group spokesman. In 1950, even though General Cevdet Sunay was not elected to a group office, his rank automatically made him a group leader.[37]

Finally, popular support serves to enhance leadership within a conspiratorial group. For example, Alparslan Turkes was mistrusted and disliked by many of the 1960 leadership cadre. He was suspected of having undemocratic personal ambitions, recruiting and organizing a personal conspiratorial organization and believed to have contacted a general after being specifically enjoined from so doing. Within the leadership core, he played an agitator's role and was the least amenable to compromise on postrevolutionary policy. Despite some group leaders' desire to remove Turkes from his leadership role, personal following within the larger group precluded such a move. Had he been expelled from the group, Turkes might have taken a large number of men with him.

Leadership Types

Although all conspiratorial group leaders are politicized, two types can be distinguished: those who are politically involved and those who are not politically involved. The politically involved view conspiratorial activity as having a broader political meaning and issues as essentially political and/or developmental in nature. Either they place their hopes in one of the existent political parties or press for formation of a new party. The latter view is often directly related to a position favoring military domination of politics. The politically uninvolved may be more concerned with status issues and favor supporting civilian political parties that recognize military needs. The latter are politically available and may be courted and captured by either of the two politicized types. The conspiratorial-group period may be one of political socialization for the uninvolved leader. The political outlook of group leaders only becomes crucial after a successful revolution, as only then can they determine the nation's political future. At that time, whether or not the leadership cadre is dominated by civilian-oriented officers or Nasserites becomes the critical variable in determining postrevolutionary national politics.

The 1960 conspiratorial group contained all three types of leaders and, from the moment the question of postrevolutionary government was introduced, internal dissension arose. Indeed, the issue was so hotly argued and the gulf between divergent opinions so great that organizational maintenance required delaying resolution of the issue until after the revolution. In consequence, when the revolutionary junta took power it was faced with the problem of defining its political role.

Ideology

None of the coteries being considered were characterized by communalities of ideology among the membership. Factors leading to conspiratorial-group formation and recruitment were less a common approach to political and developmental issues than personal and status-group alienation resulting from the impact of Democratic party policies. Consequently, group solidarity was rooted more in opposition to the government and fear of exposure than agreement on goals, strategy and tactics.

This does not mean that the conspirators were nonideological or that no common base of political perception existed. All shared in the Kemalist tradition, which had become ingrained through cultural and military socialization. However, Kemalism as an ideology was inadequate for dealing with contemporary problems and lacked a consideration of social structural and political changes that had occurred in the 30 years since its conception. Thus, while the Kemalist program propounded modernization and development through emulation of the West and persecution of religious interests, it failed to take into account critical contemporary factors such as foreign intervention in the form of economic and military assistance, the emergence of elites of wealth and multiparty politics.[38] Furthermore, there was no definitive statement on the role of social classes: Kemalism declared classes out of existence by describing the nation as a classless society. Although Ataturk had allowed urban regions to develop at the expense of the rural sector, there was no ideological statement providing a rationale for reinstituting this policy. Finally, while Ataturk had established the public sector of the economy, he failed to specify its relationship to the private sector. As an ideology, Kemalism was inadequate for providing a political and economic program suited to major contemporary issues. Lacking that, the conspirators were divided in their analysis of national ills and therapies for remedying them.

Internal ideological differences divided the group into three distinct factions. First, there were officers who were completely oblivious of ideological issues. While disgruntled and alienated from the regime, they had no program to ameliorate the national condition other than raising military salaries. Lacking an ideology, these men were available and susceptible to capture by either of the two competing ideologies.

One ideological position was rooted in support of Ismet Inonu and the Republican Peoples party as successors to Kemalism. While individual comprehension of the party's political and developmental stance varied, party affiliation led to acceptance of party ideology.

A second ideology was rooted in events that had swept the Middle East and the Islamic world since 1952—in particular, the militarization of government concomitant with the destruction of civilian political parties. Its model was not the European experience, but Nasserism in Egypt and the Ayub Khan regime in Pakistan. National ills were diagnosed as resulting from the failure of civilian politics. Caught up in the need for popular support, civilian parties could neither institute radical change nor free themselves from interest groups that had become politically entrenched during the formative years of national development. The therapy consisted, first, in destroying outmoded political parties and, second, in establishing extended military domination of the government apparatus. The rationale for military domination of politics lay in emphasis on the public-servant role of the military and lack of political entanglement with any specific class or interest group. Developmental programs were not to be predetermined, but rationally developed and implemented after the seizure of political power. In other words, the national problem was not the lack of an ideologically based program, but the identity of those controlling the government apparatus. Once power was seized, solutions would become apparent and political hegemony would make possible their implementation—in essence, a politics of *ad hoc* solutions to endemic problems.

Both major competing approaches could claim precedents in the Kemalist experience. Ataturk's seizure of political power, militarization of government and near dictatorial rule were cited as precedents for the latter view, while adherents of the Republican Peoples party identified the party and its leadership as the heirs of Kemal and the legitimate bearers of contemporary Kemalism. It was precisely these claims to the Kemalist tradition that allowed both points of view to survive and compete with one another.

Despite the common element of Kemalism, the basis of an ideology adequate for dealing with contemporary issues was not present. Supporters of the Republican Peoples party were unaware of changes occurring in party ideology leading to factionalization along lines of alternative approaches to national development.[39] Their support was for a program no longer operational. The naivete of Republican Peoples party supporters was matched by supporters of the militarization of government approach as exemplified by Nasserism. They failed to perceive essential differences between Turkish and Egyptian social structures, the strength of interest groups in Turkey and the fact that, once the peasantry had established its ability to dominate elections, it would never relinquish the vote. Given the conditions of Turkish political culture and social structure, the Nasserist approach could only be implemented at the cost of brutally suppressing the rural sector Unlike Egypt, a base of support (for military government) among a landless peasantry did not exist. The rural population was experiencing unprecedented economic growth; it was not landless, and support for the Menderes regime was unquestionable. If anything, years of military suppression of the rural population had created antipathy between the two groups that could not be overcome within a single generation.

Conspiratorial Groups and Interest Groups

By its very nature, conspiratorial involvement in politics is outside of other ongoing political processes. Lack of access to channels of political involvement, as well as illegitimacy, makes conspiratorial groups disassociated from the rest of the political milieu. Military men, shielded from unobtrusive political events and personally unaffected by political repression, are isolated from the political culture of interest-group competition. Despite all this, conspiratorial military groups may be closely bound into the political culture and interactive within it.

The conditions that elicited polarization along an urban-rural axis also provided the impetus to conspiratorial-group formation and activity. Although the identity of conspirators was secret, it was commonly assumed that a conspiratorial group existed. It is reasonable to believe that political parties acted accordingly.[40] Although there may have been no overt interaction between either political parties or interest groups and the conspiratorial group, indirect interaction did occur.

The basic problem of conspiratorial-group interaction with other political groups is super- and sub-ordination. In this instance, which of the two parties will dominate and coopt the other to its own purposes? In 1950, the Democratic party was literally able to coopt the military group represented by General Belen. The group, opposed to continued Republican Peoples party rule, found its only alternative to be support for the Democratic party. Unwittingly, the thrust of the 1950 group's political involvement was suppression of military economic interests and assistance to newly emerged elites of wealth.

The activities of the 1960 group were radically different. The conditions of group existence, lack of a single spokesman and the variety of political opinions and approaches to politics that characterized its membership precluded cooptation by any one group or party. This does not mean that they were unused by any group. The Republican Peoples party leadership was informed of group existence and activities by supporters active in conspiratorial activities. While there was no formal connection between the party and the conspiratorial group, the party did not oppose conspiratorial-group activities and viewed the conspirators as an indicator of internal turmoil caused by failure of the Menderes regime. At worst, continued conspiratorial activity might increase pressure and popular support for a new regime. Party leadership viewed the conspirators as performing a valuable service and consequently adopted a noncommittal attitude towards them.

The conspiratorial group itself was unrepresentative of any particular interest. Conspirators represented only a small segment of the military institution, and their personal interests were radically different from those of other segments of the larger institution. Thus, despite their claim to represent the military and to have military interests uppermost in mind, the conspirators' perception of military interests was limited to their own perspective.

Nor did the conspirators represent specific civilian-interest groups. They had neither affinity nor common interest with the elites of wealth, the peasantry or urban working class. Indeed, the only major interest group with which they shared important communalities was the government bureaucracy and other fixed-income, white-collar groups. However, at no point was there an attempt to join with or coopt this group and there was only minimal recognition of shared interests.

In part, the lack of affinity to any major interest group was a function of the lack of a shared ideology and approach to developmental issues. Had there been discussion and agreement on developmental issues, the adoption of a strategy of development might have aligned the conspirators with at least one major interest group, in which case the conspirators might have adopted that group as a client and fashioned a public policy designed to assist it. Lacking a shared ideology, there was no overt alignment with any of the existent interest groups.

Strategies and Tactics

Lack of channels of political involvement limited strategies of conspiratorial activity to displacement or supplantation.[41] Moreover, sentiment for removal of the Menderes regime was widespread throughout the conspiratorial group, the military and urban areas. Considering the fact of Menderes' popularity among the peasantry, displacement could only occur through resignation—which was unlikely—or a revolution; the latter alternative was chosen by the conspirators.

The question of displacement, replacing the Menderes regime with that of another party or supplantation—installing a military junta—had been an important issue of conspiratorial-group debate for a number of years prior to the coup. In general, support for either position was a function of political affiliation or nonaffiliation. Consequently, the issue was never resolved. Failure to resolve the issue effectively committed the conspirators to supplantation as a political strategy. In other words, the creation of a postrevolutionary military government stemmed more from political default than political programming.

Among the conspirators, revolutionary sentiment was not novel. As early as 1954, plans for a revolution were developed and preparations for its execution implemented. These activities were intensified in 1958 and brought to final stages in the latter half of 1959 and first months of 1960. Events within the civilian sector during the six months prior to the coup confirmed conspiratorial group opinion as to the immediate necessity for staging a revolution. These included attempts to assassinate Inonu, student riots and their suppression, declaration of martial law and mass arrests of political opposition to the government. While none of these events had direct bearing upon the major issues of the day, they were indicative of the mood of urban areas and the Menderes regime's repressive approach to politics and opposition. The brutality of Menderes' response to opposition was well advertised and served to convince even the most doubtful conspirators of the immediate need to oust the government.

Tactics used to execute the revolution fall into two categories: preparation and enactment, both of which were largely determined by conspiratorial-group organizational format. Preparation for the coup began almost six years prior to the revolt. This consisted primarily of recruitment and attempts to have members assigned to key bureaucratic positions or armed units in major political centers. The most important placement was arranging to have a conspiratorial leader assume command of the personnel section of the general staff. Control of this post made assignment of other conspirators to important command and administrative posts possible while potential enemies of the revolution were assigned to remote areas. Important positions occupied by conspirators included: commander of the presidential guard, administrative officers in the general staff, instructor at the Ankara Military Academy, executive or commanding officer of various tank and infantry units in and around the two major cities and staff officer at the general-staff communications center.

Other key positions coopted through specific recruitment included General Tacan, commander of ground forces and, after his death, Gursel, his successor. Other generals recruited were Madanoglu, commander of an infantry regiment in Ankara; Ulay, commander of the Ankara Military Academy; and, during the night of the revolution, Ozdelik, the martial-law commander of Istanbul.

Unlike civilian revolutionary organizations, the conspiratorial organization was not composed of permanent members that could be mobilized at any given time. Despite control over the personnel section of the general staff, all but the leadership group were subject to periodic reassignment out of the political centers. Only with difficulty was it possible to arrange continued assignment of group leaders in either the Istanbul or Ankara areas. Those so favored were, for the most part, upwardly mobile middle-ranking officers whose staff-occupational specialties provided sufficient rationale for continued duty in political centers and assignment to important institutional positions. It was these men who composed the leadership core of the organization and maintained organizational continuity over extended time periods.

Both fluidity and continuity of leadership are exemplified in the following: of 17 men attending the first meeting of the 1960 conspiratorial group, three later participated in drawing up final plans for the revolution. Three others would have participated, but they were stationed outside of the country or being watched by the government at the time. Of the remaining 11 officers, six were active participants from the time the group was formed through the revolt.

The fluid nature of tangential membership precluded important participation in planning and executing the revolt. Isolated from the central leadership cadre, these men were not privy to specific revolutionary plans. Indeed, when the coup occurred, most tangential members were caught unaware and had little if anything to do with its execution. Unable to mobilize a permanent revolutionary cadre, the leadership was forced to rely upon armed units that could be coopted at the point of revolution. Furthermore, many tangential members were assigned to units that would not be used in the revolution; their participation would be limited to acting as individuals and as such, they would be useless or potentially harmful. The cell organization of the group made exclusion of unwanted tangential members possible and simplified coordination of the revolt.

Limitations on available forces and centralization of government functions dictated the tactics of the revolution. Key places in Ankara and Istanbul were to be seized and communications between the political centers and the rural areas were to be severed. The latter was intended to prevent news of the revolt from reaching potentially loyal units which might provide assistance to the government. Once primary objectives were attained, Democratic party officials were to be arrested, thus immobilizing the government and acquiring potential hostages. In essence, the goal was to seize the government without, at the same time, embroiling the nation in a civil war.

Conspiratorial group strategies and tactics were based upon two premises. First, the resources available for revolutionary use were limited by the need for secrecy and the availability of armed units controllable by the movement. Second, the revolution ought not involve the total military institution or provoke intramilitary conflict. Both premises precluded widespread participation and extending armed action beyond the national political centers. Consequently, revolutionary military objectives were also limited both in number and location. The desire to avoid total military involvement was based on two considerations: first, to avoid the possibility of intra-institutional conflict stemming from witting or unwitting support for the regime and, second, to preserve the gains of the revolt from corruption or cooptation by nonrevolutionary officers.

OFFICERS AS POLITICIANS

The Turkish case provides a number of insights into military politics in developing nations characterized by similar structural, political and organizational features and may serve as a prototypic model for developing important descriptive and processual generalizations applicable over a broad spectrum of nations. The case also exposes certain confounding features of the officer corps as a social category and it is this that we will turn our attention to first.

Essentially the problem is that of delineating the officer corps as a social entity. In some respects the officer corps is a social class. Its members may have shared social status, life style and conditions, socialization experience and perception. However, large officer corps in which there are differential mobility opportunity and life style are characterized by internal cleavages creating subsegments that may be described as interest groups. While in some instances it may be appropriated to speak of the officer corps as a single entity, in most instances such generalization is unwarranted and leads to misconceptions. Specifically, as the Turkish case shows, we cannot speak of the officer corps acting in unison or overthrowing a regime; rather, particular subsegments of the officer corps may perpetrate political acts. Consequently, the focus of a theory of military politics ought properly be delineation of those groups that comprise the officer corps and specification of their political potential and social organization.

Among the different groups that comprise the officer corps in large, structurally differentiated military organizations, general officers and upwardly mobile middle-ranking officers stationed at the political center have the greatest political potential. The political potence of the former stems from established relationships with civilian political personnel and command of large troop bodies. The political potence of the latter stems from occupation of key positions within the military organization and presence at the political center. What constitutes a key position may vary from nation to nation and time to time within a given military organization. Within the Turkish military, in 1960, key positions included the personnel section of the general staff and the presidential guard; in Egypt in 1952, they were tank units stationed in the capital, while, in Greece in 1967, they were located in the intelligence section of army headquarters. We might suggest that identification of key positions within a military institution is possible if one analyzes the organization in terms of such variables as size, technological level, structural differentiation and career patterns. Important variables external to the military institution must also be taken into account. Chief among these are the status position of the officer corps and the degree of political centralization. In the Turkish instance, the root causes of the coup were changes in the social structure, while the ability of the conspirators to carry off their revolt was in part due to the highly centralized structure of Turkish government, limiting the physical scene of the revolution to key government centers in only two cities.

The different subsegments of the military also have different potential for becoming alienated from the regime and politicized. The Turkish case indicates that the greatest potential for political alienation exists among upwardly mobile middle- and junior-ranking officers and that the process of professionalization serves as one of the major sources of both politicization and alienation. In short, those most likely to form a conspiratorial group intent upon overthrowing a civilian regime are not men whose mobility is frustrated by lack of opportunity or professional skill, but those men who are most professionalized, possess the currently most-valued military skills and have the greatest mobility opportunity. For it is precisely these men who are most likely to occupy key organizational positions, suffer from perceived status deprivation, evince concern for political issues and lack access to ongoing political processes.

Lacking access to ongoing political processes, alienated, politicized middle- and junior-ranking officers are likely to form conspiratorial groups whose goals are removal of the existent regime. Once such groups are created, the members find their actions constrained by the conditions of conspiratorial-group existence. Secrecy, illegitimacy and lack of contact with political influentials pattern every facet of conspiratorial-group existence, creating tensions and dilemmas that are unresolvable within the context of the times. As a result, many issues are left unresolved and these may serve as the basis for political enmity and confrontation during a postcoup period. This suggests that the politics of postcoup military juntas may be less a function of national problems and issues than of precoup conspiratorial organization, in which case the policies of such ruling groups are, initially at least, less developmentally oriented than oriented towards resolution of conspiratorial-group problems. In most instances, this is manifested in the attempts by various junta members to gain and consolidate power within the ruling group, a process that has been noted as characteristic of newly formed military juntas.

In general, the Turkish case destroys the myth of military conspirators being tough-minded, singular in purpose and diabolically efficient. Rather, the picture is one of a highly tenuous existence under constant threat of exposure and destruction. The conspirators are neither ideologically motivated nor clear in their conception of the "good society." They are more likely to be products of larger social forces whose views are only partially fashioned prior to political ascension. Continued conspiratorial existence and success appear to depend more upon fortune and circumstance than planning and ability. Participating individuals owe their political role to things other than their ideology or personal destiny and charisma. Irrespective of how propagandists paint pictures of the leaders after a successful revolt, in reality these men are most often incompetent to fill political roles they may assume. For this reason, while military men may often seize the government, they can seldom administer it.

NOTES

1 See, for example, Reinhard Bendix, *Nation-Building And Citizenship: Studies of Our Changing Social Order* (New York: John Wiley & Sons, Inc., 1965) or Morris Janowitz, *The Military in the Development of New Nations: An Essay in Comparative Analysis* (Chicago: University of Chicago Press, 1964).

2. See, for example, Carl Leiden and Karl M. Schmitt, *The Politics of Violence: Revolution in the Modern World* (Englewood Cliffs, N.J.: Prentice-Hall, Inc., 1968).

3. On this see, Malcolm D. Rivkin, *Area Development for National Growth: The Turkish Precedent* (New York: Frederick A. Praeger, 1963).

4. For a description of the effects on local politics and civic administration see, Joseph S. Szyliowicz, *Political Change in Rural Turkey: Erdemli* (The Hague: Mouton and Co., 1966).

5. A good description is provided in Paul Stirling, *Turkish Village* (New York: John Wiley & Sons, Inc., 1966).

6. George Harris, "The Role of the Military in Turkish Politics," *Middle East Journal* 19 (1965): 54-66.

7. On this see, Abdi Ipekci and Omer Cosar, *Ihtilalin Icyuzu* [Inside the Revolution] (Istanbul: Uygun Yayinevi, 1965).

8. The process by which minority-group entrepreneurs were forced into a subordinate position is itself an interesting area of development research. In Turkey, the process was aided by the imposition of special taxes that disadvantaged minority-group merchants in competition with Turks.

9. On this see, Stirling, *Turkish Village*.

10. See, Josephy S. Szyliowicz, "The Political Dynamics of Rural Turkey," *Middle East Journal* 16 (1962): 430-32.

11. The demographic and occupational distribution of party leaders and representatives to the Grand National Assembly is discussed in, Frederick W. Frey, *The Turkish Political Elite* (Cambridge, Mass.: M.I.T. Press, 1965).

12. The best discussion of this topic is to be found in Kemal Karpat, *Turkey's Politics: The Transition to a Multi-Party System* (Princeton: Princeton University Press, 1959).

13. Irving L. Horowitz, "Party Charisma," *Studies in Comparative International Development* 1 (1965): no. 7.

14. Maury D. Feld, "Professionalism, Nationalism, and the Alienation of the Military," (Evian, France: paper presented to the Working Group on Armed Forces and Society at the Sixth World Congress of Sociology, September, 1966).

15. On this see Samuel P. Huntington, *The Soldier and the State: The Theory and Politics of Civil-Military Relations* (Cambridge, Mass.: Harvard University Press, 1964).

16. Irving L. Horowitz, *Three Worlds of Development: The Theory and Practice of International Stratification* (New York: Oxford University Press, 1966), pp. 254-71.

17. Ivo K. Feierabend and Rosiland Feirabend, "The Relationship of Systemic Frustration, Political Coercion, International Tension and Political Instability: A Cross National Study," (New York: paper presented to the Annual Meeting of the American Psychological Association, September, 1966).

18. General Gursel expressed this opinion in a newspaper interview in *Cumhuriyet*, July 10, 1960: "When I was commander of ground forces, I continued to protect the interests of the army and to struggle on its behalf. But I confess that I could not do very much because the administration had turned its back on the army. Those who felt the army's problems were few in number paid no attention to them."

19. While military salaries remained fixed throughout most of the Menderes era, between 1950 and 1959 retail prices increased 143

percent in Istanbul and 136 percent in Ankara. Other urban residents, whose income was tied to the free market, were better able to cope with the inflationary trend.

20. Georg Simmel, "The Secret Society," *The Sociology of Georg Simmel* translator Kurt Wolff, (Glencoe, Ill.: The Free Press, 1950).

21. On this see, Can Kaya Isen, *Geliyorum Diyen Ihtilal* [The Revolution that said I am coming] (Istanbul: Tan Gazetesi Ve Matbaasi, 1964); and Talat Aydemir, *Ve Talat Aydemir Konusuyor* [Talat Aydemir speaks] (Istanbul: May Yayinlari, 1966).

22. A discussion of the importance of interpersonal reliance relationships among soldiers is presented in Roger Little, "Buddy Relations and Combat Performance," *The New Military: Changing Patterns of Organization* ed. Morris Janowitz (New York: John Wiley & Sons, Inc., 1964).

23. Isen, *Geliyorum Diyen Ihtilal*, p. 91.

24. For example, two other military coups in the same region were carried out by military school cohorts. The 1952 Egyptian revolution was engineered by the 1939 graduating class and the 1967 Greek revolt by the 1941 graduating class.

25. Janowitz, citing research on Wehrmacht generals conducted by Kurt Lang, points out that politicized officers were most likely to be men whose career lines differed from traditional institutional patterns. Career deviations included numerous quasi-political assignments and rapid promotion. Morris Janowitz, *The Professional Soldier: A Social and Political Portrait* (New York: The Free Press of Glencoe, 1960), pp. 291-92.

26. On this, see the discussion of pragmatic versus absolutist political behavior in Janowitz, *The Professional Soldier*, p. 283.

27. V. Aubert, *The Hidden Society* (Totowa, N.J.: The Bedminster Press, 1965), p. 288.

28. Due to misinterpretation of a coded telephone message, the 1960 revolution commenced one hour early in Istanbul.

29. Ipekci and Cosar, *Ihtilalin Icyuzu*, pp. 159-176.

30. Simmel, *The Sociology of Georg Simmel*, pp. 345-60.

31. It is difficult to assess what, if any, relationship existed between the high command and the conspirators. A number of commentators have expressed the belief that the general staff was well aware of the existence of a conspiracy and that it could have easily destroyed the conspiratorial organization. There is, however, no evidence known to this author that directly bears on this assumption. It is, however, unreasonable to believe that so large a

group could exist for more than six years without coming to the attention of the general staff.

32. On this, see Robert Michels, *Political Parties: A Sociological Study of the Oligarchical Tendencies of Modern Democracy* (New York: Dover Publications, 1959).

33. Postcoup activities of the Turkes group indicate that this was their basic approach to resolving issues of leadership and ideology.

34. This statement may not be accurate. Ipekci and Cosar, *Ihtilalin Icyuzu*, p. 61, state that, after the 1950 election, a group of generals approached Ismet Inonu with an offer to overthrow the newly elected regime. As no specific names are mentioned and this account is not corroborated elsewhere, its veracity is questionable. However, there is no reason to believe that such an event could not have taken place.

35. Aubert, *The Hidden Society*, p. 388.

36. In 1950 and 1960, conspirators recognized the need for a senior officer to serve as titular head of the group. In 1960, attempts were made to enlist the aid of commanders of major armed units stationed outside of Ankara.

37. Ipekci and Cosar, *Ihtilalin Icyuzu*, pp. 5-17.

38. Every work on the period of the First Turkish Republic contains a discussion of the Kemalist ideology. The best source, however, is Ataturk's seven-day speech in which Kemalism is defined and elaborated. See, Mustafa Kemal, *Speech of October, 1927* (Leipzig: K. F. Koehler, 1929).

39. Final fragmentation of the Republican Peoples party was delayed until Spring, 1967 when Inonu forced splinter factions to form their own party. The new Guven (Security) party has taken a centrist position, while the Republican Peoples party has moved to the Left.

40. Menderes' distrust of the military was common knowledge. A number of commentators have suggested that his fear of military revolt prevented earlier imposition of martial law. Ipekci and Cosar, *Ihtilalin Icyuzu*, p. 154, and others have reported that a number of conspirators approached Inonu with a plan to seize the government. He is reported to have rebuffed this aproach, pointing out that, should the regime learn of party contacts with the conspirators, the results would be disastrous for both groups.

41. See, Samuel E. Finer, *The Man on Horseback: The Role of the Military in Politics* (New York: Frederick A. Praeger, 1962).

7
Political Crisis and
Military Populism in Peru

Julio Cotler

CONTEMPORARY SOCIAL MOBILIZATION AND THE
CRISIS OF POLITICAL HEGEMONY

Even though the process of social and political mobilization was initiated in its modern form during the twenties, after World War II there was a new stage in this process as changes appeared in the economic and social structure of Peru. These were characterized by the disintegration of the traditional rural world, which constituted the political base of the oligarchy, with the emergence of an intense process of urbanization involving the widening and diversification of the different sectors of society. This diversification rapidly led to a crisis of political hegemony: there was a lack of harmony among the different trends that had developed within the bourgeoisie. The latter, in turn, clashed with the interests of the popular sectors and of the politically mobilized middle sectors. These factors were at the root of the political crisis which would drag on until the establishment of the present military regime in Peru. The latter, seeking to modernize the social system, attempted to homogenize the society, recover political hegemony and make compatible different social interests, within the framework of a modern and integrated new bourgeoisie.

During the fifties, due to growing demands for raw materials by the international market—due in turn to European reconstruction,

United States expansion, and the Korean War–Peru enjoyed a
bonanza of exports equal to the value of its foreign trade during that
decade. This led to a considerable increase of individual consumption
as well as of fiscal expenditures.

At the same time, the urban population began a significant
growth, largely based on rural immigrations. Between 1940 and
1961, the population of Lima increased fourfold, attaining the two
million mark. Urban population (more than 10,000 inhabitants),
which in 1940 constituted 17 percent of the population, rose to
include 32 percent 20 years later. The voting population in 1945 had
increased fourfold by 1963.

This process of urbanization modified the traditional urban-rural
relations, previously controlled by the landowners, widening and
liberating the peasants' channels of communication. The new
immigrants served as a connecting link with the rural peasantry,
spreading new goals and values which quickened peasant
mobilization. Inflation and the growing gap between urban and rural
incomes served to stimulate desertion by the landowners and the
disintegration of the latifundium system.

New export sectors, especially that of fish flour, quickly
increased in importance. This importance derives not only from the
fact that, in ten years, fish flour has equaled copper as the main
export, but also that it developed a sizable proletarian
concentration.

Urbanization and the increase in individual consumption affected
the growth of the manufacturing sector, as well as the development
of new industries derived from mining and fishing. This whole
complex of new relationships had two important consequences at
the socio-political level: (1) it achieved a diversification of interests
at the level of the bourgeoisie, which would hinder its integration;
(2) the unleashing of the traditional rural world and of popular
urban masses which could no longer be manipulated in the
traditional repressive forms. This initiated the political crisis, with a
collision of social forces neither of which could politically control
the situation.

The dictatorship of General Manuel Odría occurred at the
beginning of this process and intended to bring about a traditional
solution. But, paradoxically, Odría only encouraged the

disintegration of those forces which sustained him, by supporting public works and industrial development.

To respond to the permanent pressure exerted by the *aprista* party, Odría sought the support of the urban popular masses, which were emigrating from the rural areas in growing numbers. Toward this goal he favored the formation of marginal neighborhoods, encouraged measures of social security and assistance, created new laws whereby the working class participated in the profits of the enterprises and granted voting privileges to literate women.

In 1955, the exporting sector of the bourgeoisie, which was being politically displaced by the new urban stratum favored by the ongoing process of change, no less than by the autonomy developed by Odría with popular support, demanded the reinstatement of a constitutional order which would ensure its political preeminence. This led to meetings at the convent of Santo Domingo de Lima, where the country's "live forces" met to find a successor for the regime. At these "talks," the different sectors of the bourgeoisie struggled to maintain or reconquer the political control which they were again losing by virtue of the military intervention that they themselves had brought about.

Two bankers emerged as candidates. It was clear that under the new circumstances, return to a constitutional order based upon an electoral process must necessarily include both the popular and *aprista* sectors. Odría asked for Apra's (Alianza Popular Revolucionaria Americana) support for Lavalle, a representative of foreign capital and of the exporting bourgeoisie, with the promise of passing a statute of political parties which would allow Apra some participation in power. Manuel Prado, who had ruled the country before and during World War II, and who represented one of the vestiges of the civilian bourgeoisie, offered Apra wide participation and political coexistence. This competition for the *aprista* vote by the two sectors of the bourgeoisie is significant insofar as it represents one more sign of the ongoing process of change in which these sectors recognize their incapacity to govern on their own and without popular support.

For the sector represented by Lavalle it was a matter of continuing to restrict political participation in order to avoid the disintegration of the traditional political framework. The sector headed by Prado, on the other hand, was seeking to coopt Apra's participation into the political game which Prado was striving to establish.

Another sign of the new winds was the confrontation of the different trends within the bourgeoisie, a process in which Prado no longer sought, as in his first government, an accommodating subservience with regard to the exporters, but, on the contrary, to make himself the directing element of the bourgeois process.

Two days before the election and while formally supporting the official candidate, Apra threw its support in favor of Prado. Thus, between 1956 and 1962, Apra's first "impossible" alliance took place: the *apro-pradista* coexistence. This government constituted the second attempt in the country's contemporary history to establish a populist government, and the first attempt in which a traditional bourgeois executive received Apra's support.

What made this *aprista* turn possible? The heads of that party would justify it by saying that it is not Apra which has changed but the structure and orientations of economic power. Indeed, foreign capital and the urbanization which it stimulated, emphasized the importance of the domestic bourgeoisie incorporated into the urban and industrial framework. While the rural sector lagged behind, the urban and industrial forces were in a clear socio-political climb.

To become incorporated into the political system, Apra had to propitiate the conditions for the peaceful coexistence of the political and economic sectors, which through negotiation would have to create conditions of stability and institutional continuity. Only in this way would Apra have a chance to attain historical significance and achieve political power through the electoral process. From here it was derived that, in order to attain such stability, Apra must abandon the radical posture that had characterized it until then and through which it had earned the qualification of "sectarian." Thus the party regulated and doused popular mobilization, incorporating it by way of consumption into the benefits of political coexistence. This brought about the demobilization of its bases, which otherwise could have broken down the institutional process with their radical demands.

But even though Apra's goals of political integration led it to modify its behavior, it could not have chosen a worse moment and partner. The process of transformation of Peruvian society overflowed once again into the leadership possibilities of neocivilianism, replicating the circumstances of the twenties.

In the mid-fifties, at the time of the new *apro-pradista* coexistence, there emerged a new urban and industrial bourgeoisie which, in close association with foreign capital, was determined to upset the sociopolitical map of the country and displace *pradismo* from its old and obsolete redoubts. At the same time, there appeared new middle and popular sectors which were disaffected from this political coexistence and which would rapidly gain significant weight in the national polity.

The changes in Apra and the country's process of urbanization created the possibilities for the formation of new political organizations which would fill the positions now abandoned by Apra. Indeed, the continuous widening of urban marginal popular sectors, and particularly of new middle sectors, politically unsocialized and deriving from different parts of the country, constituted an available population which Apra could no longer attract.

Apra, for its own part, probably due to prolonged periods of clandestine activity, had not created a process of internal mobility, of rotation of middle and executive cadres. Thus, the new groups of professionals, technicians and intellectuals emerging into the political scene in the mid-fifties, had a double reason not to join Apra: the latter's deals with a decadent bourgeoisie and the impossibility of mobilization within the diverse internal levels of the party.

There thus emerged the Progressive Social Movement, Christian Democracy and Popular Action, partially reproducing the Apra framework: a leadership of middle sectors, this time of technicians and professionals, sustained by the urban and peasant middle sectors of those areas which were not controlled by Apra and promoting a modernization from above, consisting in a change of structures which would give way to the constitution of a state representing the nation. Thus, through the enforcement of general measures such as agrarian reform, industrialization, the democratization of credit—operationalized through state planning—a national integration consisting in the reduction of social and economic distances would be brought about. These new political groups began, as did Apra, by challenging the traditional bourgeoisie's leadership capabilities, accusing it of being the cause of the country's ills, and denouncing the *apro-pradista* coexistence as immoral.

Thus a competition was created between populist parties, which, while promoting political goals that were modernizing, equivalent and within the framework of the "Western Christian" model, were supported by populations which had been incorporated into the political and economic process at different historical moments.

There is yet another difference between Apra and the new reformist groups. Whereas Apra sought to modify the country's social conditions *through* political action, that is, by means of organized popular support, the new reformist groups believed that such a change would be brought about through the implementation of technocratic measures. This difference would be of particular importance subsequently, in defining the relations of these political groups first with the bourgeoisie and later with the armed forces.

In the face of these new waves, the *apro-pradista* coexistence tried to find palliatives as long as the induced economic growth included the marginal population. The new populism, on the other hand, denounced the "archaic and negative structure" demanding "structural changes" and claimed that economic growth such as it was being realized only brought a yet more regressive distribution of social resources. Because of these pressures and in the face of the inescapable problems of urban growth and rural malaise, the government named a research committee headed by the most illustrious representative of the export sector and of the outward growth model. The committee's rulings favored private initiative and the formation of savings mutuals for the construction of urban dwellings, without state participation. With respect to the agrarian problem, the committee recommended the opening of colonization fronts in the jungles and technical assistance to small farmers to help them raise their productivity, which would help both raise their incomes and cut down food prices. In both cases, the problems of property control were eluded. The new reformist political groups, on the other hand, demanded state control of urban lands for the construction of dwellings by public agencies and the distribution of

arable lands among the peasants, with very long-term compensations.
The Cuban revolution increased the fervor of the new populism
and its university bases. New members were increasingly being
recruited among the migrants, who shifted their political
identifications to the new reformist sectors—Popular Action,
Progressive Social Movement, Christian Democracy—and to the
newly formed revolutionary Left—Revolutionary Left Movement,
Peking line of the Communist party—with the result that Apra
quickly lost its 30-year-old university support, and with it, a good
part of its middle and professional cadres.

At the same time, the problem of the International Petroleum
Company (IPC) became an object of pressure by the new reformist
sectors. They demanded a final solution to the differences which
existed regarding the legality of the title protecting that enterprise,
through nationalization and the enforcement of taxations.

Finally, the results of the typical populist policies were being felt:
salary raises, increase in public expenditures and imports, which,
without the combination of redistributive measures, brought about
an inflationary spiral and the devaluation of currency in 1959.

Under those circumstances, Prado's administration nominated the
maximum representative of the exporting bourgeoisie to head the
Cabinet of Ministers. The new cabinet enforced the classic measures
of budgetary balance and indirect tax increases, which, combined
with the raise in the value and volume of exports, temporarily solved
the situation.

This cabinet involved the alliance of various sectors of the
traditional bourgeoisie—exporting and urban and on their way
out—with the *aprista* party. Thus Apra was able to ensure an alliance
with its lifelong enemies, but its political project ended up being
absorbed by that of the oligarchy.

What Apra had hoped to gain was legitimacy, which would enable
it to achieve political power through the electoral process, thus
demonstrating that the party of the thirties was a historical fact and
that presently its leaders were "realistic" and "practical." The
conditions for the establishment of an institutional and democratic
process would thus have been ensured. The oligarchy, on the other
hand, aware of the fact that in the political game the mobilized
population must be taken into account, could for the first time

count on popular support to protect itself from changes or to adapt to them.

Under those circumstances Apra would offer two different positions: it would show its bases its classic radical traits and justify its alliance in terms of "tactics"; the reverse of the coin would be shown to the bourgeoisie, by supporting it with Apra's organizational resources and thus preparing to participate in the ensuing elections.

With the elections of 1962, in which (due to the electoral law) only one-fourth of the voting population participated, the reformist promises of Apra and Popular Action were disseminated throughout the country. The Popular Action party gathered within it the remaining reformist groups, reawakened by the Cuban event and the Kennedy reaction in the form of the Alliance for Progress. The election results brought trimuph to Haya de la Torre, but the army vetoed the choice under the disguised statement that fraud had been committed. The armed forces manifested their veto by an *institutional* coup: the three chiefs of the respective branches constituted themselves into the executive power with the intention, as they said, of reinstating the presently upset constitutional order (due to the crisis of political hegemony) and bring about the structural changes which the country required, at which time they would hand over political control to civilians. In this sense, the similarities with the present situation are complete.

This coup did not only mean the veto of an *aprista* government, but also the possibility of reestablishing an oligarchic government with Odría as president. That situation likewise anticipated the present, insofar as that institutional coup was anti-*aprista* and antioligarchic.

The year during which the military remained in power was a prelude to their present performance. They instituted planning and budgets through programs. And in order to contain peasant political mobilization in the south, which soon became linked with the emerging guerrillas, they decreed a basic law of agrarian reform, which did not involve any effective change in the situation of the peasantry.

Popular pressures and internal difficulties forced the military to hold elections, offering their support to Fernando Belaúnde. The reasons for this support were threefold: Popular Action was supporting reformist measures which would end with the traditional spectre haunting the country, that is, they would end with the oligarchic regime and the structure upon which it was based, allowing for the resolution of the hegemonic crisis. For another part, Popular Action had strong support with which it could neutralize the political emergence of the *aprista* masses. Parallel to this, the leaders of Popular Action did not purport to politically organize their popular support in order to affirm the role of the state, thus censuring the tutelary character of the armed forces. On the contrary, that popular support remained shapeless and it was hoped that the popular masses would respond to the manipulation and charisma of their "leader."

In the elections of 1963, Belaúnde won the presidency by a very small margin, without achieving a majority in Parliament. Under such circumstances and given the impossibility of an alliance between Apra and Popular Action, mainly due to the support given to the latter by the armed forces, Apra's second "impossible" alliance took place: a coalition with Odría, who once again represented the interests of the bourgeoisie. This coalition dominated legislative activities for five years, counteracting any moves by the executive to the point that political initiative originated in Parliament now became the "first power."

The Failure of the Populist Attempt

During the first three months of the Belaúnde administration—the so-called "first 100 days" during which according to pre-electoral promises the country's structural problems would be attacked—the executive took the political initiative bringing forth the reforms proposed: nationalization of the Bank of Deposits and Consignations, an agency of private banking in charge of tax collection; presentation of a law of agrarian reform by which all lands with long-term forms of payment were affected and the purchase of the Algolán estate (300,000 hectares), which was given over to the peasants. The popular euphoria favorable to Belaúnde soon manifested itself in the results of the first municipal elections to have taken place in 50 years. From 39 percent of the electorate which Belaúnde had obtained during the elections of June 1963, he obtained 49 percent in December. This euphoria increased with the creation of University Popular Cooperation, a movement in which thousands of students were mobilized in every corner of the country in order to "awaken" the peasantry and build a wide base favorable to the government and its reforms. This movement encouraged the country's general trend toward land occupation and peasant organization, especially in the more backward areas.

At this time there occurred the first confrontation between the congress and the executive, and the retaliation by the traditional bourgeoisie represented by the Apra-Odria coalition. The issues were the occupation of lands and agrarian reform. Regarding the first, the representatives of the coalition demanded the repression of the peasantry, overthrowing the first of seven ministerial cabinets. As for the problem of agrarian reform, they modified the government's proposal by eliminating from the plan the highly productive coastal estates, the best lands, devoted to cotton and sugar production, practically forcing cash payment on the value of expropriations. Finally, the establishment of the national budget became an act of political plundering by the coalition, cutting down those funds allocated for agrarian reform and thereby preventing the enforcement of that law.

The second blow against Belaúnde consisted of trimming down the funds of Popular Cooperation and accusing its leaders of encouraging the guerrilla process, claiming that elements of Popular Cooperation had maintained contacts with the new revolutionary Left and favored the occupation of lands. This reduced resources for the mobilization of peasant and student masses, while the government was made to appear responsible for the reform frustrations, this being the basic element of the political strategy of the Apra-Odria coalition.

There remained possible recourse to the government's popular support. Yet here Belaúnde's technocratic and demobilizing character was shown: faced with the need to mobilize the peasantry in order to exert pressure upon Parliament and bring about a radical agrarian reform, Belaúnde rejected that possibility and thus comprised his party's future. There then began the first of many disaffiliations by the more youthful leaders and the popular masses.

There was also the problem of the International Petroleum Company, whose "illegal" situation had been recognized by the previous government. Belaúnde, who had proposed to resolve this problem in three months, found himself trapped by his own promise. From the very first he tried to resolve the issue by negotiating with the oil company to hand over the wells of La Brea and Pariñas to the state; in exchange, the company would keep the refinery. This proposal was rejected by the company and the United States Embassy announced that, if IPC were nationalized, Peru would have to face United States reprisals and that in the meantime all economic aid from the United States government would be cancelled.

The situation with IPC further complicated the government's political game. Parliament's rejection of the agrarian and tax reforms proposed by the executive immobilized the government economically. While the coalition rejected the increase of direct taxation, which constituted 23 percent of fiscal income—a rejection that it would later use with the propagandist slogan of "no more taxes" in order to win a complementary election—it pursued, on the other hand, a definancing policy in order to incorporate its *apro-odriísta* clientele.

Given Parliament's policy and the impossibility of obtaining "soft" United States credit as long as the IPC problem remained unresolved, Belaúnde resorted to "hard" financings abroad, together with the establishment of a very liberal policy of access to foreign investments. Thus, while the coalition satisfied its constituency by means of the national budget, the executive, by means of foreign loans, set into motion the construction of public works which would supposedly replace those reforms vetoed by Parliament. The bonanza in the construction industry and speculation in real estate, both sustained by the rise in exports, coincided with a huge increase in the amount of foreign capital destined to go to industrial investments. Protected by the law of industrial promotion and on the basis of a growing urban market, foreign investments, traditionally directed to the production of raw materials for export, changed their orientation to the urban sector, promoting the new urban bourgeoisie while increasingly constraining the traditional bourgeoisie.

In the face of popular pressures (which the coalition attempted to partially incorporate in the form of a political clientele), the typical populist policies were repeated; public spending increased, causing an increase in demand without the necessary redistributive measures which would favor an increase in production and in the capacity for consumption, which again led to an inflationary spiral and a fiscal deficit. These would not be felt before the end of 1966, because the drastic increase of imports was sustained by the export bonanza, the inflow of foreign capital and the country's use of a wide margin of external credit. In 1966, the two latter resources were exhausted and inflation and foreign debts reached a critical point, making it impossible to maintain the parity of exchange.

Belaúnde went so far as to publicly declare that the devaluation of currency constituted an act of treason to the country and immediately put into the market the last $40 million from the Central Reserve Bank, obtained through a loan, in order to contain the devaluation. This influx of dollars was totally accounted for in a matter of days, as had happened with previous reserves and because of this the government was forced to effect a 40 percent devaluation of the currency. Soon after, a wave of smuggling was made public, in which prominent figures of the administration were involved, as well as high officials from the armed forces.

These events and the specific framework within which they took place increased the precarious state of the regime, bringing about dissension and resignations by the allies and reformist partisans of the government—due to Belaúnde's systematic rejection of popular mobilization as a means of regaining political initiative and bringing about structural changes. On the contrary, he underhandedly encouraged the initiation of agreements between Apra and the "Carlist monarchic" sector of belaundismo, which represented the newly emerging urban bourgeoisie, directly connected with foreign investments.

With the precariousness of the regime and public demands for a military intervention to stop institutional disintegration—which would once again eliminate the possibility for a future electoral victory by Apra—the Carlist sector of Popular Action and Apra constituted a ministerial cabinet, partially discarding the odriístas, to consolidate the government and constitute an effective populist regime. This brought about a restructuring of the political framework: Popular Action became divided, since the reformist wing saw in that act the betrayal of its original purposes. The armed forces withdrew their support (which they had been giving the government with decreasing enthusiasm, since Popular Action had become allied to Apra and had been unable to effect the proposed structural changes and, on the contrary, had accepted the maintenance of the previous regime). Thus, two elements of the political system, Odria—that is, the oligarchy—and the armed forces, the former a partner of Apra and the latter supporting Popular Action, found themselves released from obligation to coalitional politics.

The cabinet constituted by the Carlist wing of *belaundismo*, associated with Apra—which found in this alliance the leading element of the urban bourgeoisie, as opposed to what happened during the previous period with *odriísmo* and *pradismo*—received from Parliament ample powers to straighten out the country's economic situation.

This was a totally new and crucial experiment in the country's polity since, for the first time, there was a clear agreement within a new and dynamic urban bourgeoisie, despite its association with the new foreign interests, the modernizing middle-class party and with popular bases. There was thus an integration of interests among the modern, urban and industrial sectors of the bourgeoisie and of the middle class. The populist regime, forever compromised and postponed, finally seemed to be on the horizon. Apra, which had sought these allies since its inception, could now part company with the *odriístas*, an admixture of the most varied traditional elements. The emerging urban bourgeoisie could in turn count on the political support of the *aprista* popular sectors. The time had come to begin a project in which all the "modern" sectors might win, definitively discarding, both politically and economically, the crisis-laden traditional remains.

It would seem that, at that crucial moment in Peruvian history, each protagonist had found his perfect role. Apra's alliance with the new modern bourgeoisie seemed to be the final act that would give way to an exit by the exporting bourgeoisie in order that the new owners of the stage could organize the country in their image.

Thus began an irrepressible wave of reforms to reorganize and modernize fiscal policy, reforms that had been previously requested by the government without finding a favorable response on the part of Parliament.

First, the external debt was refinanced, thus alleviating the balance of payments for a couple of years; gasoline prices were increased to obtain a larger fiscal income and imports were restricted; tax collection was made more vigorous; taxes on land and stocks and bonds ownership were instituted and shares to the bearer were replaced with long-term debenture notes. There was an attempt to balance the national budget, eliminating the traditional deficit caused by the coalition. Finally, negotiations were begun toward new mining and oil investments, and Article 56 of the Mining Code was modified, granting exceptional privileges to the mining sector. The latter was due to the demands of foreign investors, as was publicly declared by the minister of the interior, and it would allow for the short-range inflow of $400 million.

But for those foreign investments to take place, and for the government to be able to count on U.S. government loans, as well as loans from those international credit agencies sponsored by the United States, a solution to the problem of the International Petroleum Company had to be found. Suddenly and strangely, after five years of unsuccessful negotiations, IPC accepted Belaúnde's original proposal of 1963: to hand over the oil wells to the Fiscal Petroleum Enterprise (EPF), annulling in exchange IPC's debt with the Peruvian government, later evaluated by the military government at $690 million. IPC would maintain ownership of the refinery, plus the granting of a concession of one million hectares in the jungle. Finally, EPF would be under the obligation to sell any amount of oil required by IPC, which would make it impossible for the former to develop its own industrial complex.

In this totally unexpected way, the so-called *Acta de Talara* was signed, to the noisy delight of the new *apro-carlista* alliance. But shortly after, the manager of EPF denounced the absence of page 11 from the *Acta de Talara*, in which, according to his declaration, oil-sale prices by EPF to IPC were specified. This generated a public turmoil, which caused the downfall of Belaúnde's penultimate cabinet. The following cabinet lasted 24 hours and was overthrown together with the president in the second institutional coup by the armed forces.

Thus the final attempt failed to constitute a populist regime that would resolve the crisis of political hegemony resulting from the society's diversification. This failure made it possible to establish a military regime which, through technocratic measures, sought to homogenize the country in terms of a modern capitalism in which the bourgeoisie would be prominent.

THE GOVERNMENT OF THE ARMED FORCES: MILITARY POPULISM

The scandals of the final months of the Belaúnde administration and the government's reorientation, caused by the new alliance between Apra and the emerging bourgeoisie, favored the direct intervention in the political process by the armed forces, thus preventing the consolidation of the populist establishment.

The armed forces saw the need to institute reformist measures that would attack the country's archaic structure and thereby neutralize the emerging popular masses—which might otherwise become an irrepressible force—while at the same time reducing foreign dependence. The institutional coup presented the armed forces with the opportunity to carry out changes which had been needed for years and which were becoming increasingly urgent for the maintenance of the social system.

The military government effected those changes the need for which Apra had formulated since the beginning. In general terms, then, all of the reformist political groups found a part of their own image realized in this government.

But because these reformist measures came from above, without considering and even rejecting popular participation, the government had to adopt an ambiguous posture to avoid incurring the displeasure of those reformist sectors. The same situation developed with regard to the investors and the bourgeoisie, from whom support was hoped for, despite reforms which would affect them.

From the time of the proclamation of the "revolutionary government of the Armed Forces" it was clear that the government was headed by officials with modernizing and nationalistic purposes·

In that proclamation, the connivance of native sectors with foreign interests which impeded the country's development was denounced, establishing the urgency for structural transformations which would modify the country's condition of dependence. Yet at the same time, the new rulers invited the foreign investors to exploit the country's natural resources, emphasizing the new administration's recognition of international treaties and its inclination to maintain itself within the "Western Christian system."

In spite of its modernizing and nationalistic tendencies, the new administration's ambivalence and indecision was clear: on the one hand it was willing to modify the relations of dependence, and on the other favored the country's further mining and industrial exploitation by foreign capital. One week after the institutional coup, the military initiated, with the intervention of IPC's oil complex and of all its subsidiary activities, a trend which was to intensify that contradiction, while at the same time it would compel them to dissipate the ambiguities.

With this military intervention, the new government cut the gordian knot that tied Peruvian polity. The armed forces legitimized their political intervention, while at the same time curbing the *aprista* rise which had developed due to the institutional deterioration of the Belaúnde government. The military's political legitimation not only stopped Apra's rise to political power, but also that of Apra's new allies, the urban bourgeoisie which was the intermediary of foreign capital. In order to neutralize this situation, the new government justified its position by stating that the situation with IPC was a unique case which did not include the remaining foreign enterprises.

A new expression of military nationalism was manifested in the presentation of their government plan, which constituted a typical version of the development program of the United Nations Economic Commission for Latin America (ECLA). This plan, which was not too far removed from the projects of the reformist and nationalist parties and groups from the middle sectors, such as Christian Democracy, Progressive Social Movement and the dissident wing of Popular Action, constituted the basis for support which these groups began to give to the military government following the nationalization of IPC, while the investors on all fronts were receding in their activities, aggravating economic contraction and urban unemployment.

Due to U.S. reaction to the IPC expropriation, there emerged among the reformist middle sectors a general current of opinion toward the new government which was increasingly supportive, together with the definitive neutralization of those sectors which had been removed from political power. The U.S. government's reaction to the IPC expropriation was not long to come. The latter informed the Peruvian government that it had six months in which to pay the amount of the expropriation, or otherwise it would have to face the enforcement of the Hickenlooper Amendment, ignoring the Peruvian position in the matter. This amendment considers two types of sanctions: one provides for the suspension of governmental financial assistance, which was in fact already suspended at that time and had been the basis for political blackmail to the previous government. The other type of sanction eliminated the possibility of the inflow of Peruvian sugar to the United States market. In the Peruvian case, this second sanction would be affecting 50 percent of sugar production and would have a negative effect on the country's economy, in the amount, directly or indirectly, of $120 million as well as on the employment situation of 45,000 unionized workers (*apristas* in the majority).

The military reacted to the U.S. position in a highly unusual manner in terms of contemporary Peruvian political life. The Peruvian Chancellery, traditionally passive and following United States norms, rejected the United States threat, considering that the problem was one between the country and *one* United States enterprise—which had behaved incorrectly—and denounced the action as coercive.

In order to find a solution to the Peruvian-American conflict and avoid new difficulties in Latin America, expectantly watching the new behavior of a military government, the United States proposed to initiate negotiations and thereby justify the future postponement of the application of the Hickenlooper Amendment. The acceptance of this proposal by the Peruvian government and the arrival of the U.S. presidential envoy created some uneasiness among the officialdom, where the opinion was spreading that there was going to be a "sell-out." This uneasiness was picked up by the government and quickly discarded by official statements declaring that the problem with IPC was not negotiable, and that the United States envoy was simply coming for information.

Simultaneously with this situation, the Peruvian Chancellery opened up two fronts to obtain alternative resources in its diplomatic confrontation with the United States. To the wave of propaganda by IPC, denouncing the alleged injustice committed against it, Peru responded with an unsuspected initiative in its foreign relations, mobilizing public opinion and Latin American governments in its favor, since the latter had an interest in the solution of the conflict insofar as it affected U.S. investments in their respective countries.

At the opening address of ECLA's conference in Lima, the president emphasized the nationalistic traits of his regime, denouncing the U.S. government's political intromission in the internal affairs of the country and placing particular emphasis on the existing relation between underdevelopment and external dependence. Similarly, at the meeting of the Coordinating Executive Committee for Latin America (*Comité Ejecutivo Coordinador de América Latina*—CECLA), in Viña del Mar, the Peruvian chancellor had a motion approved expressing the rejection by all Latin American countries of credit with "strings attached" and of United States political intervention in the relations between Latin American governments and United States enterprises. Finally, the CECLA document, partly inspired by the Peruvian events, demanded U.S. recognition of the fact that U.S. loans and investments in Latin America caused the latter's decapitalization.

For another part, the chancellery reopened negotiations—initiated during the *apro-carlista* period of the previous administration—with the Soviet Union and other Eastern European countries, establishing diplomatic relations with them, in order to obtain new possibilities of exchange and financing as well as the support by that bloc with regard to diplomatic and eventual economic assault by the United States. Peru also requested, with the same purpose, that it be admitted as an observer at the meeting of the nonaligned countries. In the meantime it was rumored that if the United States were to apply the Hickenlooper Amendment, Peru was prepared to denounce such behavior before the Organization of American States and the United Nations. For this, Peru had requested and received the support of Latin America and the Socialist bloc and it was preparing in the same spirit to participate at the Belgrade meetings. In other words, the chancellery mobilized new pressures upon the United States and rejected closed-door negotiations with that country. Thus the pressures reverted upon the United States; internally in Peru this situation was established as a model in terms of the possibilities which Belaúnde might have developed in a U.S. liberal juncture during the Kennedy administration.

At that point an incident opened up a new front of diplomatic confrontation with the United States. Californian fishermen who had made incursions into the Peruvian coast were captured and forced to pay a fine, similar to what had been happening for years, for not having obtained a fishing license within the 200 miles which Peru, together with Chile and Ecuador, had declared territorial waters. Californian interests, which recognized only up to 12 miles as territorial waters and had long been denouncing without too much success the situation maintained by the three countries, associated their own claims to those of IPC. The United States fishermen aroused their country's public opinion in terms of the affront of having U.S. ships captured. This was happening soon after the capture of the U.S.S. *Pueblo* by North Korea.

The fishermen requested that the Pelly Amendment be applied to Peru, establishing the suspension of military aid and they proposed the suspension of purchases of Peruvian fishing products in the eventuality of discrepancies between the Peruvian and U.S. legislatures. The impact of this measure upon the Peruvian economy would have been, as in the Hickenlooper case, quite serious. Fish flour, which contributes almost one-fifth of the total value of Peruvian exports, destines 50 percent of its production to the North American market.

Contrary to expectations, the Peruvian government reacted immediately and directly, denouncing the fact that with the application of the Pelly Amendment the United States broke with what had been established in the 1952 bilateral treaty of military assistance, thereby expelling U.S. military missions. Further, the Peruvian government declared that it considered Nelson Rockefeller's visit to Peru as unnecessary. The latter had just begun a tour of Latin America as President Nixon's special envoy, to listen to the grievances and recommendations of Latin American governments in order to delineate a new U.S. policy with regard to Latin America.

While the military government had the tacit support of the population in its foreign policy and maintained those sectors affected by the military coup neutralized, the "internal front" was growing weaker. This was partly a result of the devaluation, but also of the government's foreign policy, which led the bourgeoisie and foreign investors to limit their activities until the government had defined its policies, solved its differences with the United States and returned to "normal" paths. The reformist sectors, while dazzled by the foreign policy, were disconcerted and uncertain as to the government's definitive direction.

Since its inception the military government exhibited a technocratic and authoritarian character. Its first performances were related to the "moralization" of the country, that is, the judgment of those mainly responsible for the country's economic and political condition—seeking to affect the leaders of the previous regime. Yet curiously, those actions were not as arbitrary as might have been expected. Those accused of economic crimes and of crimes against the public faith were turned over to the judiciary, political parties were not persecuted, Apra and its labor unions had complete freedom of action and its leaders publicly expressed their views against the new government. Further, individuals who had been accused by the government were freed by the tribunals. In this way, the government tried to avoid confronting public opinion and creating a focus of opposition. Nonetheless, the only freed persons who had been deported for having denounced alleged internal divisions within the armed forces, demanded and obtained from the tribunals to declare grounds for *habeas corpus*. This ruling the government refused to accept.

To bring some order to the country, the government decreed the reorganization of the public administration, which Parliament had already previously approved but not executed. Some departments were eliminated, others were divided and four new ones were created which considerably widened public functions. Changes were introduced in the laws regulating the departments which were one-century old and restricted the state's activities. All key positions in public agencies were filled by officers from the different branches of the armed forces.

The president built around himself the Corps of Officers Advisors to the Presidency, which was the redoubt of the developmental colonels. This was the political body in charge of analyzing and operationalizing social-structural reforms and its president belonged to the category of a minister without portfolio.

In order for the military government to maintain its institutional link with its base of sustenance and to do justice to its title—Government of the Armed Forces—the three ministers of the respective branches were at the same time their general commanders. Similarly, the National Intelligence Service of the Armed Forces and the state security division initiated a program of censorship of personnel of the public administration. This was the first time in the nation's history that the public administration was in so complete a condition of dependence with regard to the armed forces.

This reorganization of the public administration, which was considered fundamental by the armed forces insofar as it clearly established the new operational bases, was carried out together with a fiscal reorganization, as part of the task of balancing the national budget, eliminating the severe deficit and cancelling the internal public debt.

These moves, which at first caused an economic recession, sought to create a conservative image in the eyes of foreign investors and financers, insofar as they were an attempt to stop inflation. On these premises and seeking to encourage investments, energize economic activities and inspire the confidence required by the ideologues of an open economy, each ministry called meetings with the "productive forces" of its sector—the managers and delegates of labor organizations—in order to achieve interaction between the plans of the government and those of the private sector, as well as listen to the concerns of the workers. These meetings, which indeed served to open up new channels of communication, were nonetheless associated with reformist measures which, in addition to the foreign policy, only increased the investors' confusion, as they continued to postpone the expansion of their activities. This situation, which in turn affected urban unemployment, forced the government to adopt new reformist measures to satisfy both popular demands and those of its own developmental orientations, seeking the support of the peasantry, the urban marginals and the urban middle sectors. In view of the bourgeoisie's retreat and the government's own nationalistic aspirations, it needed to build up a popular foundation.

One of the reformist measures that disconcerted investors was the "nationalization" of the Central Reserve Bank, since the delegates of private banking had previously constituted the majority of its management with the result that those organizations managed the country's monetary policy. Another such measure was the "Peruvianization" of banks. These were forbidden to hold foreign capital in excess of 25 percent, thereby preventing the increasing participation of foreign capital in private banking. The banks were also limited in the distribution of their investments, with the requirement that beyond a certain limit they were forced to invest in projects established by the state. This measure was intended to favor the domestic financing bourgeoisie which was in a state of prostration.

Regarding agriculture, the respective ministry expropriated the agricultural enterprise of Cerro de Pasco, the country's largest, of 260,000 hectares. This eliminated the conflict that had plagued the area for the past decade and paved the way for a new law of agrarian reform. The government presented for public consideration a project for a new code governing offshore rights, as opposed to what it had done earlier with the university law which had been decreed without consultations.

The new code governing offshore rights, which replaced one dating from the turn of the century, proposed in its first article that all waters were state property and rejected "acquired rights" of estates which, on the basis of this old precept, had achieved the monopoly of coastal lands. The fact that the government submitted this proposal to discussion raises the thought that military developmentalism, confronted with the National Agrarian Society, will end up being absorbed by those interests. It must also be added that there are ideological differences among the ministers-generals, thereby creating a conflictive situation within the government. These differences seemed to be resolved with the ouster of the minister of agriculture.

These divisions correspond to the different versions of

development that the reformist sectors and the exporting bourgeoisie had been bringing forth for the past 40 years. These ideologies can be broken down into two basic points of view: One emphasizes change in the relationships of power, while the other sees the axis of change in the problems of production and productivity. The first considers that only a redistribution of resources among the marginal population will achieve an increase in the capacity for consumption which in turn will increase production. The second position proposes an increase in the productivity of enterprises, ensuring through their capitalization the progressive economic incorporation of the population and an increase in consumption. The problem of economic concentration and the consequences derived from this position, attacked by the reformists, are, according to its supporters, political and not technical arguments.

Thus certain class conflicts and their respective ideologies were projected in the midst of the government. In this particular case, the dilemma was whether to introduce reforms and create a new type of power relations or to favor the productivity of the lands of the sugar and cotton barons; becoming associated with the power that they mobilized.

While the project for a new code governing offshore rights was being archived, due to internal and public differences regarding "acquired rights," a series of events related to the educational problem would cause the government to take the developmental and reformist path, defeating the "productivist" trend by decreeing on June 24, Day of the Indian, a law of agrarian reform proposing a substantive modification not only of the agrarian structure but of society as a whole.

The events that made it possible for the reformist line to impose itself upon the traditional line originated in two resolutions by the Ministry of Education. Since the early sixties, there took place among university students the emergence of a radical political perspective, which they tried to disseminate among the urban and rural popular sectors. This radicalization was not confined to the public universities but had also spread to the private schools. For a long time official publications had demanded effective action that would reduce the task of the universities to preparing technicians and professionals for industry, agriculture and commerce. It was within this framework that the Minister of Education of the military government, in an authoritarian and technocratic move, passed a law that would "reestablish the principle of authority" and remove politics from the university.

The university law, while it introduced "modern" changes to academic organization, also granted unusually wide attributions to the rector (university president), while drastically cutting down student participation, which had been largely responsible for changes in university orientation. The law allowed for the expulsion of students and teachers dedicated to "partisan political activity," considered the setting of student fees in accordance with their means, and finally it adjusted the institutional pace of the university centers to the development plan for the country as a whole. In other words, the government sought to modernize the institutional structure while restricting political participation.

On the other hand, the Minister of Education issued Special Decree 006 whereby secondary education remained only partially free of charge. This was a blow against one of the most important aspirations of the upwardly mobile popular sectors, both urban and rural. As was to be expected, this control to social mobility would have tragic consequences. One such result was the outbreak of violence in the city of Huanta with an outcome of several dozen dead and wounded. Huanta was taken over by thousands of peasants led by students who had come together for educational reimbursement. A few days prior to this event, in Lima, the students of the Agrarian University and later those of the Catholic University were severely attacked by the police after the students of the Catholic University had staged a small demonstration downtown. The attack also affected the rector of that university as well as some of the teachers. Reaction would be swift to come and the cardinal formally protested this affront.

Thus, the radicalized students who sought to retrieve their lost power and join the peasantry in order to widen the conflict within a revolutionary perspective, independent of military nationalism, brought the government to a crisis, while the traditional bourgeoisie was preparing to step forward as savior of the country and of military integrity.

The generals showed, just as they had done in terms of foreign policy, an unsuspected political dexterity. After the first of the student incidents, at the Agrarian University, the president showed up unexpectedly to arrange dialogue with the students. After the attack on the Catholic University and its rector, the latter was invited by the president to give him satisfaction, while at the same time the entrance by the public forces into the confines of the university was regulated with a judicial order. Immediately after the minister of education accepted many of the modifications of the university law proposed by the national council of the Peruvian University. Finally, with regard to the outbreak of violence at Huanta, the minister of energy and mines, a well-known developmentalist, made public statements in terms of the identity of interests between the students and the armed forces in the sense of promoting changes that would drastically affect the social structure. The law of agrarian reform, which had been under study, was passed after an uninterrupted debate which lasted 15 hours. The modification of Decree 006, which had caused the tragedy of Huanta, was likewise passed.

The military government tried to create a source of support from among the different middle and popular social sectors, discarding repression as a basic political instrument. In this respect it would be sufficient to compare the performance of the Peruvian government with that of the Brazilian government, for example.

In his message to the nation announcing the agrarian reform law, the president recognized the injustice and exploitation to which the peasant was subjected and the urgent need to eliminate peasant marginality, which would in turn allow for the industrial development of the country. He called for the cooperation of the popular and middle sectors (peasants, workers, white collars, students and professionals) to bring about the agrarian reform. He warned that the government would "crush" any attempt to undermine this reform and ended quoting Tupac Amaru, the agrarian leader who had been the forerunner of Peruvian independence: "Peasant, the boss will no longer eat out of your poverty."

Internal reaction was not long in appearing. All the reformist groups found in the law of agrarian reform an echo of their own voices. Haya de la Torre had no further comment but to say that this reform was the goal toward which Apra had struggled for 40 years. Favorable international reaction would likewise provide warm support to the military government. In terms of Latin America, the Peruvian government generated even greater interest.

In the United States, a few commentators said that, except for a few aspects, this was the law that best corresponded to the purposes of the Alliance for progress. Simultaneously with the passing of the law of agrarian reform all discussions regarding the expropriation of IPC were silenced, steps were initiated to annul the Pelly Amendment and negotiations were begun on the problem of the 200-maritime-mile limit. That is, relations with the United States took a new turn.

The new agrarian reform law attacked the agrarian sector of the bourgeoisie head on and ended by destroying its weakened political bases. The law affected all the lands in the nation. Production units became cooperatives or peasant communities. Thus sugar cane plantations were changed over to a cooperative regime. This was the answer to the problem of compatibility between reform and high levels of production. Eight enterprises controlling approximately 90 percent of the sugar production were taken over the day after passage of the law.

Cash payment for those lands affected by the agrarian reform, according to the law, amounted to a maximum of about $2,500, and payment for the industrial plant to about $23,000. The remainder would be cancelled out in the form of debentures and nontransferable bonds with terms of 20, 25 and 30 years.

Just as the law imposes the cooperative organization of salaried workers in modern estates, it also emphasizes the creation and strengthening of peasant communities in the traditional areas of the country. The term "peasant communities" includes the Indian communities and those formed around the laborers of the traditional estates. In both cases communal lands are considered inalienable and transfer or inheritance of plots is forbidden——the lands being returned to the communities after use.

In order to stimulate the development of cooperatives and peasant communities, public agricultural credit had that same order of priorities, so as to transform them into modern enterprises fully incorporated into the urban economic circuit.

Aside from the cooperatives and peasant communities, there were provisions for medium and small independent owners. Maximum acreage allowed for these was flexible and in accordance with zone requirements. The maximum limit for agricultural lands was 150 hectares and for the cattle-raising properties of the sierra sustained by natural grasslands, the limit was 1,500 hectares. The law also established that individual plots were required to have a minimum extension of three hectares.

Despite the drastic nature of the law of agrarian reform, it favored the shifting of agrarian capital to industrial capital. Individuals holding bonds derived from the agrarian reform were allowed to invest them for up to 50 percent of their value in industrial installations, which would be financed by the state in accordance with the plan for development, with the requirement that the remaining 50 percent be deposited in cash.

The operation of agrarian reform sought, among other things, to undermine the basis of sustenance of the *apristas* residing in the sugar plantations. Not only was the reform of those plantations begun, but it also attempted to build "agrarian reform defense fronts," rallying the peasantry for the support of this operation and, at the same time, to support the government's general policy.

The *apristas* took the position that those organizations divided the workers and competed with the trade unions. They therefore initiated a campaign toward the purpose that the workers should participate in the general process of the agrarian reform through their trade unions. With this move they were attempting on the one hand to maintain the trade unions (which some official spokesmen had considered unnecessary given the new conditions) and on the other to assign them new functions eliminating the need for the agrarian reform defense fronts as well as attacking one of the weakest points of that law, the lack of peasant participation.

The agrarian-reform measures, following the technocratic version dear to reformist military and professionals, considered that to bring about the transition from plantation to cooperative or peasant community, the state must delegate the managerial functions of the enterprise to an intervenor and a group of professionals. These would replace the figure of the boss and his administrators, while the peasantry would passively conform. As in the case of university reforms, there was a rejection of the active and autonomous presence of the population affected by the changes.

As a result of growing protests against this technocratic mode of domination, the military government exhibited once again the new political style it had established. The government picked up those criticisms and introduced some changes, at least in the case of the sugar plantations, by including two working-class delegates in the committees of intervention. This kept the conflict in a state of suspension.

The law of agrarian reform constitutes an "omnibus" law: it seeks to pacify the peasant masses and eliminate the possible operational basis for another guerrilla attempt; likewise, it attempts to undermine the *aprista* bases and the rural political mobilization of that party generally; it provokes a state of confusion among the fragmented Left; it eliminates the rural sector of the bourgeoisie, which had been the most important obstacle for the development of the country and for social homogeneity. With all this, the government obtained the support of the reformist middle sectors.

Within an international framework, this law presents the paradox of a military government—traditionally associated with reactionary ideologies—effecting measures of a reformist nature, thus altering the existing stereotype regarding dictatorial governments in Latin America.

The law of agrarian reform presents a social model as its goal: cooperative and communal enterprises, in which self-management substitutes private control; small- and medium-sized independent peasants who, together with the cooperatives and the communes should have access to credit, modern technology and the urban market, which would be characterized by the development of an industry established in consideration of the national interest and whose owners would have been shifted from agricultural to urban functions. The model suggests a *social homogenization* based on modern terms—urban and industrial, fully capitalistic—which would stimulate the development of a strong *national* industrial bourgeoisie and resolve the problem originated with the crisis of political hegemony.

In order to acquire a growing and self-sustained rhythm, this development had to take into consideration national interests and not restrict itself to considerations of consumption of the middle and higher sectors, as in the case of the traditional industrialization by import substitution. The development of this orientation is conditioned by the existence of wide markets, which explains the increasing interest in Andean integration and the development of the more dynamic sectors of the economy with no impairment to criteria of international competition. The realization of this project requires an orientation exclusively in the interest of the country, without the interference of international conglomerates. This can only be achieved through the state.

This policy led to the formation of three well-defined entrepreneurial sectors: the state sector, which would be in charge of basic industrial development, the domestic private sector, which in association with foreign investments would develop the consumption industry; and the foreign sector, which would specialize in mining, the source of national savings. From this outline, the following hypothetical development of the model might be attempted: this industrial development would allow for the absorption of underemployed urban labor, creating a new social dynamic which would gradually minimize the excessive role of foreign capital and the export of raw materials; thus creating increasingly wide margins of national autonomy.

Further, in order to avoid a subsequent polarization of classes, which might posit the social conflict at a different and sharper level, there would be an attempt to "democratize capitalism," through the participation of the working class both in the profits and in the management as part of the reform of the enterprise. This would achieve a balance between a capitalist and a socialist system, through participation which constitutes the new version of a corporate regime.

This model of development for Peruvian society has made it possible for different sectors of the various social classes to become integrated around the rulers, molding a political system which we have called military-populist.

The remainder of the traditional urban bourgeoisie, which had never been able to reemerge due to the weight of the exporting bourgeoisie and of foreign capital, found in the nationalist orientations of the military the possibility of realizing its civilian project. The new entrepreneurial sectors gradually realized that this government, while it attacked the traditional bases of the bourgeoisie, also offered them the possibility of becoming the leading element in the country's economy; thus granting the middle sectors a support which they had never before had in the state. The reformist middle sectors, constituted by professionals, projected upon the government their technocratic aspirations of leadership which would ensure them a pre-eminent role in the society.

The armed forces, for their own part, partially participated in the aspirations of these sectors. Insofar as their tutelary role was being questioned by the *aprista* popular mobilization and a revolutionary outcome was anticipated, the armed forces found in economic development a source of internal security. The theme of the relationship between development—as the integration of state and nation—and internal security would be expressed on various occasions to build up the military nationalism and justify the shifting of its technical and organizational capacity to the development of the country.

The measures adopted by the government, especially the more significant ones such as the expropriation of the International Petroleum Company, the law of agrarian reform and the bold confrontation with the United States, had a wide repercussion among the urban popular sectors and the rural modern sectors, eliciting an admiration and support which resulted in the formation of a national-populist consciousness. Likewise, the importance accorded by the government to the "young towns," a new designation for marginal neighborhoods, manifested by a strong policy of assistance to those centers and further supported by a law favoring the expropriation of rustic lands destined to this population has elicited the sympathy of this important sector toward the government.

A victory in international sport competition would unleash such a manifestation with a spontaneous celebration in which, for the first time in the country's history, there was a national identification that went beyond social barriers. The lack of political channels to express the popular satisfaction with the country's new image and the opening up of new possibilities, gave way to this kind of manifestation. This support would be felt again in October 1969 when on the celebration of the first anniversary of the IPC expropriation, proclaimed the day of "National Dignity," the president and his cabinet paraded through the solid *aprista* north, receiving a tumultuous support the magnitude of which had never before been seen, except for Haya de la Torre at the very peaks of his electoral campaigns.

There thus emerged a front of class integration with popular support, that is, a populist front headed by the armed forces.

Several observations are necessary to distinguish this brand of populism from those which developed in Argentina with Perón, in Brazil with Vargas and in Venezuela with Democratic Action. The populist regime has been characterized by the mobilization of the popular bases by means of a party which thus manipulated the masses to carry out a bourgeois policy. In the Peruvian case, this latter circumstance is not present and it is hard to believe that it might be. The armed forces constitute the political basis of sustenance of the regime, which explains the government's interest in appearing as a bloc with no fissures. The possibility of creating a political party, which would mobilize the popular masses, would produce a partisanship within the armed forces that would split this unity. This explains the government's insistence in presenting itself as "apolitical" and reinforce its identification as military.

From this circumstance and the tacit refusal to seek a popular mobilization, which might exceed tolerable limits for the armed forces, there results a contradiction that will undoubtedly be the bottleneck of the populist regime which the military are attempting to establish. There is a well-known positive correlation between social and economic modernization, on the one hand, and political participation, on the other. From this it is possible to foresee the origin of a conflicting situation, insofar as the government should continue its reforms while simultaneously seeking to curb political mobilization.

While the government is achieving the integration of different social sectors around itself, due to the reforms which it is carrying out, on the other hand it tries to make this support fragmentary and shapeless, since its organization might compete with the initiative and management of such reforms.

Regarding the agrarian reform, for example, the government

considers itself in charge of indicating with the intervenors under its command, the moment, place and manner of the transfer of lands, without taking into consideration peasant initiative, which is restricted to acceptance of bureaucratic dispositions. (A few days after the law of agrarian reform was passed, a small group of peasants from the district of Puno tried to begin the agrarian reform by its own initiative and was quickly repressed.)

The same situation prevails in the case of university reform. The law tends to the organizational modernization of the ancient Peruvian university; yet at the same time it seeks to drastically limit the participation of the sectors involved. This is the paradox of university reform without university participation. In the case of the "young towns," the situation is similar. The National Office of Young Towns, headed by a bishop and staffed by high officials and the new technicians—sociologists, engineers and economists—is in charge of determining the work to be done in the marginal neighborhoods as well as the part to be played by the population. Popular mobilization is understood in this case, as with Belaúnde and his Popular Cooperation, as the dwellers' participation in the building of streets, sidewalks, sewers and so forth.

THE CONTRADICTIONS OF THE REFORMIST POLICIES OF THE GOVERNMENT OF THE ARMED FORCES

For the realization of its nationalist and modernizing project, the military government is confronted with various problematic situations whose method of solution could seal the structure of Peruvian society for a long time. These problems hinge mainly around the government's economic policy, but their formulation and resolution involve the structure of social relations and the future development of the country.

The burden of the external debt was oppressive and the economic contraction initiated with the devaluation of 1967 was becoming increasingly severe. Foreign capitalists held out with their investments, hoping that the government would revert its trend, and seeking to stop those governmental reforms which went against their own interests. As had been expressed earlier by the sugar lords regarding the application of the law of agrarian reform to their properties: "Will this not lead to the destruction of all juridical security without which the investments that the country needs cannot be attracted? Those who are receiving guarantees today—as did not many years ago the sugar producers—will they not be paralyzed by the fear that tomorrow those guarantees might be plainly and simply annulled and that the fruits of investments and efforts should be expropriated in exchange for papers?"

The application of the agrarian reform and the announcement of new reforms were increasingly limiting the government's possibilities. The economic sectors linked to important capital were determined that as long as the Peruvian government did not resolve its differences with the United States government and did not undertake firm measures to ensure the investors not only of the modification of effected reforms, but also the elimination of announced projects of reform in the cities, enterprise and the fishing complex, it was improbable that any new investments should be made.

Confronted with this dilemma, the government adopted certain measures that were incompatible with its nationalistic project. Following the policies of Belaúnde's last cabinet, the government eliminated the fiscal deficit, prolonged the validity of measures drastically restricting imports and maintained a limited type of exchange control. While the first two measures allowed for the control of inflation and sustained the value of currency, thereby presenting an image of prudence and moderation, they also contributed to intensifying economic recession, with the consequent aggravation of unemployment forecasting a confrontation with the urban population.

Nonetheless, the government tried, by means of repeated invitations and the offering of guarantees, to attract new foreign investments, particularly in the field of copper, repeating again the policies of Belaúnde's last cabinet. It would seem that the logic underlying the application of this strategy followed the same reasoning as that of the modernizing ideologues of recent years: the arrival of those new foreign investments would offer assurances to the remaining investors, creating a current that would resolve the problems of the balance of payments, of economic contraction and unemployment, while at the same time offering the fiscal means for the financing of the agrarian reform and industrial development, goals regarding which the country was firmly committed due to the signing of the Andean pact. Ultimately, then, the inducement for modernization and social homogenization would have to come from foreign capital, which in time would allow for the widening of the margins of autonomy.

This policy conflicts with the realization of reforms such as those proposed by the government, insofar as no investor would be willing to run such a risk. This was the aspect of political blackmail which jeopardized the government's project, aside from the weakness and intrinsic contradiction of resorting to foreign capital to bring about national development. This brought into the horizon a new political crisis, since the foreign investors called upon to realize the national project would be in charge of energizing the model; but, to effect the needed investment they would in turn demand the disruption of that model. Once again in Peruvian history, foreign capital would be in control.

There is a basic contradiction between a reformist policy and one of fiscal austerity; no less than between a reformist policy and the inflow of new investments. Even though austerity seeks to stimulate investments, these are curbed by the reforms which, in turn, cannot be implemented due to fiscal austerity and the lack of investments.

Aside from those reforms attacking the oligarchic sector of the bourgeoisie, the government has suggested its intention to "democratize" the control of resources manipulated by that sector and foreign investments, in order to ensure distributive growth and eliminate the possibility that the concentration of those resources should lead to a sharpening of social conflicts, as well as to avoid the possibility that those sectors should constitute themselves into a competitive power vis-a-vis the state.

This reformist intention, associated with the traditional measures of economic stabilization of the military government, produced a paralyzation of economic activity manifested in the lack of investments and in a growing malaise. This placed the government in a very tight spot, since it compromised the support it was seeking from different sectors, while on the other hand it was trying to avoid any confrontation casting doubts on its legitimacy.

The government has indicated its intention to reform the fishing sector—whose exports have grown enormously. This might take the form of either cooperatives or of distribution of production quotas, in order to break the monopolistic power created in this branch of production. There is also the plan to reform the banking system, which aside from the "Peruvianization" to which it had been subjected, might have to undergo a compulsory distribution of credit, by economic sectors and by quotas, among the large, medium and small entrepreneurs, as well as the possibility that the state bank might receive private deposits. The tax system would also be affected, with the purpose of shifting the largest proportion to direct taxation. There have also been talks of enterprise reform, to establish working-class participation or certain forms of "popular capitalism," through the distribution of shares among the workers, which would affect managerial action. Finally, there is a possibility of modifying mining policies, in terms of an increase in taxation, the constitution of mixed societies, or both.

While on the one hand the new entrepreneurial sectors of the bourgeoisie are supported by a developmental government, on the other they anticipate vague threats on the part of the government. This leads them to paralyze their activities until the picture becomes clearer. At the same time, the support they offer to the government's new measures acquire an ambivalent connotation.

To this must be added that foreign investments have come to a sharp stop. This was caused by the nationalistic measures adopted by the Peruvian government, such as the nationalization of IPC, the chancellery's reaction to the threats of the United States government and the problems that emerged, also with the United States, regarding the protection of the 200-mile limit off the Peruvian coast from Californian exploitation. Finally, the Peruvian demand to establish a new mining policy with a significant increase of state participation in the profits derived from new wells and from the aggregate value of mining exports.

In sum, the government demands the acceptance by the bourgeoisie and foreign capital to rules which it seeks to impose, after having modified the rules that they had established, yet without specifying the nature of the new rules.

The results are obvious. Both native and foreign entrepreneurs withdraw from making new investments, partly due to the economic recession brought on by the government, but especially to wait for the specification of the new rules to be imposed by the government. But at the same time this waiting period functions as a pressure upon the government, establishing a new relationship with the latter and thereby achieving the indefinite postponement of some reforms or at least reducing their radical elements.

Once again the government had to define its policies around a specific problem: whether the country was capable or not of achieving autonomous development. For the bourgeoisie the answer was definitely negative. The military, while realizing that the country was not ready for a total disengagement, believed that the state must be put on the road toward such a goal.

In other words, the government recognized the pragmatic need for Peruvian dependence upon the United States. But at the same time it sought to obtain the greatest possible number of advantages within a relationship of dependence with regard to foreign capital. This was what they wanted and to a large extent it was what they achieved.

The military government announced that it was planning an expansion of the budget for 1970, and that it would make possible a greater availability of funds destined to the growth of the private economy. The most feared reforms, such as that of enterprises, were postponed; an agreement was reached with foreign capital; and the state was offering an important line of credit destined to industry and public works.

INTERNAL CHANGES WITHIN THE ARMED FORCES

In this presentation of the Peruvian political situation, emphasis has been placed on an anti-mass mobilization element as defining the government of the armed forces. This trait does not explain why the armed forces reacted to mass mobilization with a developmental and populist trend. They might just as well have responded with conservative and fascistic manifestations.

The reasons which may be given to explain the new behavior of the armed forces refer to the change in the relationships between the bourgeoisie and the middle sectors, as well as to the change within the armed forces, regarding the role that they had to fulfill to relegitimize the social system.

The social origin of the army's officials, the most important branch of the armed forces, plays an important role to explain the relations between the latter and the polity. The majority of the army's officials come from the rural middle sectors of the country. In this sense, their origins are the same as those of the leaders of the *aprista* party during the twenties.

We sustain the hypothesis that while the *aprista* leaders originated from rural middle sectors in a condition of crisis and displacement, due to the incorporation of new modes of organization of property and of production, the origins of the military, on the other hand, have their roots in established positions associated to the dominant regime instituted by the government of Leguia, in which the landowners performed a repressive role to contain peasant mobilization.

Up until a few decades ago, the possibilities for social mobility in the country were very limited, mainly due to the open nature of the economy and the slow urban and industrial development. The elitist recruitment and orientation that have characterized the university, together with the lack of opportunities for graduates lacking any meaningful family connections, did not provide the means for those rural sectors to fulfill their aspirations of social mobility. This was not the case in the military career.

In a closed society such as the Peruvian, in which birth strongly conditions an individual's future, the armed forces constitute the only channel favoring the criterion of achievement for social promotion.

While the bourgeoisie overlapped with the oligarchy, that is, the traditional export sector, and constituted the undisputed leading element, the middle sectors were weak and completely dependent upon the former for their existence. In this sense, the middle sectors identified with the oligarchy and confronted the popular masses in order to maintain the symbolic order which they shared with the bourgeoisie through the armed forces.

But since the fifties, certain changes began to take place, producing the internal differentiation of the bourgeoisie and the breakdown of its hegemonic character, together with the disintegration of the traditional rural world and the widening and differentiation of the middle and popular sectors which, associated with the social and political mobilization, caused the political system to enter into a process of crisis characterized by the breakdown of the relationship of dependence of the middle sectors with regard to the oligarchy.

The disintegration of the bourgeoisie and the parallel differentiation of the middle and popular sectors allowed for the creation within the latter of foci of political autonomy which, in tune with the new times, sought to become fully incorporated into the political mainstream with the support of the popular strata, trying to eliminate those traditional sectors of the bourgeoisie standing in their way. University students, the Church and the army thus emerged with radical, modernizing and nationalistic traits. It is not a simple coincidence that when the armed forces tried to achieve the modernization of the country and the elimination of the traditional sectors of the bourgeoisie, the "young Church" exhibited solidarity with the urban marginal population. Nor is it a simple coincidence that the main developmental military should have declared that their objectives were the same as those of the revolutionary students.

We thus encounter the paradox of the middle sectors, always considered as dependent upon the oligarchic bourgeoisie, which attempted to break the spectre of archaic social relations, as well as supporting the modification of the relations of dependence abroad. The crisis of the political hegemony and the failure of the political parties led by the middle sectors left an open door for other institutional elements grouping these sectors to emerge politically.

Together with this differentiation of the bourgeoisie which allowed for the relative autonomy of the middle sectors, within the armed forces there occurred organizational changes that encouraged a change of perspective among its executive ranks.

In 1952, with the beginning of the cold war, bilateral treaties of defense and mutual help were signed between the Latin American countries and the United States. This enabled the armed forces to intensify their professionalization and technification in order to become true "occupation armies" that would contain the revolutionary processes.

As a result of United States assistance, Peruvian officials began to travel to the United States, particularly for study and training from an organizational, technical and military point of view and to be capable of managing such enormous enterprises as the army, navy and air force. This training has become of such importance that it constitutes a requirement to achieve promotion to the higher ranks.

Together with the formation of intermediate cadres, one-year courses for general officers were organized at the Center for High Military Studies (CAEM) on subjects referring to the relationship between the armed forces and society. This relationship suggests the study of such problems as those which interested Prussian militarism and which have never ceased to be the center of interest of military institutions stimulated by international rivalries. We are referring to the relationship between military power and its social infrastructure. In the Peruvian case, this kind of interest led to the consideration of economic underdevelopment and the planning of growth, at a time when the simple use of the term "planning" was considered taboo by the oligarchic press. The armed forces' interest in military logistics would enable them to include economic planning within their concerns. This initiated during the decade of the fifties a developmental consciousness within the armed forces (and especially within the army) which had its first fleeting surge to power with the establishment of the military junta in 1962.

8
External Political Socialization as a Source of Conservative Military Behavior in the Third World

Miles D. Wolpin

The term military aid generally evokes images of such weapons as tanks, aircraft, or ammunition. Similarly, training is commonly perceived as a process of transferring technical expertise in the handling of men or equipment. Less widely known is the fact that Western nations, and particularly the United States, have gradually incorporated political indoctrination into the technical training programs for officers from the Middle East, Africa and Latin America. In the discussion that follows, we shall examine the evolution, purposes and impact of such-directed political socialization. Before doing so, brief mention will be made of several theoretical and methodological problems that are relevant to the analysis of these relationships.

A concomitant of the behavioral revolution in political science since World War II has been the emergence of several semiautonomous subdisciplinary areas. Despite the empirical aspirations of many specialists, much effort has been invested in scholastic model building and conceptual frameworks for analysis. As one experienced scholar has observed, the:

so-called revolutionary transformations in comparative politics of the last two decades have involved, among other things, a proliferation of macro-theories of politics, political systems and political behavior. Many, perhaps most, such "theories" are of extremely dubious value. . . . There has occurred an alarming neglect of the political process, itself, and of key institutions directly involved in the policy-making process. The need is, therefore, great for a return to a segmented and partial-systems approach to both theory and research.[1]

The most productive micro or segmented approach has been survey research. Hence, systematic correlation of interview replies with independent variables is commonly viewed as the scientific method for the study of institutional relationships and policy-making processes.

Attitudinal statements derived from this strictly empirical approach often are only tenuously related to overt behavioral patterns. Although this linkage problem is affected by a variety of factors, a major one is the assumption of respondent veracity. Philip Converse has reported, for example:

> that a large proportion, apparently approaching 50 percent of respondents in a sequence of national panel studies are individuals with no real attitudes on the matter in question . . . [who] felt obliged to try a response to the item despite our generous and repeated invitation to disavow any opinion where none was felt. This seems to be explained by the fact that "the attitude questionnaire is approached as though it were an intelligence test, with the 'don't knows' and 'can't decide' confessions of mental incapacity."[2]

If interviews can elicit the articulation of behaviorally irrelevant attitudes at the mass level, they are even more likely to inspire deceptive expressions of intent by self-conscious political elites. This would be particularly true of American and foreign military officers who have been involved in the overthrow of civil governments in the Third World. Given their need to secure the acquiescence of attentive publics and/or potential rivals, "any serious claimant to power, regardless of his antecedents, associations, or intentions, will justify his claim by professing profound concern for national independence, for popular aspirations, for social justice and for economic development."[3]

To mendacity must be added the ambiguities occasioned by multiple motives and divergent goals of the factions that frequently coalesce during a successful military conspiracy. Professional interests may interact with personal antipathies, nationalistic or anticommunist sentiments within a political tradition that recognizes the armed forces as exercising a veto or orienting role for the system in question. Without denying this complexity or the occasional utility of publicly declared goals, the most reliable explanation of military intent can be arrived at by focusing upon subsequent policies as the point of departure. For this to be manageable at the partial-systems level, it is advisable to limit one's focus to particular types of behavior. To the extent that a pattern of goal-directed conduct can be ascertained, it is reasonable to ascribe or impute motives.

Eric Nordlinger has recently correlated various indices of economic development during the 1957-62 period with the incidence of military rule in Africa, Asia and the Middle East. Except for those polities characterized by negligible middle classes, most military regimes have exerted a conservative impact upon their societies. Where the middle class exceeded 10 percent of the population, it was assumed that a concomitant of this societal differentiation was the existence of lower-class interest groups which occasioned some conflict and a threat to the material privileges of both the military and the middle class. The conservative role of these armed forces was explained by: (1) military internalization of professional norms emphasizing order, hierarchy, discipline and so on; (2) perceptions of trade- or peasant-union demands upon the military share of the national budget; (3) generalized lower-class claims against middle-class privileges. According to this class model, reference-group identifications of the officer corps with the middle classes exerted a significant, though secondary, reinforcing influence. The first two factors were regarded as crucial.

A similar explanation has been proposed to account for conservative interventions in Latin America by José Nun and Martin Needler. The latter used a longitudinal analysis to assess the incidence of conservative/reformist coups between 1930 and the mid-sixties. To explain the increasing ratio of rightist interventions, Needler notes their proximity to elections in which populist forces were either victorious or appeared to be on the verge of triumph.[4] This finding is consonant with Nordlinger's model because of the rapid growth of the middle classes that accompanied the import-substitution expansion associated with the Great Depression and World War II years. The thesis of middle-class reference groups as a source of coups when the former are confronted by lower-class mobilization within a relatively stagnant economic context is most forcefully presented by Nun.[5] The persuasiveness of his explanation is heightened by the failure of the developmental model to fully account for militarism in such relatively advanced countries as Brazil and Argentina during the past decade.

Multiple motives which may accompany hostility to egalitarian mass mobilization are quite consonant with a class-reference-group model. This is especially true of Kling's emphasis upon upward individual-mobility aspirations in stagnant neocolonial economies as it is for such variables as prestige attainment ambitions, personal antipathies, tradition and institutional interest.[6] Yet, except when the first or last of the forementioned are defined as requiring stylish consumption patterns, most of these aspirations and simple opportunism can be reconciled with either conservative or leftist interventions. Hence, they cannot in themselves explain those coups which are associated with a distinct ideological change in public policy.

One factor which most analysts of military roles in the underdeveloped areas ignore or de-emphasize is the external-reference-group identification with the officer corps of a metropolitan power.[7] Given the generally conservative and authoritarian attitudes of Third World and Western military officers,[8] it is probable that their propensity to intervene against radicals or populists is significantly increased by ideological indoctrination and interface relations in the course of training abroad. "Narrowly conceived, political socialization is the deliberate inculcation of political information, values, and practices by instructional agents who have been formally charged with this responsibility."[9] A recent study by Price suggests that both intentional as well as nondirected political socialization in British military academies powerfully reinforced institutional grievances in predisposing the military to seize power in Ghana five years ago.[10]

This chapter will focus upon directed political socialization at United States military installations for officers from Third World countries. The military assistance program (MAP) of the United States has trained more than 320,000 foreign military men since 1950; in excess of 50 percent are "officers, the majority from the emerging nations."[11] Before assessing the validity of our hypothesis that this program has exerted a moderate, though nonetheless significant influence upon the ideological behavior of ex-training officers, the MAP will be described and set functionally within a broader or systemic framework.

It is our contention that since the last decade of the nineteenth century, the United States has sought an open door for its investors in the Far East, Latin America, the Middle East and, most recently, in Africa.[12] Noncommunist nationalists and social radicals have been actively opposed since the military counter-insurgency campaign against Aguinaldo's Philippine rebels following the war with Spain. This pattern of foreign policy was manifested by opposition to Article 17 of Mexico's 1917 Constitution, in sanctions against Cárdenas in 1938, Perón in 1946, and through the overthrow of such radical nationalist leaders as Mossedegh, Lumumba, Sukarno and Sihanouk.[13] During the cold war era, the option of a neutralist or nonaligned foreign policy has been a sine qua non for expropriating Western investment interests and instituting major egalitarian social reforms, since the latter tend to undermine investment incentives.

Although the U.S. foreign aid program has, during the sixties, been rationalized as intended to promote a world safe for freedom and democracy, such goals seldom govern or are related to amounts appropriated by Congress for particular countries.[14] Nor are they evidenced by the pattern of U.S. support for authoritarian military regimes—this stance having antedated the cold war. And if one discounts public relations releases, there is abundant evidence in U.S. congressional testimony by both executive officials and congressmen to the effect that America is hostile to noncommunist leftism, expropriation, revolution, extremist nationalism, nonalignment, etc. For the purposes of this analysis, conservative military interventions will be those which are directed against either expropriation or neutralism.[15] As a caveat, it should be added that there are many political decisions by regimes in the underdeveloped areas concerning which the United States is either indifferent or assigns a relatively low priority. We do not suggest that the MAP is an instrumentality designed to secure complete integration into an empire similar to that of ancient Rome, or France more recently. Nor, on the other hand, is it limited to socializing foreign officers against nonalignment and socialism. Distinct complementary objectives include diplomatic support, intelligence facilities, communications installations and base rights, and so on. Naturally, these are incidental to a policy of containing communist social systems that have been particularly effective in closing the door on drainage of development capital by foreign corporate interests.[16]

Since World War II, one of the major threats to American corporate investments has been the rise to power of nationalist regimes pursuing socialistic policies in the Third World. Our problem is to assess the effectiveness of the training-induced relationships in preventing the emergence of such governments on one hand and in deposing them or forcing moderation of their policies on the other. Because of data censorship and the multiplicity of variables which are often operative, it is not possible to measure the effectiveness of this foreign-policy instrumentality with any precision. Even if the vital interpersonal relationships were not systematically concealed, the immensity of the research effort would mandate nothing short of a Defense Department-financed task force.

We shall therefore be compelled to rely upon a number of partial indicators which can support only the most tentative conclusions. They are based upon the classification of interventions in the Middle East, Africa and Asia during the post-World War II period. Between January 1, 1946, and December 31, 1970, there were 14 radical and 15 conservative coups.[17] In addition, there were 44 interventions which we have excluded. These will not be considered in the following discussion since they were judged to have been primarily motivated by discontent associated with such nonideological matters as budgetary apportionment, personal antagonism, upward-mobility aspirations, dominance ambitions, inefficacy or corruption of the civil regime, ethnic rivalries, and so on. While ideological factors were often present, we may not always have correctly concluded from subsequent policies that they were appreciably less significant than the forementioned motives.[18]

During the decade of the sixties, Washington's decision to expand and systematize MAP political indoctrination was accompanied by a sharp rise in ideological coups. Thus, of the 29 which occurred between 1946 and 1970, 20 were effectuated during the last ten years of the period. That this marked increase cannot be solely attributed to the emergence of new nations after 1959 is suggested by the fact that all 29 took place in but 20 countries of which at least 16 were independent for part or all of the earlier period (1945-59).

The widening appeal of nationalism in the underdeveloped areas was reflected by a substantial shift in the ratio of conservative to radical interventions. During the 1946-59 period, six of the nine ideological coups were conservative, while 11 of the 20 during the decade of the sixties were radical. Leftist appeal to officers was due in part to the patent inability of their societies to develop under a regime of capitalism and surplus drainage by Western centers. In some cases it was sparked by an often-related desire to be more independent of Western tutelage and chauvinism. Success for nationalistic officers—as transitory as it frequently is—requires balancing the West against the East to obtain external aid with minimal restrictions. Thus, very few of these countries received military aid from but one side in the cold war ——only two regimes obtained such assistance from the East and Egypt while not receiving any from the West for a period of several years. Significantly, within from three to five years both Sudan and Algeria experienced radical—but not communist—coups. In such cases and elsewhere, if only Eastern aid were accepted, environments characterized by widespread economic stagnation, poverty and economic exploitation provide powerful reinforcement for the acceptance of radical goal orientations. This is particularly true when the local bourgeoisie is nascent and marginally organized (See Table 1).

The limited medium-term counterrevolutionary effectiveness of Western military assistance is evidenced by the fate of those nonaligned nations which accepted not only Eastern (most often Soviet or Czech) military aid, but also training and equipment from one or more capitalist donors.

If we restrict our comparison to those Eastern-supplied Third World countries that received U.S. military aid,[19] an equally pronounced medium-term counterrevolutionary trend is evidenced. While all of these countries received U.S. aid, many also maintained similar ties with other Western nations (See Table 2).

Similar relationships are apparent if we examine those underdeveloped countries which have not received Eastern or neutral military aid prior to the ideological coups. Here, the counter-revolutionary impact of Western ties is modest and slightly longer-range in nature (see Table 3). The secular decline in the incidence of ideological coups manifested above and in Table 4 reflects the long-term receptivity of civilian political sectors to Western and U.S. reinforcing input constraints. These probably reduce radical threats to military values and privileges.[20] Again, the relationship is somewhat stronger for those states receiving U.S. military assistance. Here the conservative/radical ratio for less than nine years is 1/1, while a more favorable 3/1 is associated with the maintenance of such relationships for ten years or longer. Similar essentially long-term effects are manifested by arranging the date by length of Western aid where all have also accepted Eastern and/or neutral assistance (see Tables 5 and 6). For nine years or longer the C/R ratio is 9/5, while it is only 7/8 for the shorter period. Again, there is slightly greater effectiveness for MAP recipients, and this extends to both medium- as well as long-lead times.[21]

If we can hypothesize that the stability or slight decline in the number of conservative interventions is attributable to the simultaneous penetration of civilian sectors whereby the internal power balance is mobilized against radical groups, how can we explain the marked decline in radical military interventions? The relationships structured by MAP training not only aid conservative officers in suppressing radical conspiracies but the process of ideological indoctrination progressively denudes radical factions of potential sympathizers within the military establishments. As conservative ideological cohesion—even when weakly internalized on an individual level—is enhanced, the prospects for radicals are appropriately diminished. The decline in Tables 3 and 4 is more impressive than in 5 and 6 where competing though not especially efficacious Soviet training is operative. More definitive evidence of

MAP effectiveness is provided by comparing the proportion of a nation's armed forces trained by the United States with the incidence of ideological interventions. Although somewhat crude as a measure, it does allow ex-trainees to rise through the officer ranks as the armed forces of most countries increased in size.

For those nations with less than one percent CONUS-trained, the ratio of C/R interventions is 6/5, while where it exceeds one percent, the corresponding ratio is 6/1. The relationships are almost identical if we add those trained overseas to the CONUS figures for each country (see Table 7).[22]

We have not dealt with Latin America because of an excellent longitudinal analysis by Martin Needler in 1966. Examining an area where a higher ratio of officers are U.S.-trained than elsewhere in the underdeveloped world, Needler found a pronounced decline in the percentage of reformist coups. While the definition of reformism used in Table 8 may include some interventions which would not warrant a radical designation, his data are consistent with our hypothesis and support the conclusion of John J. Johnson "that without the military, every government in the Latin American orbit would be further to the left than it is now."[23]

Space limitations here preclude a survey of statements by adivisory committees, congressmen, military writers and scholars who conclude that the MAP *has been effective* in terms of increasing the responsiveness of Third World officers to U.S.-policy goals.[24] There are a plethora of more sweeping allegations by Defense Department officials and military officers associated with this external political socialization endeavor. The following statement by Grand Pre is fairly typical of this genre:

> Actions which we take in the future—or choose not to take—will be based on their understanding—or mis-understanding—of our society. . . . Lt. General Robert H. Warren, Deputy Assistant Secretary of Defense for Military Assistance and Sales, recently stated that, although he places a high priority on contacting and influencing leaders in foreign societies, "long experience has indicated that *training* is one of the most productive forms of military assistance investment, in that it fosters attitudes on the part of the trainee which lead to better mutual understanding and greater co-operation. . . ."[25]

External political socilization is an imperfect and only moderately effective means of mobilizing bias against radical nationalists in underdeveloped countries. An awareness of this limitation may have occasioned the addition of a soft sell on U.S. free enterprise to the traditional negative anticommunism which characterized the indoctrinational aspects of MAP during the late fifties and early sixties. A distinction was wrought between progressive U.S. capitalism and the visibly poor performance of bourgeois elements in most backward lands. As the gap continues to widen between the economic growth of the metropolitan centers and the underdeveloped areas, pro-American military elites may increasingly reject their own nationally oriented bourgeoisie in favor of the modernizing transnational corporate conglomerates. By strengthening their reference-group identifications with the ideological frontier orientation of the U.S. officer corps, the United States increases the likelihood that Third World military elites will contribute to the integration of their economies into a semistable world order whose basic parameters are defined by U.S. developmental needs.

These external inputs and their reinforcing effect upon conservative military behavior do not occur in an environmental vacuum. The fact that in stagnating economies with no colonial dependencies, blue-collar sectors are often mobilized by unintegrated radical elites who have not been suborned or socialized to middle-class identifications, may well signify a genuine threat to the professional budgetary aspirations of the officer corps. Also supportive of conservative militarism is the recruitment of officers from bourgeois and socially mobile lower middle-class elements. As in other societies, such persons frequently are avid to distinguish themselves from the unkempt lower orders. A recent study of mass attitudes in Chile, for example, found that middle-class psychological identification correlated much more strongly with hostility to political radicalism than such demographic variables as occupation, income or even education.[26] Given the status insecurity and nonspartan social privileges (servants, resorts, limousines, clubs, and so on) of military officers in many of these societies, it is little wonder that MAP indoctrination has attained a moderate degree of success. José Nun emphasizes:

... the special vulnerability of the Latin American middle class in the face of the imperialistic strategy of the Cold War. The vulnerability corresponds to the worsening of the relations of this class with the popular sectors and for this reason, systematic anti-Communism appears as the type of rationalization most suited to its interests. Furthermore, the middle class, as a consequence of the lack of hegemonic vocation on the part of its various factions, achieves only a precarious unity on the basis of negative principles. It is opposed to corruption and it is opposed to Communism, without realizing that corruption is a function of the irrationality of the system it is helping to preserve and that Communism is the name that its fears give to the desire of the popular sectors for a better way of life.[27]

An almost identical distinction between ideological perceptions and systemic functions—but one which emphasizes external linkages—was tendered two years before Nun's by Irving Louis Horowitz.

While each of the Latin American miliatry elites might employ such themes to justify its own behavior ... basically they represent supposed United States needs in the area. This supposition is in itself the most decisive aspect of the present situation—namely, the breakdown of neocolonialism and its replacement with imperial politics of a more classic vintage. The present turn to counterinsurgency as a style of politics marks a return to military solutions of economic problems, rather than economic solutions to military problems. While the form of colonialism may be classical, the content is quite new....[28]

In arguing for the utility of a class model in assessing certain types of military interventions, we recognize that a majority have been largely devoid of ideological goals. Many coups must be explained by other variables. If for a moment we ignore those which are unique to particular conspiracies (i.e., opportunism, personal antipathy, and so on), the general pattern of military intervention can be explained by two factors which are ubiquitous in underdeveloped areas: (1) Kling's emphasis on the paucity of alternative upward mobility channels in stagnating neocolonial economies; (2) Nun's emphasis on the failure of civilian elites to assume leadership in modernizing military technology and imposing professional norms upon officer corps—thus causing officer corps to develop a type of institutional inferiority complex. As contrasted with the historic pattern in the NATO community, such a self image is translated into respect for civilian supremacy while being simultaneously buttressed by extramilitary avenues for upward mobility. Although we are ignoring national and regional differences, it can be argued that in general this predator model of military establishments contributes to an explanation of the lack of legitimacy with which Third World officers view civilian supremacy. When one couples de facto military supremacy (not autonomy) with the accretion of material privileges and middle-class identifications, it becomes immediately apparent why these officers find American indoctrination and social hospitality to be so congenial. The consequential reinforcement contributes to a definition of atheistic communism that indiscriminately includes all egalitarian elements that can be perceived to threaten officer privileges, military supremacy, the modernizing oligarchic classes or their capitalist benefactors in the developing North Atlantic community.

The widening gap between the economies of the Third World and the metropolis in conjunction with the patriotic role orientations of military officers—especially when they are exposed to radical nationalist ideas—will ensure that the process of neocolonial subjugation is imperfect at best. There will always be some officers who for patriotic or a combination of this and less noble motives assume the mission of struggle against dependency, underdevelopment and oligarchic class dominance. But even in cases such as the recent Peruvian coup, they may be outnumbered by colleagues who are genuinely friendly to the United States and receptive to foreign investment.[29] There have been very few leaders like Yon Sosa in Guatemala or Camaano in the Dominican Republic and their insurgencies have in most instances been suppressed by pro-American military establishments. No Left-socialist or communist interventions have been successful in any long-term MAP country.

TABLE I

CONSERVATIVE/RADICAL INTERVENTIONS IN COUNTRIES RECEIVING EASTERN AND WESTERN MILITARY AID

Years of Eastern Military Aid	Interventions Conservative	Radical
0–4	0	2
5–8	4	1
9–12	1	1
TOTALS	5	4

TABLE 2

CONSERVATIVE/RADICAL INTERVENTIONS IN COUNTRIES RECEIVING EASTERN AND U.S. MILITARY AID

Years of Eastern Military Aid	Interventions Conservative	Radical
0–4	1	1
5–8	5	1
9–12	0	1
TOTALS	6	3

TABLE 3

CONSERVATIVE/RADICAL INTERVENTIONS IN COUNTRIES RECEIVING WESTERN MILITARY AID ONLY

Years of Western Military Aid	Interventions Conservative	Radical
0–4	2	3
5–8	2	4
9–12	4	1
13–22	1	1
TOTALS	9	9

TABLE 4

CONSERVATIVE/RADICAL INTERVENTIONS IN COUNTRIES
RECEIVING U.S. BUT NOT EASTERN OR NEUTRAL MILITARY AID

Years of U.S. Military Aid	Interventions Conservative	Radical
0–4	1	1
5–8	3	3
9–12	2	0
13–20	1	1
TOTALS	7	5

TABLE 5

CONSERVATIVE/RADICAL INTERVENTIONS IN COUNTRIES
RECEIVING WESTERN AND EASTERN OR NEUTRAL MILITARY AID

Years of Western Military Aid	Interventions Conservative	Radical
0–4	4	4
5–8	3	4
9–12	5	2
13-22	0	1
TOTALS	12	11

TABLE 6

CONSERVATIVE/RADICAL INTERVENTIONS IN COUNTRIES RECEIVING
U.S. AND EASTERN OR NEUTRAL MILITARY AID

Years of U.S. Military Aid	Interventions Conservative	Radical
0–3	2	1
4–7	5	4
8–11	3	1
12–15	1	2
16–22	2	0
TOTALS	13	8

Although congressional restrictions have been imposed upon the military assistance program since the Vietnamese campaign began to appear hopeless, most of these have simply made it easier for liberal congressmen to criticize exercises of executive discretion. The Symington Amendment to the Foreign Assistance Act of 1967 directs the president to terminate economic aid if a country is diverting funds "to unnecessary military expenditures, to a degree which materially interferes with its development." And the Conte-Long Amendment to the same act ends grant aid if underdeveloped recipients—with certain exceptions—purchase "sophisticated weapons without a determination by the President of the United States that such transactions are in the American national interest."

There have been some genuine changes in recent years. Due to the weakening of the U.S. dollar, the Nixon administration has attempted to substitute military credit sales for grant aid. Recently, two Defense Department associated specialists warned that this may be self-defeating and therefore dysfunctional:

> The substitution then of credit sales for grant aid is no panacea. . . . It exacts a price in terms of reduced economic growth, diplomatic problems of transition, and the reduction of U.S. control of military forces in the recipient countries.[30]

The authenticity of this apprehension is suggested by Horowitz's conclusion several years earlier that "what has taken place in increasing degrees is the external or foreign management of internal conflicts in Latin America. . . ."[31] And a considerable body of data which tends to substantiate Horowitz's assessment has been assembled by his former student John Saxe-Fernández.[31]

In the short run this tendency and the diversion of Food for Peace aid has enabled client regimes to continue receiving almost the same number of training spaces as they had prior to the enactment of statutory limitations upon military grant aid. According to the comptroller general of the United States, it is unlikely that there has been any substantial decline in military aid.[33] In the long run there is some danger in this shift away from grants. Another defense establishment expert has noted in a slightly different context:

TABLE 7

CONSERVATIVE/RADICAL INTERVENTIONS IN COUNTRIES HAVING DIFFERENT PROPORTIONS OF CONUS TRAINEES FY 1950-69

CONUS[a] Trainees (1950-69) as Percent of Armed Forces Manpower (1968)	Interventions	
	Conservative	Radical
0.00–0.49	3	2
0.49–0.99	3	3
1.00–1.99	3	0
2.00+	3	1
TOTALS	12	6

[a]Continental U.S. Command.
Sources: U.S. Department of Defense (1970:17); Sellers (1968).

TABLE 8

SUCCESSFUL LATIN AMERICAN COUPS: 1935-64

Characteristics	1935-44		1945-54		1955-64	
Reformist	8	50%	5	23%	3	17%
Low in Violence	13	81	15	68	6	33
Overthrew Constitutional Governments	2	12	7	32	9	50
Around Elections	2	12	7	32	10	56

Source: Needler (1966).

To the extent that aid is stepped up by Washington it may be as a result of competition with Western nations, not the Soviet Union, for the United States sometimes finds it more difficult to exert pressure against Latin American countries receiving aid from U.S. allies, such as France, Germany or the United Kingdom.[34]

The overcommitment of U.S. resources and enemy capabilities in Vietnam may then result in a slight erosion of American hegemony within the Western world. If so, it will not be with the willing acquiescence of the Nixon administration, which has been seeking—in accord with the recommendations of the Rockefeller Report—to increase military assistance training.[35] Other changes are in line with what public relations experts call a low profile. This explains the contemplated transfer of U.S. Southern Command (SOUTHCOM) functions to the Norfolk headquarters of the North Atlantic Command because "the maintenance of a large military command structure in Latin America, whose commander in chief is a frequent visitor to the countries of the region is seen by critics as too conspicuous and implies Washington's total blessings on regimes that may not be based on popular trust and confidence.[36] Along similar lines, the Rockefeller Report advised that Military Missions and Advisory Groups (MILGRP) be reduced in size and visibility. Officers should not appear in public wearing uniforms and the missions would not be called permanent. In addition, it counseled a change in name from "military assistance program" to "Western Hemisphere Security Program." The manipulation of symbols to conceal asymmetrical relationships has also been reflected in the proposal to rename the United States Army School of the Americas as the Inter-American Defense Academy.

Future research might well assess the effectiveness of such facades upon various attentive publics. Of more direct relevance to our hypothesis that external socialization by the West in general and the United States in particular measurably affects conservative role-playing by officer corps in the Third World would be a detailed analysis of the training, engendered personnel relationships and the prior socialization of coup leaders. Military journals and newspapers in such countries could be examined, or the academic profession might request that the Defense Department publish the names of all ex-trainees. Investigation must also focus upon external sources of humanities and social science curricula utilized by military academies and staff colleges in the underdeveloped areas. Marital patterns and other social interaction between officers and the middle sectors would also help to better test the class model as developed by Kling, Nun and Nordlinger.[37] This is on the assumption that primary relationships and recent socialization experiences exert a more significant impact upon political behavior than do social origins or other reinforcing or antithetical environmental factors.

NOTES

1. Joseph La Palombara. "Macrotheories and Microapplications in Comparative Politics: A Widening Chasm," *Comparative Politics* 1 (1969): 52-78.

2. William R. Schonfeld, "The Focus of Political Socialization Research: An Evaluation," *World Politics* 23 (1971): 571.

3. W. W. Rostow as quoted by Eric A. Nordlinger. "Soldiers in Mufti: The Impact of Military Rule upon Economic and Social Change in the Non-Western States," *American Political Science Review* 64 (1970): 1134.

4. Martin C. Needler, "Political Development and Military Intervention in Latin America." *American Political Science Review* 60 (1960): 616-26.

5. José Nun, *Latin America: The Hegemonic Crisis and the Military Coup* (Berkeley: University of California, Institute of International Studies, 1969), Politics of Modernization Series, no. 7.

6. Merle Kling, "Toward a Theory of Power and Political Instability in Latin America," in *Latin America: Reform or Revolution?* eds. James Petras and Maurice Zeitlin (New York: Fawcett, 1968).

7. Of the 73 studies annotated by Peter Riddleberger no more than five held that external military training exerted a significant influence upon indigenous political roles. Sixty-five items completely ignored such inputs. See Peter B. Riddleberger, *Military Roles in Developing Countries: An Inventory of Past Research and Analysis* (Washington, D.C.: American University, Special Operations Research Office, 1965), AD463188.

8. On this see such authors and research as Edwin Liewen, *Generals Versus Presidents* (New York: Praeger, 1964); Harold A. Hovey, *United States Military Assistance: A Study of Policies and Practice* (New York: Praeger, 1965); James Clotfelter, "The African Military Forces," *Military Review* 48 (1968): 22-31; and Martin C. Needler, "The Latin American Military: Predatory Reactionaries or Modernizing Patriots?" *Journal of Inter-American Studies* 11 (1969): 239-42.

9. Greenstein as quoted by Schonfeld in "The Focus of Political Socialization Research."

10. Robert M. Price notes that "the individual trainee is isolated from his past reference and membership groups, that is, from the sources of social and psychological support for his previous beliefs. He is enmeshed in a network of new membership groups, characterized by high levels of cohesiveness and a reinforcing ideological homogeneity.... The training process undergone by the officer corps of many of the new states is such as to produce reference-group identifications with the officer corps of the ex-colonial power and concomitant commitments to its set of traditions, symbols and values." Robert M. Price, "A Theoretical Approach to Military Rule in New States: Reference Group Theory and the Ghanian Case," *World Politics* 23 (1971): 399-430.

11. Donn R. Grand Pre, "A Window on America—The Department of Defense Information Program." *International Educational and Cultural Exchange* 6 (1970): 86-93.

12. Historical studies providing substantive bases for this view have been published by a number of authors. See, among others, Walter La Feber, *The New Empire* (Ithaca, N.Y.: Cornell University Press, 1963); Lloyd C. Gardner, *Economic Aspects of New Deal Diplomacy* (Madison, Wis.: University of Wisconsin Press, 1964); and Gabriel Kolko, *The Roots of American Foreign Policy: An Analysis of Power and Purpose* (Boston: Beacon Press, 1969). In the words of two Defense Department-associated scholars, "the major long-range task in the underdeveloped countries appears to be less that of the development of military capabilities than the promotion of conditions of general material and psychological well-being and satisfaction with Western political approaches to economic development. The latter goal requires ... internal security, technical development, and political development ... military personnel influence all three areas as they attempt to provide military assistance." Theodore R. Vallance and Charles D. Windle, "Cultural

Engineering," *Military Review* 43 (1962): 62.

13. Instructive sources on such U.S. interventions are, Robert F. Smith, *The United States and Cuba: Business and Diplomacy, 1917-1960* (New Haven: College and University Press, 1960); Kolko, *The Roots of American Foreign Policy*; and Gardner, *Economic Aspects of New Deal Diplomacy*, among others.

14. R. A. Packenham, "Political Development Doctrines in the American Foreign Aid Program," *World Politics* 18 (1966): 194-235.

15. As used here, conservative does not necessarily imply opposition to all social change or technological modernization. It may be defined as encompassing at least one, though generally several, of the following policy orientations: (1) high priority to the protection of domestic and foreign property holdings in profitable areas; (2) de facto refusal to redistribute existing wealth in favor of the blue-collar workers or peasant sectors; (3) opposition to publicly owned and controlled enterprises when generous tax privileges or other subsidies will induce private investors to assume responsibility for the undertaking; (4) anti-Communist suppression; and (5) advocacy of a de facto pro-Western foreign policy.

16. Although the posture of antagonism which dates from the 1917 anti-Bolshevik allied invasion of Russia has often been articulated and perceived in purely ideological or normative terms, the latter have always been operationally defined within a framework characterized by open-door constraints. The absence of establishment outrage over torture in Brazil is only superficially inconsistent with the numerous denunciations of Cuban revolutionary justice in 1959 and the subsequent elimination of a free press in that country. On the basic class nature of cold war antipathies as well as the role of foreign investment as a net expropriator, rather than a source of capital for underdeveloping areas, see David Horowitz, *Empire and Revolution* (New York: Monthly Review Press, 1969); Pierre Jalee, *The Pillage of the Third World* (New York: Monthly Review Press, 1968); and Andre G. Frank, *Latin America: Underdevelopment or Revolution* (New York: Monthly Review Press, 1970).

17. Algeria R(7/62); Burma C(9/58); Cambodia C(3/70); Congo (B) R(8/63); Congo-Katanga C(9/60); Egypt R(3/54); Ghana C(2/66); Greece C(4/66); Indonesia C(3/66); Iran C(8/53); Iraq R(7/58), C(2/63); Jordan C(4/57); Laos C(1/60), R(8/60), C(4/64); Libya R(9/69); Mali C(11/68); Pakistan C(10/58); Somali R(10/69); South Yemen R(5/68); Sudan R(10/64); Syria C(3/49), R(2/54),

C(9/61), R(2/66); Thailand C(11/51); Zanzibar R(1/64)–R = radical; C = conservative.

18. Our classifications were based upon policies pursued or objected to as reported by the *New York Times*, periodicals and scholarly publications. When clear evidence of such conduct was lacking, statements by coup leaders and deposed politicans were relied upon. "Conservative" is defined in note 15. The converse is radical for our classificatory purposes.

19. We are now excluding a small number of countries that were militarily aided by East and a Western nation other than the United States.

20. The creation or maintenance of a favorable internal power balance is furthered by strengthening political parties, the provision of economic aid, cultural exchange programs, educational modernization, diffusion of propaganda, organizing peasant unions and cooperatives and so on. A variety of U.S. governmental entities, official agencies and international organizations contribute to this counterrevolutionary institution-building process which parallels the MAP.

21. In tables 5 and 6 several of the countries did not receive any military aid from non-Western or non-U.S. sources.

22. This is our best indicator and not merely because it would survive a statistical test. Quite simply, it avoids the problem of countries that despite long-term aid relationships have sent relatively small numbers of officers for training. Hence, the earlier, secular tables did not distinguish high-impact from low-impact penetration. If we had, it is virtually certain that the conservative interventions ratio would be highest for countries with the largest proportion trained over the longest period.

23. John J. Johnson, *The Military and Society in Latin America* (Stanford: Stanford University Press, 1964), p. 143.

24. Some of these assessments have been referred to or quoted in preceding sections of this chapter. Others, along with a few dissenting views, appear in Miles D. Wolpin, *Military Aid and Counterrevolution in the Third World* (Lexington, Mass.: D.C. Heath, 1973), ch. 7.

25. Grand Pre, "A Window on America," pp. 87-89. He goes on to note that "nineteen of the countries receiving military assistance are currently governed by military or ex-military officers. Five of them received training in the United States. . . . Others have deputies who have trained here . . . . Twelve of the 19 countries have

cabinet ministers who received military training in this country. . . . In Peru, 11 cabinet ministers received military training in the United States.

"Nearly 200 U.S.-trained military officers occupy executive or legislative positions in their governments, are presidents of major industrial firms, or are chiefs or deputy chiefs of their respective military departments.

"Over 600 others are senior commanders within their military service; and more than 1,200 fill key staff positions in their military departments."

26. Alejandro Portes, "Leftist Radicalism: Chile: A Test of Three Hypotheses," *Comparative Politics* 2 (1970): 254-68.

27. Nun, *Latin America*, p. 55.

28. Irving L. Horowitz, "The Military Elites," in *Elites in Latin America*, eds. Seymour M. Lipset and Aldo Solari (New York: Oxford University Press, 1967), p. 179.

29. U.S. House of Representatives, *Reports of the Special Study Mission to Latin America on Military Assistance Training and Developmental Television. Submitted by C.J. Zablocki, J.G. Fulton and P. Findley to the Subcommittee on National Security Policy and Scientific Developments of the Committee on Foreign Affairs. 91st Congress (May 7, 1970).* (Washington, D.C.: Government Printing Office, 1970), pp. 9-10, 18-20; and Richard L. Clinton, "The Modernizing Military: The Case of Peru," *Inter-American Economic Affairs* 24 (1971): 45-64.

30. Harold M. Hockman and C. Tait Ratcliffe, "Grant Aid or Credit Sales: A Dilemma of Military Assistance Planning," *Journal of Developing Areas* 4 (1970): 461-76.

31. Horowitz, "The Military Elite," p. 180.

32. John Saxe-Fernandez, "The Central American Defense Council and Pax Americana," in *Latin American Radicalism: A Documentary Report on Left and Nationalist Movements*, eds. Irving L. Horowitz et al. (New York: Random House, 1969).

33. William C. Selover, "U.S. Food for Peace Converted to Armament," *Christian Science Monitor* (January 8, 1971); and Drew Middleton, "Thousands of Foreign Military Men Studying in U.S.," *New York Times* (November 1, 1970).

34. Stephen P. Gilbert, "Soviet-American Military Aid Competition in the Third World," *Orbis* 13 (1970): 1127-28.

35. U.S. Senate, *Rockefeller Report on Latin America. Hearings before the Subcommittee on Western Hemisphere Affairs of the*

Committee on Foreign Relations. 91st Congress (Washington, D.C.: Government Printing Office, 1969), pp. 8-11, 35-6, 45, 85-6, 120-1; and U.S. House of Representatives, *Report of the Special Study Mission*, p. 29.

36. Ibid., pp. 20-22.

37. For a summary of available empirical studies on Latin America see Nun, *Latin America*, pp. 17-20. Nun singles out a comprehensive investigation by José Luis de Imaz "of Argentine generals, brigadier generals, admirals (in which) Imaz finds that only 23 percent of the examined sample are descended from traditional families. According to his estimates, 'seventy-three percent of the brigadier generals and generals studied came from families of well-to-do bourgoisie, 25 percent from the lower middle class, and only 2 percent from families of worker origin.' Even though his category 'high middle-class or well-to-do bourgeoisie' is extremely wide, and includes big landowners as well as professionals, industrialists are considered to belong to the 'high' class. Still, it is irrefutable that two-thirds of the body of officers come from among the members of the middle class."

9
Revolution From Within?
Military Rule in Peru Since 1968

Luigi R. Einaudi

In 1871, Karl Marx wrote to Ernst Kugelmann that the fate of the Paris Commune demonstrated that henceforth popular revolutions could not succeed without first smashing the increasingly powerful repressive arm of the modern bureaucratic state: the armed forces.

In 1954, the dominant elements of the Guatemalan military, acting with the support of the then foreign policy of the United States, helped to overthrow the elected government of Colonel Jacobo Arbenz and reversed what was becoming an increasingly radical agrarian reform program.

In 1959, a triumphant Fidel Castro took what he considered the first key steps toward consolidating his power by declaring himself commander-in-chief of the Cuban armed forces and placing his brother and his most trusted guerrilla commanders in charge of a program of restructuring the Cuban officer corps, thereby ensuring himself against internal counterrevolution. Only then did he turn to the agrarian reform that was to prove the symbol of the Cuban revolution.

In 1968, in direct contrast to these previous events and to the generalizations commonly drawn from them, Peru's armed forces, acting (in exemplary bureaucratic fashion) under the command of the military chief of staff and the commanders of the three services, seized power from an elected but ineffective liberal democratic regime, nationalized without compensation the local subsidiary of

Standard Oil of New Jersey and set under way a revolutionary process that has included Latin America's most radical agrarian reform since Cuba.

What makes these Peruvian events doubly puzzling is that the revolution was led by many of the same officers who in 1965 had destroyed in blood the guerrillas of the Movement of the Revolutionary Left (MIR) led by Luis de la Puente. Could it really be, as Fidel Castro colorfully put it last August with his characteristic sense for the jugular, that "the fire has broken out in the firehouse"?

This chapter seeks to address Castro's question about Peru by looking first at the firehouse and then at the fire. First, it considers briefly the military forces of Peru and their political behavior, which have so strikingly contradicted the stereotypical view of the military as committed to the preservation of the status quo through repression. It then considers even more briefly some of the innovations the military government has attempted to bring to Peru since 1968 and concludes in suggesting some implications of these events for strategies of change in general.

MILITARY SOURCES OF
THE 1968 REVOLUTION IN PERU[1]

The evolution of the political style of the Peruvian military is complex and halting, as befits the behavior of an organized bureaucracy in a rapidly if unevenly developing society. Nonetheless, events since October 3, 1968, mark a qualitative shift in military participation in politics from a generally cautious political stance, dedicated primarily to arbitrating between the policies and leaders advanced by civilian political groups, to an even more dominant role, placing military leaders directly in policy-making positions to the point of virtually excluding civilians. Military rule, previously generally conservative and caretaking in style, now claims to be revolutionary and is introducing innovations in public policy that, when considered in the past, were regularly rejected.

The origins of this pronounced leftward shift in the style and substance of military political activity are rooted in a complicated combination of institutional military factors, of personal experiences of members of the military officer corps (particularly in the army) and of the course of Peruvian society in recent decades. What happened may be summarized at one level by saying that military leaders began to perceive national security problems as extending beyond conventional military operations. They did so in large part because many of the existing social and economic structures seemed so inefficient or unjust as to create the conditions for, and give legitimacy to, revolutionary protest and hence constitute a security threat. Even conservative officers came to feel that these conditions could ultimately become a threat to the military itself as an institution.

In the late 1950s and early 1960s, Peruvian officers increasingly saw their society caught up in a fundamental, long-term crisis that threatened them both as military men and personally as members of an often hard-pressed middle class. Land invasions, guerrilla movements and acts of political terrorism were seen as the top of an iceberg of inexorably mounting social pressures caused by exploding populations that would, in the long run, overwhelm traditional social structures. Military officers in the national war college, the Center for Higher Military Studies (CAEM), increasingly studied a wide range of social problems. These included questions of land reform, tax structure, foreign policy and insurgency, and involved the formulation of policies and reforms the military felt necessary to ensure stability. The result was that military policy became much more closely linked to political policy than it had been in the past.

The guerrilla experience of 1965, though successfully controlled in military terms, underscored to the military the importance of social change. It also raised fundamental doubts about the capacity of civilian-directed efforts to achieve that change—despite the fact that the military junta of 1962-63 had helped install Fernando Belaúnde as president with the hope that he would prove to be a successful reformer. By 1966, military men were ready to perceive Belaúnde as a failure, the more so as many of them envied the power and activity of the civilian professionals around Belaúnde, many of whom were financially rewarded beyond the highest expectations of general officers yet were often far less competent.

The impotence of the Belaúnde government, together with the continuing presence of the aging and by then largely complacent *apristas*, heightened the military's anger. Their frustration was continuously fed by incidents of social rejection by the pretentious "whiter" social elites of the coastal cities and by the antimilitary arrogance of the United States, whose efforts to promote the Alliance for Progress often appeared to many army officers as anti-Peruvian meddling limited to the defense of U.S. economic interests.

These shifts are of sufficient interest to warrant their more detailed examination, in both theory and practice, from the viewpoint of the Peruvian military leadership: traditional military resentment of civilians, plutocrats and foreigners became focused increasingly on organized political parties, which were in turn viewed as hopelessly committed to an unjust social, political and economic order. These views, together with the wider concerns over economic backwardness and social instability, gradually permeated the training and operations of two major institutions: the military schools and the military intelligence services.

THEORETICAL PERCEPTION OF THREATS: THE MILITARY SCHOOL SYSTEM AND CAEM

Ever since the founding of the Center for Military Instruction (CIMP) and CAEM in the first years after World War II, military education had improved and expanded to include socioeconomic concerns.[2] CIMP opened in 1948; it pulled together military education under a single command, laying the basis for greatly expanded emphasis on continuing post-Academy training. CAEM, which opened in 1950, offered a one-year course largely devoted to social, economic and political problems to selected classes of colonels and generals. Moreover, officers were encouraged to follow specialized military or civilian courses both in Peru and abroad, usually at government expense. Members of the officer corps had studied military affairs in Europe and the United States since the turn of the century, often winning recognition as the best foreign students. In the 1950s and 1960s, Peruvian officers studied economics under United Nations auspices with ECLA in Chile, attempted unsuccessfully to import the Belgian Catholic sociologist Frère L.J. Lebret to teach and made innovative policy suggestions to the conservative Prado government, some of whose members in turn became concerned at "communist" infiltration of CAEM.

As Whyte and Flores have suggested, most Peruvians do not believe that success in life is based on merit.[3] In the military, however, the emphasis on professional training and education in the promotion process, particularly since World War II, has made its members perhaps the most merit-oriented within the state bureaucracy, if not the entire society. All navy and air force officers and more than 90 percent of all army officers are Academy graduates. The continuing value of education in the Peruvian military career may be inferred from the fact that, of the division generals on active duty between 1940 and 1965, no fewer than 80 percent had graduated in the top quarter of their class at the Military Academy. In addition, the expansion and improvement of advanced military training after 1945 introduced a new element of competition into the officer corps and improved the life chances of officers previously stymied by the promotion system's dependence on class standing at the time of graduation from the Military Academy. The final Academy class standings, determined on the basis of combined academic and discipline performances, were often stifling to bright men who were deficient in discipline or conduct. These were, in the 1950s and 1960s, given new chances to prove themselves in advanced education, much as the development of the air force had in the 1920s and 1930s provided an outlet for energetic and talented officers who had been "burned" in the regular army.

CAEM is probably the most important center for the development of Peruvian national security strategy.[4] Many of the changed military perceptions have crystallized in CAEM studies and class exercises. Of the first 19 cabinet ministers after the 1968 revolution, 13 were CAEM graduates, including the prime minister and the chief of the Council of Presidential Advisors (COAP). The director of CAEM is a general appointed by the Joint Command of the Armed Forces, and he has a small staff, three departments and three directorates under him. The departments include the deputy director, who is in charge of administration and through whom the three directorates report, the Academic Council, made up of the heads of the directorates and selected professors and, finally, an

optional body called the Consultative Council, which may be
convened at the director's discretion to study special problems. Of
the directorates, the Academic Directorate is responsible for plans,
academic programs and the actual content of instruction. To it are
assigned the students, mainly officers in the rank of full colonel,
known as participants. The Directorate of National Strategy and
Special Studies handles contemporary problems of national security,
special problems and the strategies of foreign powers, including the
United States. The third directorate, Research and Development, is
concerned exclusively with the future.

CAEM courses in 1970 opened with an introductory study of
methodology, sociology and similar general principles.[5] This was
followed by the first major curriculum segment, the study of
national reality. This segment of instruction was followed by the
analysis of national potential, defined as constantly moving and
changing. The contrast between reality and potential establishes
national objectives, which are to eliminate the differential between
the two. National problems are studied from economic, social,
military and psychological viewpoints, each of which was
represented in the second major part of the course, the study of
national strategy. National strategy consists of the actual programs
designed to attain national objectives. The final portion of the
course is devoted to individual case studies. These studies, drawn up
by the participants in CAEM, benefit from the experiences not only
of the military participants but of the civilian as well. Although
occasional civilian students attended CAEM classes as early as 1961
and 1962, it was not until the mid- and late sixties that the numbers
became significant on a routine basis. In 1971, 16 students out of 43
were civilians.

CAEM has consistently taught, since its founding in 1950, that, in
accordance with Article 213 of the Peruvian Constitution, the
military must defend national sovereignty. Specifically, this is
defined as an obligation to increase Peru's capacity to maneuver
vis-à-vis the outside world, and particularly the United States.
Recognition of the Soviet Union, coupled with some trade, is in
harmony with this interpretation of the constitutional mandate.
Similarly, the constitutional prescription for the maintenance of
order is now interpreted at CAEM as the need to ensure an order

conducive to national well-being, that is to say, the well-being of all Peruvians, not just of the dominant social classes.

To argue in favor of economic development and social justice is not, however, to have a clear plan for how to bring them about. Military men have a powerful impulse to see politics in a fundamentally apolitical light. This contradiction is exemplified in the opening paragraph of the action program adopted in 1944 by a secret military lodge, the Revolutionary Command of Army Officers (CROE):

> CROE has no political implications of any kind. It is a revolutionary organization of the officers of the Army who aspire to lead the country within a democratic and strictly constitutional order.[6]

The failure to realize that revolution involves politics, though a generation old, is still typical, as is CROE's stress on the need for "morality" in public life. As recently as 1970, General Velasco was proclaiming that he was a soldier and a revolutionary, not a politician.[7]

To say that the traditional military prescription for good government is morality, discipline and patriotism is to be reasonably close to fundamental old-line military attitudes. There has also always been some tension, however, between these views of politics and the military's sense of inferiority in cultural and social matters. "When a general met an ambassador, he turned red in the face and trembled," said a former minister of war, one of Peru's leading military intellectuals.[8] Traditionally, the thought persisted that successful politics might require more than could be brought to it by the military.

Peruvian officers' attitudes toward civilians and politics have historically combined into a powerful dislike for civilian politicians. Their attitude toward politics, taken with the self-image of discipline and efficiency, leads some officers to believe that they are the elect and must lead the nation. Typically, however, these same attitudes also lead to another and somewhat contradictory sense of contempt for officers who "play politics" within the military, thus undermining discipline and efficiency. With these conflicting

attitudes to overcome, even among their fellow officers, it is little
wonder that military leaders who ultimately do assume national
leadership tend to be both tactically astute and politically tough.

The military's proposed solution to these conflicts has generally
been apolitical: officers should be better trained. CAEM, whose
directors have proudly proclaimed it to be not a school for
presidents but definitely a school for statesmen, has not only
improved military training but retained the traditional military
prescription for national health, adding only technology. And the
means by which to instill morality, discipline, patriotism and
technology remains one of the traditional panaceas of the Peruvian
military: education. As with other military attitudes, the origins of
this emphasis on education are to be sought in a mixture of
institutional and social factors. The importance of education to the
promotion process (a step that has revolutionized the military career
since the 1930s) reflects, among other things, the concerns of men
sensitized by the knowledge that low social standing and limited
finances had, during their adolescence, precluded their attending
civilian universities.

Even at CAEM, politics in Peru, and especially good government,
was still seen in the early 1960s as imponderable, fraught with
difficulties and beset by devils. Bolívar's statement that he had
"ploughed the sea" in trying to govern reflects a common military·
attitude. "So long as Peru does not have programmatic and
well-organized political parties, the country will continue to be
ungovernable."[9] This ungovernability, however, was not attributed
to the traditional and well-known civilian defects alone:

> The sad and desperate truth is that in Peru, the real powers are
> not the Executive, the Legislative, the Judicial or the
> Electoral, but the landowners, the exporters, the bankers, and
> the American [U.S.] investors.[10]

And the oligarchic and foreign devils are joined by the Apra party—a
form of national cancer, according to the same military planners.

Despite their hostility to politics and the tendency to
oversimplify complicated issues for the sake of action, Peruvian
military leaders have frequently demonstrated considerable

flexibility and political skill. That some officers are capable of being *criollos* (clever and sometimes unscrupulous realists) does not alter their suspicion that political compromise is fundamentally a betrayal of military values, but it may enable them to put some of their theories to a rather effective test.

PRACTICAL THREAT PERCEPTION: GUERRILLAS, INTELLIGENCE ORGANIZATION AND PETROLEUM

The military education system, as we have seen, developed some interesting doctrines. It nonetheless took the guerrilla campaigns of 1965-66 to force social theory out of the schools and into the barracks, thereby making the political immobilism and economic decline of the late 1960s a matter of urgent military concern. In the summer of 1965, two separately organized guerrilla fronts opened in the central and southern Andes with ambushes of police units. Within a month, the outbreaks had led to the displacement of the relatively ineffective rural police by a joint military command and martial law in the affected areas. This in turn led to the discovery of other fronts still in the process of forming in other parts of the country. Within six months, despite forebodings in elite political circles about revolution in the Andes, the military forces completely eliminated the guerrilla pockets and almost entirely wiped out the MIR leadership. And they did this without forcing a change in government and without the prolonged suffering and mounting casualties characteristic of other cases of political violence (Guatemala and Colombia among them).[11]

Containment of the guerrilla threat also confirmed the military in their commitment to reform. The guerrillas had chosen for their headquarters a remote mountaintop called Mesa Pelada near the Convención Valley in the province of Cuzco, where the famous Trotskyist labor organizer Hugo Blanco had successfully organized peasant unions in the early 1960s before his capture in 1963. But the Convención Valley had also been the scene of construction of a penetration road from Colca to Amparaes by military engineer battalions and the site of a pilot agrarian reform program by the military junta of 1962-63. The failure of the region's peasants to provide significant support to the insurgents appeared in military circles to confirm the wisdom of the earlier reform policies.

The sense of success was tempered by fear of a recrudescence of violence. If a handful of radicalized urban intellectuals could keep thousands of troops busy for months, what would happen if popular forces and the peasantry were enlisted in future disorders? The Ministry of War's published account of the guerrilla campaign concluded that Peru had entered a period of latent insurgency.

Nor was this a matter to be readily resolved with foreign assistance. Guerrilla war had proved the undoing of France, first in Indochina and then in Algeria. French military operations had been observed by Peruvian officers with French training and connections. Later Vietnam proved to be the Achilles' heel of the United States, demonstrating the difficulties that irregular warfare could create even for the world's foremost military power. The conclusion that the fate of these two historic military mentors seemed to suggest for Peru was that internal subversion would have to be controlled by Peruvians alone, if indeed it could be controlled at all.

The latent insurgency dilemma appeared to open many officers to the idea that Peru needed agrarian reform combined with industrialization, or, in the more abstract language of the Ministry of War, a "general policy of economic and social development."[1 2] According to this view, similar to the McNamara-Rostow thesis that violence springs from economic backwardness, conditions of injustice in the countrywide needed to be removed so that the absentee landowner and his local henchmen no longer would exploit and oppress the rural peasant masses, whose marginal living conditions were making them potential recruits for future subversion and movements against military and governmental authorities.

Elimination of the latent state of subversion now became the primary objective of military action. In a formal intelligence analysis by General Mercado, the man who was to become Peru's foreign minister after the 1968 revolution, the "latent state of subversion" was defined as the presence of communist activity exploiting national weaknesses. This communist activity, which took a variety of forms—military, political, economic and social—was containable for the present. But the existence of national weaknesses continually threatened to point the balance against the forces of progress and order. National weak spots were defined, in General Mercado's remarkable statement of this theory, to cover a wide range of organizational, economic, technical and political elements. His list of national weaknesses included fiscal crises, scarcity of trained personnel, resistance to change by privileged groups, inadequate scientific and technical development, lack of unity and coordination of efforts, absence of effective international security cooperation, lack of governmental control and communication with the rural areas and, finally, lack of identification by the population with national political objectives. The reforms introduced by the revolutionary military government that took office less than a year after Mercado's article had appeared were largely meant to offset these weaknesses.

But threat perceptions, fear, and antisubversive warfare were not the only wellsprings of action. Genuine compassion for the conditions of the rural population was quite common among officers who had served in rural areas during regular tours, as well as during the guerrilla campaign, and who often found emotional and ideological support for such feelings in paternalist Catholic social doctrines, which stressed that every man had a right to an existence offering material and spiritual dignity. In fact, there can be little doubt that among the major intellectual and moral forces impelling the largely Catholic military to action were the progressive priests and scholars who in the 1960s helped move the hierarchy of the Church in Peru to reorient its political participation in the direction of greater social justice for all Peruvians, including the poor.[14]

Communists, of whatever variety, were not the only enemies of order and security in Peru. Many officers, accustomed since the War of the Pacific in 1879 to seeing external enemies exploit internal weaknesses, had come to believe that the United States, in alliance with Peru's oligarchy, favored Peru's continuing in a state of underdevelopment. This view associated the United States with Peru's vulnerability to subversion as well as to more traditional external threats. The Belaúnde government had been strongly supported by most military men as a reformist movement dedicated to national progress. Its fumbling, which some attributed to American interests, only added to this theorizing, which to outsiders sometimes seems to verge on paranoia.

"Foreign interests, the oligarchy, and the decrepit politicans in their pay" was the way President Velasco was later to characterize this new subversive force, or *antipatria*, in a speech commemorating the takeover of the International Petroleum Company.[15] Although one result of studying political and social problems may be to realize their complexity, another may be to undermine the credibility of solutions advanced by political parties, thereby weakening the claim of civilian leadership to sole legitimacy. The legitimacy of civilian leadership was further eroded in Peru during the 1960s by the information collected through the increased activity of military intelligence services. The military command developed evidence of the corruption and compromises that were the daily fare of Peruvian politics. Even normal political compromise finds little acceptance in the military's values, as we have already discussed. Peruvian politics have never been very clean. Yet not every form of misconduct provokes indignation. A particularly messy smuggling scandal broke under the Belaúnde administration in early 1968. Smuggling, to military people, was sufficiently common not to be in itself cause to unseat Belaúnde. But in the context of the payment by private interests of contributions to political parties and leaders, of continuing inaction on basic reforms and of congressional privilege, it was enough to lead increasing portions of the military, including nationalist elements in the intelligence services, to side with Catholic priests and others who denounced corruption in government.

All of these complicated matters were involved in the explosive petroleum issue that came to a head in the proposed Talara Agreement of 1968 and provided the immediate impetus behind the overthrow of Belaúnde and the installation of the government that still rules Peru today, two-and-one-half years later. This is not the place to review the petroleum affair,[16] except to point out that the debate over IPC became pivotal in helping to associate the United States government with the Peruvian and American private interests that military officers were already increasingly perceiving to be inimical to Peruvian security and development.[17]

As General Arturo Cavero[18] later explained to a group of visiting American military officers, threats to the internal security of Peru could originate in the plotting of groups opposed to peaceful revolution as well as in the efforts of groups who sought to impose revolution by violence. General Cavero, who is now the director of CAEM, spoke when relations with the United States had improved from their low in early 1969, when application of the Hickenlooper Amendment seemed imminent, threatening to cut U.S. economic assistance and sugar quotas in response to the IPC nationalization. But Cavero began his remarks to the U.S. officers by pointedly quoting from General Mercado's speech before the United Nations in April of 1969:

> The threat has varied over time. At first it was narrowly military in nature. Then new and subtler psychological and ideological threats arose against the security of each country. Today we face a new threat: economic aggression. Just as we fought against the violent aggression generated by guerrillas and by different forms of terrorism, so we are now fighting against economic aggression.

Cavero's U.S. military audience could not have had doubts about the direction of these remarks. Nor could they have had much doubt that the Peruvians meant what they said: In May 1969, less than a year before, Peru's military government had expelled the U.S. military missions from Peru.[19]

For a combination of reasons, then, many officers, particularly in the army, moved in the late 1960s toward an authoritarian preemption of what had traditionally been nationalist and left-wing positions, especially on petroleum and agrarian reform. But unlike the Left, most of whose leaders dreamed of guerrillas or elections—they imposed their views under the aegis of a nationalist military dictatorship pledged to the nonviolent restructuring of Peruvian society.

REVOLUTION IN LATIN AMERICA IN LIGHT OF THE PERUVIAN EXPERIENCE

The military government that ruled Peru since October 1968 has clearly unleashed a process that is reshaping Peruvian society. Whether this process is called a revolution or not is partly a matter of perspective. For some, no process that is essentially nonviolent, or

that leaves many traditional institutions formally intact, or that is
led by military forces, or that is not led by a Communist party, can
be called a revolution. And it is difficult to quarrel with such
viewpoints because the Peruvian government is led by the military,
has avoided political repression, is willing to accept the Catholic
Church and to defend private property, and has only the support,
not the leadership, of the Communist party.

The real point is that while revolution can be *defined* in many
ways, it is important not to lose sight of the social and political
reality with which words are meant to deal. And the process under
way in Peru today is clearly unprecedented. Parliament may return;
some future government may decide to pay Standard Oil an
indemnity for the Talara Oil Fields formally operated by the IPC
and now administered by Petroperú; some of the military ministers
who have fought corruption may succumb to the temptations of
power.

Yet should all this happen, Peru will still have changed in ways
this writer considers decisive. The government has gone well beyond
attempts that tinker with the status quo so as to modernize it or
otherwise render it less objectionable. The agrarian reform begun in
1969 with the productive coastal estates turned into cooperatives,
the passage of the water rights law and the subjection of new
investment to the establishment of workers' communities for
profit-sharing under the terms of the new industrial, fishing and
mining laws, are acts whose impact are more than legal.[20] They
affect the fabric of Peruvian life in many ways that cannot be
reversed by changes in government or new laws.

It is not yet entirely clear what that impact will be. It is also
difficult to identify who will be favored most by the process under
way. If the middle classes and the foreign investors can take heart in
the thought that the government does not in principle oppose the
idea of private profit or property, the lower classes can also take
heart in the government's willingness to recognize violent seizures of
public lands for the purposes of private home construction by the
landless poor and in the government's attempt to limit profits and
ensure their equitable distribution.

Let us suppose, however, that much will go wrong, and also that
some social sectors will profit considerably more than others in the

changes under way. Let us even suppose that the one-third of Peru that is Indian in culture and life style profits least, directly, from what is now happening. Should we then argue that this is no revolution, or that this is just another military dictatorship to be opposed by all progressive and civilized people?

This writer would argue that three major points should be borne in mind in seeking the answer:

First, a great deal has already been done for Peru under present historical circumstances. Peru has not only one-third of its population unable to speak Spanish (and thus not easily mobilizable for national political—even revolutionary—purposes), but it has twice the population spread over ten times the territory with one-fifth the television sets per capita that Cuba has. Revolution in Peru, Cuban-style, would seem difficult even if a charasmatic leader and an obligingly terrifying (and foolish) foreign enemy could be found.

Second, the changes that have taken place in Peru have come from within the system, not from outside it. Since the Cuban revolution, and especially since the rise of guerrilla movements, much attention has focused on outside strategies of change. Little hope was expressed for political leaders following inside strategies of change, that is, utilizing traditional institutions like the military or the Church for innovative political ends.

Third, we should not assume that because of the relative success of the Peruvian military and the relative failure of Ché Guevara that inside strategies will work where outside strategies have failed, or, alternatively, that the military has in the current decade become an inevitable force for progress. In the first place, the limits set by bureaucracy, internal divisions and resource scarcity may in the long run produce a conservative reaction within the military even in Peru, where the process of military reorientation toward structural change has gone very far.[21] And finally, as our Peruvian case study has also made clear, those military intellectuals who argued for the inside strategy and for revolution from within gained their audience among their fellow officers and comrades-at-arms not just because they were working within an institution with a highly developed educational system but also because young civilian students and intellectuals gave their lives in following an outside strategy, and their sacrifice gave the "insiders" a chance to make their views felt.

NOTES

1. The discussion that follows is largely drawn from Luigi R. Einaudi and Alfred C. Stepan III, *Latin American Institutional Development: Changing Military Perspectives in Peru and Brazil.* (Santa Monica, Cal.: Rand, R-586, 1971).

2. For a sketchy summary of the structure and function of military educational institutions, emphasizing the role of General José del Carmen Marin in the founding of CAEM see Luis Valdez Pallette, "Antecedentes de la nueva orientación de las Fuerzas Armadas en el Perú," *Aportes* 19 (January 1971).

3. William F. Whyte and Graciela Flores, *Los valores y el crecimiento económico en el Perú* (Lima, Peru: Senati, 1963).

4. National planning, conceived less as general theory and more as related to immediate government policies, is carried out elsewhere, of course, primarily at the National Planning Institute (INP), originally established with mixed civilian and military personnel by the 1962 military junta. Civilian institutions, including universities and the research-oriented Institute of Peruvian Studies (IEP), are important primarily through the impact on CAEM doctrine achieved through individual faculty members.

5. The information in this and the preceding paragraph is partially based on an interviw with General Augusto Freyre García, director of national strategy and special studies at CAEM.

6. Villanueva provides a complete text in an appendix. See Victor Villanueva, *La tragedia de un pueblo y un partido* (Lima, Peru: 1956).

7. Juan Velasco Alvarado, *Speech delivered in Trujillo (October 11, 1969)* (Lima, Peru: Oficina Nacional de Información, 1969), p. 36.

8. General José del Carmen Marín, who made this particular comment to the author in 1964, was referring to the 1930s primarily. By the 1960s and 1970s, partly because of Marín's efforts as an educator and more importantly because of the strengthening of the military as an institution, these roles were frequently reversed.

9. CAEM (Centro de Altos Estudios Militares), *El estado y la politica general* (Chorrillos, Peru: 1963), p. 89.

10. Ibid., p. 92.

11. The official account of the campaign was published by the Peruvian Ministry of War. See Ministerio De Guerra, *Las guerrillas en el Perú y su repressión* (Lima, Peru: 1966). For an intelligent analysis by one of the few surviving leaders see Hector Bejar Rivera, *Perú 1965: apuntes sobre una experienca guerrillera* (Havana, Cuba: Casa de las Américas, 1969).

12. Ministerio De Guerra, Las guerrillas, p. 80.

13. Edgardo Mercado Jarrin, "Insurgency in Latin America—Its Impact on Political and Military Strategy," *Military Review*, March 1969, pp. 10-20.

14. Luigi R. Einaudi et al., *Latin American Institutional Development: The Changing Catholic Church* (Santa Monica, Calif.: Rand, M-586, 1971), pp. 51-55.

15. Juan Velasco Alvardo, *Mensage a la nación dirigido por el Señor General de División Presidente de la República, desde Talara, en el primer aniversario del día de la dignidad nacional* (Lima, Peru: Oficina Nacional de Información, 1969).

16. Goodwin describes the intricate historical and legal background of the La Brea and Pariñas deposits, and the incredible ineptitude that marked the company's and Belaúnde's dealings with each other. See Richard Goodwin, "Letter from Peru" *New Yorker* (May 17, 1969).

17. Perhaps even more than the fishing industry (in which Peru now competes with Japan for world primacy), petroleum fits the category of a basic national resource. Contrary to some suspicions in the United States at the time that President Velasco had been irresponsible and unrepresentative, he almost certainly acted with broad military support in the IPC case. As early as February 5, 1960, the Joint Staff, over the signature of the Commanding General of the Army, publicly recorded its belief that the La Brea and the Pariñas agreements were harmful to national sovereignty. That it took nearly nine years to put belief into practice is a sign of institutional caution rather than individual recklessness. An "inside dopester" account of the political history of the petroleum issue from the Peruvian perspective, of additional interest because shortly after writing it its author moved from the conservative newspaper *El Comercio* to the directorship of the Government Information Bureau run by the presidency, is Augusto Zimmerman Zavala, "La historia secreta del petroleo," *El Comercio* Lima, Peru (August 29, 1968).

18. Arturo Cavero Calixto, "Threats to the National Security of

Peru and Their Implications for Hemispheric Security." Chorrillos, Peru: lecture delivered at the Centro de Altos Estudios Militares (CAEM) (April 1970).

19. The immediate cause of the expulsion was an attempt to retaliate for prior U.S. suspension of military sales (imposed in accordance with the requirements of the Pelly Act as a result of the perennial tuna disputes). The departure of the missions was also delayed proof of the deterioration in both political and military relations between the two countries during the mid- and late 1960s. See Luigi R. Einaudi, *Peruvian Military Relations with the United States* (Santa Monica, Calif.: Rand, P-4389, June, 1970).

20. The purposes of these and other laws are detailed by the chief of the Presidential Advisory Committee (COAP), General de Brigada E. P. José Graham Hurtado, *Filosofía de la Revolución Peruana* (Lima, Peru: Oficina Nacional de Información, April 14, 1971). Luigi R. Einaudi, "The Military and Progress in the Third World," *Foreign Service Journal* (February 1971).

21. Einaudi, "The Military and Progress."

10
Militarization, Modernization and Mobilization: Third World Development Patterns Reexamined

Irving Louis Horowitz

To be seriously involved in Third World studies obviously requires a studied concern about the role of militarism. I have emphasized the military element far more than many researchers from the "advanced" Western nations. On the theoretical side, this stems from my assessment of C. Wright Mills and an extension of the analysis he offered in the *Causes of World War Three* (1958), and somewhat later the kind of thinking I did in writing *The War Game* (1963). I applied to the international arena a belief in the centrality of the military pivot that most social scientists restrict to the national arena. So much so, perhaps, that I have been targeted as being a military determinist in my analysis of the Third World and the developing regions. While this appellation is incorrect, it is fair to say that for me the role of the military is considerably higher and more autonomous than most development analysis tends to admit.

On the practical side, in terms of the Third World as such, my interests have moved from the notion of the military as the mark of sovereignty to the whole process of the militarization of society as a result of increased activities by the armed forces in the political sector. My point of view can be described negatively as a counter-Janowitz position. Janowitz speaks of the civilianization of the military as a result of the interpenetration of military and civic activities.[1] In my view his causal model is largely erroneous. In capsulated form, the sequence is the other way around: the civilian sectors, especially the political-bureaucratic sectors, tend to become militarized, rather than the military sectors tending to become civilianized. To be sure, this proposition, no less than its counter, has a certain "chicken and egg" property. There is no point in dwelling on causal issues abstractly. Whether society is becoming militarized or civilianized by increased political participation of the armed forces must be judged empirically. However, it is a potentially fertile contribution to the developmental literature to attempt a reorientation away from the idea of a civilian model.

After settling to my own satisfaction that Third World patterns move from civilian to military modes; and that these define political orientations rather than the other way around, my attention was drawn to the military of Latin America.[2] Those who are familiar with the Lipset-Solari volume on *Elites in Latin America* realize that there are certain peculiarities in my chapter vis-à-vis the rest of the book.[3] One "innovation" is that it is the only chapter to deal with the interpenetration of an advanced society with the so-called underdeveloped societies. The model of autonomous elites does not merely stem from the internal functioning of the national military, it derives from the international complex of military systems and military networks. Just as one can speak of an international economy, or an international policy, or as Rosenau might say, linkages between polities, one is entitled to speak of linkages within the military framework.[4] In the Panama Canal Zone, on any given month of any given year, there will be a clustering of national military regimes from nearly every nation of South and Central America. They are coordinated, rationalized, legitimized, funded and oriented by the United States Military Assistance Program (MAP) to create a larger network of military cover for whatever regime or whatever power base is operative within the area. In the Western world or the Western Hemisphere, obviously, the key relationship is between the North American military and the South American military. It would be foolish to talk about the military elites of Argentina or the military elites of Brazil without dealing with the interpenetration of elites. Training programs, cadre leadership schools: these organizational forms involve more than just national-sectoral ties of patterns, the elites are partially defined by international power relations as these evolve in such conduits as the U.S. Army School of the Americas (USARSA) and the

Inter-American Air Force Academy (IAADA) among other sponsored military subagencies.[5]

The most advanced point my analysis took me to was an awareness of how decisively the role of militarism in the Third World is anchored to tasks of internal repression rather than those of international guardianship. But while this properly directs our attention toward the connection of the military and the state, it does not explain why the political apparatus and the economic establishments should be so supportive, and indeed even underwrite, militarization—particularly since such a course of action is so often extremely perilous to politicians and men of wealth in particular.

A continuing source of concern for those working in the area of comparative international development is the ever-widening disparity between political democracy and economic development. This disparity has been dealt with usually in what might be termed a *necessitarian* framework by scholars like Heilbroner who assert that a choice has to be made between political democracy and economic development.[6] In point of fact what is really being claimed is that no choice exists at all. Economic growth is a necessity, whereas political mobilization is declared to be a luxury. The mark of sovereignty, the mark of growth is, in fact, developmental, and therefore is said to offer no real volition and no viable option.

On the other hand, there are economists and sociologists like Hoselitz[7] and Moore[8] who have taken what might be called a "libertarian" point of view. They claim that the disparity between democracy and development is real enough, but that the costs of development remain uniformly too high in the developing regions. Therefore, it is more important to preserve and enhance democracy than any irrational assumptions that development is either a mark of sovereignty of the necessary road to economic development. Underlying such thinking is a political determinism no less dogmatic, albeit far neater to advocate than the economic determinism under attack.

By now this argument of the sixties has a somewhat arid ring. The assumptions are either that development is necessary and we can do nothing about the costs involved, or that democracy is a categorical imperative and we must curb whatever developmental propensities we have to preserve this supreme good. Rather than penetrate the

debate at this level, since the premises are either well known or well
worn by this time, we should perhaps turn the matter around and
inquire what has, in fact, been the relationship between political
democracy and social and economic development over the past
decade, and what are the dynamics in this Third World network of
interrelationships?

The first observation that has to be made is that the process of
comparative development includes a wide and real disparity between
democracy and development. There exists a relatively high
congruence between coercion and even terrorism and development,
and a far lower congruence between consensus and development. In
part, our problem is that middle-class spokesmen of the Western
world have often tended to identify a model of consensus with a
model of democracy, and both become systematically linked to
what has taken place in North America and Western Europe in the
last 150–200 years: that is, a model of congruence in which political
democracy and economic growth move toward the future in
common unison. The very phrase "political economy of growth"
gives substance to this "bourgeois" model of development. When
faced with the necessity of playing a role in the Third World and
performing certain activities economically, politically and socially in
terms of the inherited model, what is retained in the rhetoric no
longer can be sustained in performance. What one is left with, and
why it has been difficult to confront so much theorizing on
development, is a democratic model at the rhetorical level that is
different from the capitalist model at the functional level. Further,
there is a strong propensity, once this ambiguous model is accepted,
to avoid coming to grips with the role of high coercion in achieving
high development.

On examining the available data here I will restrict myself to the
non-Socialist sector, in part because there is a problem of data
reliability, and also because Socialist systems have their own peculiar
dynamic in relation to development and democracy that require a
different set of parameters to explain relationships. Further, since
there is a bias already established which equates Socialist systems to
high political coercion, it is instructive to see how capitalist systems
stand up to such coercive strains. Developmentalists are already
prone to employ a Stalinist model as the basic type of socialist

option. Thus there is no problem in conceptualizing the relationship between coercion and development as a natural one when it comes to the Socialist sector. However, when we turn systems around and look at that Western or capitalist sector of the developmental orbit, then because in the absence of the same kind of coercive model there are great problems conceptualizing Third World tendencies.

When the word *democracy* is herein referred to it will be defined in terms of (1) multiparty operations under (2) civilian regimes. Those two variables are key. There is no point in cluttering matters up with rhetorical theorizing about nice people who do good deeds. Simply put, democracy refers to multiparty control of politics on one hand and civilian bureaucratic administrative control on the other. This definition is bare-boned and obviously subject to refinement. However, when talking about a military leadership or a military regime we can be equally simple (hopefully not simple-minded). Military government ranges from outright rule of the armed forces without any civilian participation to coparticipation by civilians under military domination and control. It will usually signify a single-party structure rather than a multiparty structure in the legal-superstructural aspects of political life.

The data herein examined is drawn from reports issued by the Organization for Economic Cooperation and Development.[9] It concerns growth rates of the total and per capita GNP output between 1960 and 1967 and on average per annum and per capita GNP in 1968 for selected developing countries. The information, although provided randomly, does break down into three large clusters: (1) There are those countries that are single party, under military rule, which have high developmental outputs and a high GNP rate over the decade. (2) There are at the opposite end of the spectrum those countries that are democratic (or relatively democratic) and have low GNP levels. (3) There are a clustering in the middle of approximately 20 nations that do not reveal any consistent pattern in terms of problems of conflict and consensus in development. It is not that they violate any model construction, as remain undecided—significantly uncommitted at economic levels and in political techniques for generating socioeconomic change.

PATTERNS OF MILITARIZATION AND DEVELOPMENT

Let me outline three national clusterings and see what the results are at the factual level. Such material is a useful place to start in this most dismal science called development.[10]

In the high developmental, high militarization cluster, there are the following nations: Israel, Libya, Spain, Greece, Panama, Nicaragua, Iraq, Iran, Taiwan, the Ivory Coast, Jordan, Bolivia, Thailand and South Korea. Even a surface inspection indicates that this is hardly a lineup of democratic states. Let us directly examine the GNP figures, so that some sense of the extent of the aforementioned correlation can be gauged. On an annual percent increase over the decade the figures are as follows: Israel, 7.6; Libya, 19.2 (there are some special circumstances related to oil deposits in Libya but nonetheless the figure is impressive); Spain, 5.9 (an interesting example since it is a long-militarized European mainland country); Greece, 7.5 (with no slow-up in sight under its present military regime); Nicaragua, 7.5 (one of the most "backward" countries in Latin America from a "democratic" point of view); Iraq, 6.9; Iran, 7.9; Taiwan, 10.0 (a growth figure that even the Soviets have recently marveled at); Ivory Coast, 7.5 (by all odds, one of the most conservative regimes in Africa and boasting the highest growth rate on the continent in the sub-Sahara region); Jordan, 8.8; Bolivia, 4.9 (a long way from the old Socialist days of high foreign subvention); Thailand, 7.1; South Korea, 7.6. This is a most interesting lineup. One would have to say that those with democratic proclivities and propensities must face the fact that high development correlates well with high authoritarianism. Whether this is because authoritarianism quickens production, limits consumption or frustrates redistribution is not at issue. The potential for growth under militarism remains an ineluctable fact.

Let us turn to the other end of the spectrum. These are relatively low GNP units: Venezuela, Argentina, Uruguay, Honduras, Ghana, Guatemala, Brazil, Dominican Republic, Senegal, Ecuador, Tunisia, Paraguay, Morocco, Ceylon, Kenya, Nigeria, Sudan, Uganda, India and Tanzania. Within a Third World context and without gilding the lily, and admitting that there are exceptions in this list like Paraguay, this second cluster in the main represents a far less militarized group of nations than the first list presented. It is instructive to list their GNP per capita annual percent increase: Venezuela, 1.0; Argentina, 1.2; Uruguay, -1.0 (which is one of the most democratic, one of the most liberal countries in South America); Honduras, 1.8; Colombia, 1.2; Ghana, which exhibits no percentile change over time in the whole decade; Guatemala, 1.9; Brazil, 1.2 (increasing, however, under military rule from 1964 to 1968); Dominican Republic, -7; Senegal, 1.2; Ecuador, 1.1; Tunisia, 1.5; Paraguay, 1.0; Morocco, 0.3; the Philippines, 1.0; Ceylon, 1.3; Kenya, 0.3; Nigeria, 1.6; Sudan, 1.2; Uganda, 1.2; India, 1.5; Tanzania, 1.2. The data plainly yield that the low rate of development intersects with the nonmilitary character of political mobilization in this second group of nations. Low militarization and low development are only slightly less isomorphic than high militarization and high development.

There is a most important middle group of nations. They do not partake of the nations that reveal extensive polarities in GNP. Further, they exhibit different kinds of transitory patterns of political systems. Chile, for example, has 2.4; Jamaica, 2.1; Mexico, 2.8; Gabon, 3.2; Costa Rica, 2.4; Peru, 3.2; Turkey, 2.7; Malaysia, 2.5; Salvador, 2.7; Egypt, 2.1; Pakistan, 3.1; Ethiopia, 2.7. Many of those nations have relatively stable GNP figures over time and do not easily fit the description of being depressed or accelerated in GNP rates. They are also the most experimental politically—at least during the 1960s. Certainly, experimentation (both by design and accident) characterize countries like Pakistan, Egypt, Costa Rica and Chile. It is not entirely clear what this middle cluster of nations represents, or whether these trends are politically significant. Yet, they do represent a separate tertiary group and should be seen apart from the other two clusters of nations.

The critical level of GNP seems to be where levels of growth are under two percent, and where there is high population growth rate which more or less offsets the GNP. Under such circumstances, it is extremely difficult to achieve basic social services for a population, or maintain social equilibrium. For example, in India, if there is a 1.5 level of growth of GNP and a 2.4 level of population growth per annum, there is an actual decline in real growth rates. This is how economists usually deal with the measurement of development. It may be faulty reasoning to accept *ex cathedra* this economic variable as exclusive, yet this measure is so widely used that the GNP provides a good starting point in our evaluation. The fit at the lower end of the model is not as good as at the upper end. Statistically, it is necessary to point out that militarized societies like Argentina and Brazil are not doing all that well economically. However, Latin Americans have a kind of "benign" militarism, a genteel quality that comes with the normalization of political illegitimacy. Thus, Latin American military regimes, in contrast to their African and Asian counterparts, have many exceptional features that account for why the fit of the model is better at the upper end of the GNP than at the lower end.

Before interpreting such information further, it seems that the many nations clustering in the middle are also carriers of experimental political forms like single-party socialism, communal living, socialized medicine, etc. The "ambiguous" nations also reveal an impressive movement towards some kind of democratic-socialism that somehow eludes electoral definitions. In other words, the experimental forms seem to be clustered in that middle grouping, whereas the nonexperimental nations tend to be polarized, just as the GNP itself is polarized.

The most important single conclusion is that the political structure of coercion is a far more decisive factor in explaining the gross national product than the economic character of production in any Third World system per se. Without becoming involved in a model of military determinism, the amount of explained variance that the military factor yields vis-à-vis the economic factor is much higher than the classical literature allows for. If we had comparable data for the Socialist countries and if we were to do an analysis of the Soviet Union over time, then we would see that there is a functional correlation between the coercive mechanisms that a state can bring to bear on its citizenry and the ability to produce high economic development, however development is defined, and ignore the special problems involved in definitions based upon the GNP. For example, one problem in GNP is the development of a cost-accounting mechanism whereby education is evaluated only by cost-factors in input rather than output, whereas in goods and commodities you tend to have a profit-margin built into the GNP figure. But such variations are true across the board; therefore, special problems involved in using the GNP formula are cancelled out in the larger picture. But the main point is that the element of coercion is itself directly linked to the character of military domination, while the specific form of the economy is less important than the relationship between military coercion and economic development.

Those critics in the West who celebrate progress as if it were only a matter of GNP cannot then turn around and inquire about the "quality of life" elsewhere.[11] Developmentalists cannot demand of foreign societies what they are unwilling to expect from their own societies. Too many theorists of modernization ask questions of the quality of life of countries that themselves ask questions about the quantity of life. The military is the one sector, in most parts of the Third World, that is not absorbed in consumerism and commodity fetishism. It is not a *modernizing* sector, but rather a developmental one. In so far as the military is autonomous, its concern is nation building: highway construction, national communication networks, etc. It creates goals that are not based on the going norms of commodities that characterize the urban sectors of most parts of the developing regions. The functional value of this model is that the linkage between the military and the economy is unique. The military is that sector which dampens consumerism and modernization and promotes, instead, forms of developmentalism that may move toward heavy industry and even heavy agriculture rather than toward automobiles and televisions. This is a critical decision in nearly every part of the Third World. Because the military most often will make its decision on behalf of industrialism rather than modernism, it generates considerable support among nationalists and revolutionists alike. This is a big factor in explaining the continuing strength of the military in the Third World.

The data clear up a number of points. They help to explain why many regimes in the Third World seem to have such a murky formula for their own economy or polity. For example, despite the brilliance of Julius Nyerere[12] it is exceedingly difficult to determine the political economy of Tanzania. One reason for this is that there is a powerful military apparatus in nearly every expanding nation of the Third World. And this military structure, if it does not share in national rule directly, is directly plugged into the nation as an adjudicating voice between the political revolutionary element and the bureaucratic cadre.

To appreciate the role of the military'in developing nations we must go beyond the kind of economic definitions that have been employed either in Western Europe or in the United States. The murkiness of the Third World at the level of economics is in fact a function of the lack of clearly defined class boundaries and class formations. A critical factor is not so much social structure as social process. There is stability over time in these regimes. The political regime, the civilianized political regime, tends to be much less stable than the military regime. This is slightly obscured by the fact that in many of these nations there are coups within the coup, i.e., inner coups within the military structure that function to delegitimize civilian rule altogether. But these processes do not obscure the main fact that the military character and definition are not altered. For this reason, the relationship between military determinism and high economic growth tends to be stable over time—precisely to the degree that civilian mechanisms are found wanting.

Philips Cutright came to this conclusion through an entirely circuitous and different route. He examined a mass of information on health, welfare and security and found that the contents of the national political system usually become stabilized at that point in time when basic socioeconomic needs are satisfied.[13] Further, there is no mass mobilization beyond such a point in time. If socioeconomic needs are satisfied within a Socialist regime, then the Soviet system is stabilized. If such social needs are satisfied during a capitalist regime, then the capitalist system becomes permanent. If they are satisfied during an outright military dictatorship, then outright military dictatorship becomes normative and durable. In other words, the satisfaction of basic social services and economic wants is a critical factor beyond which masses do not carry on active political struggle. This quantitative support for the Hobbesian thesis on social order in the Leviathan has not been lost on the leadership of Third World nations, which continue to see the military as a stabilizing factor in economic development.

MILITARISM AS STABILITY

If this foregoing analysis is correct, and if the military is able to solve these outstanding problems at the level of the GNP, we should be able to predict its continued stability. Since basic social services will be resolved at a particular level of military rule, political struggles will cease to assume a revolutionary character in much of the Third World. In point of fact, the character of Socialist politics does not determine the strength of political behavior, but rather the other way around. The critical point in the Soviet regime comes at a time of Stalinist consolidation. During the 1930s the Soviet regime achieved internal stability. The contours of socialism in Russia were thus fixed, some might say atrophied, at this specific historical juncture. True, certain adjustments have had to be made, certain safety valves had to be opened to prevent friction or crisis. The Soviet Union exhibited a move from totalitarianism to authoritarianism. However, basically the political organization is set and defined. There are no opposition movements in the Soviet Union, since there are no mass movements at the level of social discontent.

Similarly, in the United States, the point of resolution emerged when the political democracy became operational. Therefore, it continues to be relatively operational 200 years later, even though great pressures have been brought to bear on the federalist system in recent times. Many Third World areas are stabilized at that point when military intervention occurs. When the initial revolutionary leadership vanishes (or is displaced) and when the bureaucracy and the polity are both bridled and yet oriented toward common tasks, the military becomes powerful. This is also the moment when economic growth charts start rocketing upwards. Therefore it is no accident that this is also a moment at which fervor for political experimentation declines. What we are confronted with is not simply transitional social forms, but permanent social forms.

The trouble with most general theories of development is that they postulate conditions in the Third World as transitional when they fail to coincide with preconceived models. We are told in effect that military regimes in the Third World are a necessary transition of "political economy."[14] Socialist doctrines of development often employ the same teleological model of politics for explaining away uncomfortable situations. Marxists declare that everything is in transition until achieving the height of socialism. Everything else is either an aberration, deviation or transition. The difficulty with teleological explanations is that they work from the future back to the present, instead of taking seriously the present social structures and political systems that exist in the Third World.

From an empirical perspective, social science determines what is meant by stability over time in terms of survival rates. Therefore, on the basis of this kind of measurement, the kind of network that exists in the Third World is, in point of fact, stable. What we are dealing with in many Third World clusterings are not simply permutations or the grafting on of other social system parts. Third World systems are not simply transitional or derivational, they have worked out a modality of their own. Let us proceed out one step further in the characterization of militarism and modernism. Going over the basic data presented, we can observe that the Third World, on the whole (and in particular those nations which exhibit a pattern of high economic growth during military rule), has accepted a Leninist theory of the state, and at the same time has rejected a Marxist theory of economics. That is to say, it accepts the need for political coercion as a central feature of Third World existence, but at the same time denies Socialist principles of economic organization.

The military state model is invariably a one-party model. Interparty struggle and interparty discipline vanish. The party apparatus becomes cloudy as to its gubernatorial, bureaucratic and even political functions. The Leninist model is decisively emulated. The party serves the nation, but with a new dimension: the party also serves the military. The traditional Leninist model has the military politicized to the point of serving the ruling party. In the Third World variation, the political elites become militarized to the point of serving the ruling junta. And this reversed role of military and political groups is a decisive characteristic of the Third World today.

The economic consequences of this sort of Third World neo-Leninism is an acceptance of some kind of market economy based on a neocapitalist model. This process might be called, "one step forward, and two steps backward." Any series of national advertisements will point out the low-waged, obedient-worker syndrome of many new nations. The model being sold to overseas investors by Third World rulers is in large measure (whatever the rhetoric socialism may dictate) a model built on production for the market, private consumption and private profit, and on a network that in some sense encourges the development of differential class patterns within Third World nations. But to gain such capitalist ends, the political participatory and congressional model common in northern and western Europe and the United States is rejected. There is no reason why this sort of system is transitional. On the contrary, given the conditions and background of underdevelopment, the kind of revolution made, the historical time of these revolutions and the rivalry between contending power blocs, this nco-Lcninist polity, linked as it is to a neocapitalist economy, is a highly efficacious, functional and exacting model of the way most societies in the Third World have evolved in terms of political economy.

It might well be that with a greater amount of accurate data, this theory of the militarization of modernization will require modification or even abandonment. However, the *prima facie* evidence would seem to indicate otherwise. More countries in the Third World have taken a sharper military turn than anyone had a right to predict on the basis of prerevolutionary ideology of postrevolutionary democratic fervor. Therefore, the overwhelming trend toward militarism (either of a left-wing or right-wing variety) must itself be considered a starting point in the study of the Third World as it *is*, rather than how analysts might want it to become.

This is not a matter of either celebrating or criticizing the good society or how Third World nations have fallen short of their own ideals. Few of us are entirely happy with any available system of society, and being critical of societal systems is a professional and occupational hazard. It is, however, not something that one would simply use as a proof that the system is unworkable. Indeed, what is revealed by the foregoing analysis is that the Third World has evolved a highly stable social system, a model of development without tears that forcefully draws our attention to the possibility that the Third World, far from being transitional or disappearing, far from being buffeted about, is becoming stronger, more resilient and more adaptive over time. The widespread formula of military adjudication of political and bureaucratic strains within the emerging society is an efficacious model for getting the kind of mobilization out of "backward" populations that at least makes possible real economic development. It might happen that the strains in this military stage of development become too great, and the resolution itself too costly to sustain real socioeconomic stability. However, at that point in the future, the Hobbesian laws of struggle against an unworkable state will once more appear and we shall know the realities of the situation by the renewed cries of revolution—this time against internal militarists rather than external colonialists.

NOTES

1. Morris Janowitz, *The Professional Soldier: A Social and Political Portrait* (New York: The Fress Press of Glencoe, 1960).
2. Irving Louis Horowitz, *Three Worlds of Development: The Theory and Practice of International Stratification* (New York and London: Oxford University Press, 1966).
3. Seymour Martin Lipset and Aldo Solari (eds.), *Elites in Latin America* (New York: Oxford University Press, 1967).
4. James Rosenau (ed.), *Linkage Politics: Essays on the Convergence of National and International Systems* (New York: The Free Press, 1969).
5. Clement J. Zablocki, James G. Fulton, and Paul Findley, Reports of the Special Study Mission to Latin America on Military Assistance Training and Developmental Television. (Washington, D.C.: U. S. Government Printing Office, May 7, 1970).
6. Robert Heilbroner, *The Great Ascent* (New York: Harper & Row, 1963).
7. Bert Hoselitz, *Sociological Aspects of Economic Growth* (Gencoe, Ill.: The Free Press-Macmillan, 1960).
8. Wilbert E. Moore, *Order and Change: Essays in Comparative Sociology* (New York: John Wiley & Sons, Inc., 1967).
9. Edwin M. Martin, "Development Aid: Successes and Failures," *The OECD Observer* no. 43 (December 1969) :5-12.
10. Ibid.
11. Chester L. Hunt, *Social Aspects of Economic Development*

(New York: McGraw-Hill Book Company, 1966).

12. Julius K. Nyerere, *Freedom and Socialism* (*Uhuru na Ujamaa*) (London and New York: Oxford University Press, 1968).

13. Phillips Cutright, and James A. Wiley, "Modernization and Political Representation: 1927-1966," *Studies in Comparative International Development* vol. V, no. 2, 1969-70.

✗ 14. Warren F. Ilchman, and Norman Thomas Uphoff, *The Political Economy of Change* (Berkeley and Los Angeles: University of California Press, 1969).

INDEX